THE COMPLETE
BOOK OF FRIENDS

THE COMPLETE BOOK OF FRIENDS

comprises

THE BOOK OF FRIENDS, Volume 1
MY BIKE & OTHER FRIENDS
JOEY

Henry Miller

THE COMPLETE
BOOK OF FRIENDS

a&b

This edition published in 1993 by
Allison & Busby
an imprint of Wilson & Day Ltd
5 The Lodge
Richmond Way
London W12 8LW

Published in 1988 by
W.H. Allen & Co. Plc

Book of Friends was first published in 1976;
My Bike and Other Friends was first published in 1978;
Joey was first published in 1979

Drawings throughout by Henry Miller

Printed and bound in Great Britain by
Cox & Wyman Ltd, Reading, Berkshire

ISBN 0 85031 852 1

Contents

BOOK ONE

Book of Friends

Stasiu

He was the very first friend in my life.
A friend from the street, where we first met, in that glorious
Fourteenth Ward I have written about so glowingly. We were
both five years old. I had other little friends in that neighborhood
beside Stasiu of course. It has always been easy for me to make
friends. But Stasiu was my real friend, so to speak, my pal, my
buddy, my constant companion. Stasiu was what his parents
called him. None of us dared call him that because it made him a
"Polak" and he didn't want to be thought of as a Polak. His name
was Stanley and Stasiu is the affectionate diminutive for Stanley. I can still hear his aunt calling in her sweet staccato voice—
"Stasiu, Stasiu, where are you? Come home, it's late." I will hear
that voice, that name, until my dying day.

Stanley was an orphan who had been adopted by his aunt and

uncle. His aunt, a woman of enormous proportions with breasts like cabbages, was one of the sweetest, kindest women I have ever known. She was a real mother to Stanley, probably much better than his own mother would have been had she lived. His uncle, on the other hand, was a drunken brute who owned the barber shop on the ground floor of the house we lived in. I have the most vivid and terrifying memories of him chasing Stanley through the streets with an open razor in his hand, cursing him at the top of his lungs and threatening to cut his head off.

Though Stanley was not his son, he too had an unbridled temper, particularly when one teased him. He seemed to have no sense of humor whatever, even later when he had grown up. Strange, now that I think of it, that "droll" was one of his favorite words. But that was much later, when he had dreams of being a writer and would write me lengthy letters from Fort Oglethorpe, or Chickamauga, when serving in the cavalry.

Certainly as a boy there was nothing droll about him. On the contrary, his expression was usually glum, morose, downright mean at times. If I angered him, as I did occasionally, he would chase after me with clenched fists. fortunately I could always outrun him. But these chases were long and full of terror, for I had an unholy fear of Stanley when he lost his temper. We were about the same size and build, but he was much the stronger. I knew that if he ever caught me he would beat me to within an inch of my life.

What I did on these occasions was to outdistance him and then hide somewhere for a half-hour or so before sneaking home. He lived at the other end of the block in a shabby three-story building much the same as ours. I had to be wary sneaking home, for fear he was still on the lookout for me. I didn't worry about meeting him the next day because these rages of his always subsided in due time. When we met it would be with a smile, a wry one from Stanley, and then we'd shake hands. The incident would be forgotten, buried—until the next time.

One might wonder how I became such good friends with a kid like this, who on the whole was a rather unsociable lad. It's hard for me to explain myself, and perhaps it's best I don't try. Maybe even at that early age I felt sorry for Stanley, knowing he was an orphan, knowing his uncle treated him like a dog. His foster parents were poor too, much poorer than my parents. There were many things I owned, toys, tricycle, guns and so on, to say nothing of the special privileges that were granted me, which made Stanley jealous and envious. He was particularly annoyed, I remember, because of the beautiful clothes I wore. It didn't matter to him that my father was a boss tailor, rather well-to-do for that time, who could afford to indulge his fancy. Myself, I was rather embarrassed and often ashamed of wearing such sumptuous raiment when all the kids I associated with were virtually in rags. These duds my parents thought looked so fetching on me made me look like a little Lord Fauntleroy, which I hated. I wanted to look like the rest of the gang, not like some freak from the upper classes. And so, now and then, the other kids would jeer at me as I walked hand in hand with my mother, and call me a sissy, which made me wince. My mother of course was insensitive to these gibes and to my feelings as well. She probably thought she was doing me a great favor, if she thought about it at all.

Already, at that tender age, I had lost all respect for her. On the other hand, whenever I went to Stanley's home and met his aunt, that delicious hippopotamus, I was in seventh heaven. I didn't realize it then, but what made me so happy and free in her presence was that she was affectionate, a quality I didn't know mothers were supposed to possess in dealing with their off-spring. All I knew was discipline, criticism, slaps, threats—or so it seems as I look back on this state of my life.

My mother, for example, never offered Stanley a huge slice of rye bread smeared with butter and sugar, as did Stanley's aunt when I visited his home. My mother's greeting to Stanley

9

usually was: "Don't make too much noise and be sure to clean up when you've finished playing." No bread, no cake, no warm slap on the back, no 'how's your aunt' or anything. Just don't make a nuisance of yourself was the idea she conveyed. Stanley didn't come very often to my home, probably because he sensed the unfriendly atmosphere. When he did it was usually because I was convalescing from some illness. I had all the child's illnesses, by the way, from chicken pox to diphtheria, scarlet fever, whooping cough, the measles and what not. Stanley never had any illness that I knew of. One couldn't afford to be ill in a poor family like his.

And so we often played on the floor below, where my grandfather sat on a bench making coats for my father, the boss tailor of a Fifth Avenue establishment. We got along well, my grandfather and I; I could communicate better with him than with my father. By comparison, my grandfather was a cultured gentleman, who spoke a beautiful, impeccable English which he had learned during his ten years in London as an apprentice. It was a pleasure, when the holidays were on and all the relatives gathered together, to hear my grandfather discourse on the state of the world, on politics—he was a Socialist and a Union man—or to listen to his tales of adventure as a boy when wandering through Germany in search of work. As Stanley and I played parchesi or dominoes, or some simple card game, my grandfather would hum to himself or whistle a tune from some German song. It was from his lips that I first heard *"Ich weiss nicht was soll es bedeuten das Ich so traurig bin..."* He had one song called "Shoo-fly, don't bother me," which he sang in English and which always made us laugh.

There was one game we played with toy soldiers and cannons which roused us to fever pitch; we would shout and scream with excitement as we battered the enemy to pieces. The racket we made never seemed to disturb my grandfather. He went right on sewing and pressing his coats, humming to himself, getting up now and then to yawn and stretch. It was a back-breaking business sitting on a bench all day making coats for my father, the boss tailor. Now and then he would interrupt our play to ask us to go to the saloon at the corner and fetch him a pitcher of lager beer. He would always offer us a little, very little, saying it would not harm us.

If I were not in good enough condition to play games I would read to Stanley from one of my fairy tale books. (I knew how to read before going to school.) Stanley would listen for a while and then beat it. He didn't like to be read to. At that age he wasn't much of a reader; he was too healthy for such a pastime, too restless, too full of animal spirits. What Stanley enjoyed, and I too when I was well, were rough games in the street, and we knew many of them. If football had been the rage then, as it is now, he might have become a football player. He liked "contact" games in which you shoved the other fellow about or knocked him flat on his ass. He liked to use his fists too; when he got angry and put up his dukes it was always with his tongue sticking out, like a viper. Because of this habit he often bit his tongue, which would set him to howling and scowling. Most of the kids on the block were afraid of him, except for one little Jewish boy whose big brother had taught him the manly art of self-defense.

But about my apparel—I have to use a high-falutin' word for it. One day when my mother was taking me to the doctor, me rigged out again in some outlandish costume, Stanley planted himself square in front of my mother and exclaimed: "Why does he have to get all these fancy things? Why don't somebody dress me up like that?" Upon saying which he turned his head away and spat. It was the first time I saw my mother soften up. As we walked on—she was carrying a parasol, I remember—she looked down at me and said hurriedly: "We'll have to get something nice for Stanley to wear. What do you think he'd like?" I was so bewildered by this about-face that I didn't know what to answer. Finally I said: "Why don't you get him a new suit?" That's what he needs most." Whether Stanley ever got the suit I don't recall. Probably not.

There was another boy in the neighborhood whose parents were very well-off and who always used to dress him up in grand style. They even had him wear a derby on occasion, along with a little cane. What a sight in that poor neighborhood! To be sure, he was the son of a Congressman, and a spoiled brat to boot. All the kids made fun of him and would tease him unmercifully, trip him up if they could, call him filthy names, imitate his mincing gait, and make him miserable in every possible way. I wonder what because of him in later years. With a start like that it seems to me it would be hard for anyone to become anything worthwhile.

In addition to his other qualities Stanley was also a good liar and a thief. He stole barefacedly from the fruit and vegetable stands and, if caught red-handed, would invent a pitiful story about his folks being so poor that he never had enough to eat.

One of the special privileges I enjoyed, one which Stanley never shared with me, was to attend a matinee vaudeville show every Saturday at a local theater called "The Novelty." I was about seven years old when my mother decided to let me enjoy this privilege. First, of course, I had to do some chores—wash dishes, scrub the floor and wash the windows. I was then given a dime to buy myself a seat in the gallery—"nigger heaven," we called it. I usually went alone, unless my little friends from the country happened to be visiting us.

Though Stanley never got inside a theater, the two of us usued to enjoy an imaginary spectacle at a burlesque house nearby called "The Bum," a name invented because of its evil reputation. Saturday nights we would first inspect the billboards displaying the soubrettes in tights, then take a stand near the box office, hoping to catch some dirty jokes the sailors might make as they stood in line for their tickets. Most of the jokes were over our heads, but we got the drift of them nevertheless.

We were inordinately curious to know what went on in there when the lights went up. Did the girls really strip to the waist as they said? Did they throw their garters to the sailors in the audience? Did the sailors take the girls to the nearby saloon after the performance and get them drunk? Did they go to bed with them in the rooms above the saloon from which there always came great sounds of merriment?

We would question the older boys in the street about these matters, but seldom got satisfactory answers. They usually told us we were too young to be asking such questions, and then they would laugh in a most significant way. We knew a little bit about the fucking business because there was a girl named Jenny, just a wee bit older than us, who would offer her body to any and all of us for a penny a crack. This performance usually took place in Louis Pirossa's cellar. I don't think any of us really got it in her. Just to make contact sent shivers up and down our spines. Besides, she always remained in a standing position, which is not the best position for beginners. Mere urchins that we were, we referred to her among ourselves as a whore. Which did not mean that we treated her badly. It was simply that we marked her out as different from the other girls in the neighborhood. Secretly we admired her for her boldness. She was a very likeable girl, rather good-looking and easy to talk to.

Stanley didn't figure strongly in this cellar game. He was shy and awkward, and, being a Catholic, felt guilty for committing a grave sin. Even when he grew up he was never a lady's man, never a skirt chaser. There was something austere and severe about him. I am certain that he never went with a girl until he ran into the woman who was to become his wife, and to whom he remained faithful. Even when he joined the cavalry and wrote me long intimate letters about his life in the barracks he never spoke of women. All he acquired in those four years with Uncle Sam was how to roll the dice and guzzle it. I'll never forget the

13

night I met him in Coney Island upon his release from the service. But that's for later ...

Summer nights in New York, or Brooklyn, as it happened to be, can be wonderful when you're a kid and can roam the streets at will. On a very hot night, after we had worn ourselves out playing "cops and robbers," say, we would finally settle down on Stanley's doorstep, eating cold sauerkraut and frankfurters which he would swipe from the icebox. We could sit there talking for hours, it seemed. Though Stanley was rather the silent type, with a long, thin face rather dour in expression—something on the order of Bill Hart, the cowboy idol of the silent screen—he could also talk when in the mood. At seven or eight the man who was later to write "romances," as he called them, was already recognizable. To be sure, he didn't talk love, but the ambience in which he set his little tales was poetic, imaginative and romantic. He was no longer the street urchin looking for trouble, but a dreamer longing to escape from his narrow environment. He loved to talk of far-off places like China, Africa, Spain, Argentina. The sea had a special appear for him; he wanted to be a sailor when he came of age and visit these strange, distant lands. (In another ten years he would be writing me about Joseph Conrad, his favorite author, who was also a Pole but who had chosen to write in English.)

During these talks on the doorstep he was indeed another Stanley. He was softer and gentler. Sometimes he would interrupt himself to tell me of his uncle's cruelty, show me the welts on his back, where his uncle had beaten him with the razor strop. I remember him telling me how furious he made his uncle by refusing to cry; he would simply clench his teeth and scowl, but never let out so much as a whimper. It was typical of Stanley. That's how he went through life, taking his punishment but never showing what he felt. It was a tough life from the very start and it ended as miserably as it had begun. Even his "romances" were doomed to failure. But I am getting ahead of myself ...

14

Born in America, Stanley nevertheless had many of the characteristics of an immigrant. For example, he never spoke Polish in front of us though we knew he did at home. If his aunt spoke Polish to him before us he would answer in English. He was ashamed to speak Polish in our presence. There was something slightly different about his use of English compared to ours; he did not use the gutter language we indulged in with the same ease or fluency as the other boys. He was also more polite than we were and showed respect to adults, whereas we other kids seemed to enjoy being vulgar, disrespectful and careless about our speech. In other words Stanley had good manners even though he was just a gutter snipe like the rest of us. Stanley hadn't cultivated these habits, they were a result of being brought up by people from the Old World. This touch of refinement in Stanley was something of a joke to us, his friends, but we never dared mock him because of it. Stanley not only could hold his own with the best of us but, as I said before, when irritated or offended he was a holy terror.

There was another thing about Stanley I should touch on—his jealousy. While still living in that same neighborhood I became acquainted with two youngsters my own age who lived in the country, as we called it, though actually it was a suburb of Brooklyn. Every now and then my parents invited these boys to stay with us; later on I would visit them—"in the country." Joey and Tony were their names. Joey soon became one of my great friends. Stanley, for one reason or another, didn't show much warmth toward my new-found friends. He made fun of them at first because their ways were different from ours. He pretended that they were stupid and too innocent—country bumpkins, in other words. The truth was that he was jealous, particularly of Joey whom he sensed I had a great affection for. It was as if Stanley and I were blood brothers and no one had the right to come between us. It was true, of course, that there was no other boy in the neighborhood about whom I felt as I did about

15

Stanley. His only rivals were older boys, whom I regarded as my idols. I was a hero worshiper, a born hero worshiper, no doubt about it. And I still am, thank God. Not Stanley, however. Whether it was because he was too stiff-necked, too proud to bow his head, or just plain jealous, I can't say. He had an eye for the flaws and failings in others and was rather good at lampooning and ridiculing those he disliked. All his efforts were in vain where my idols were concerned. To me, no matter what anyone said, my idols were made of pure gold. I saw only their virtues; if they had any defects I was blind to them. It may sound rather ridiculous, but I believe I see things in very much the same way today. I still look upon Alexander the Great and Napoleon as extraordinary human figures, men to be admired no matter what their faults. I still think reverently of Gautama the Buddha, Milarepa, Ramakrishna, Swami Vivekananda. I still adore such writers as Dostoievsky, Knut Hamsun, Rimbaud, Blaise Cendrars.

There was one older boy whom I regarded not as a "hero" like the others but more as a saint—not a Saint Augustine nor a Saint Bernard, but a Saint Francis. That was Johnny Paul, an Italian born in Sicily. To this very day I think of Johnny Paul with the utmost tenderness, sometimes, to be frank, with tears in my eyes. He must have been eight years older than Stanley and I, which is a great deal in the calendar of youth. As best as I remember he delivered coal for a living. He was of dark complexion with very bushy eyebrows set above two dark, glowing eyes which burned like hot coals. His clothes were always dirty and ragged and his face covered with soot, but he was clean inside, clean as a hound's tooth. What got me about him was his tenderness, his soft, melodious voice. The way he would say, "Hello Henry, how are you today," would melt me. It was the voice of a compassionate father who loved all God's children. Even Stanley had to succumb to his charms which were nothing more than a fundamental good nature and a humility that was utterly sin-

16

cere. Stanley even liked the fact that he was a "wop," whereas Louis Pirossa and some of the other "wops" were beneath Stanley's attention.

When one is seven or eight an older boy can play a great role in one's life. He is a father without being a father; he is a companion without being a pal or a buddy; he is an instructor without the forbidding lineaments of a teacher; he is a father-confessor without being a priest. He can mold a boy's character or set him on the path, so to say, without being meddlesome, pompous or sententious. All these things Johnny Paul was to us. We adored him, we hung on every word he said, we obeyed him and we trusted him. Would that we could say the same of our own fathers, our own teachers, our own priests and counselors!

Sitting on the doorstep in the cool of the evening Stanley and I often wracked our brains to explain to ourselves why Johnny Paul was so different from the other young men his age. We knew that he had had no schooling, that he couldn't read or write, that his parents were of very humble origin, nobodies so to say, but not trash. Where did he get his good manners, his kindness, his gentility, his forbearance? For, above all things, Johnny Paul was a tolerant individual. He had the same regard for the worst among us as for the best; he played no favorites. What a great, great thing this is, especially if one has been reared among narrowminded, prejudiced, bigoted individuals, as most of our elders were, including the hypocritical minister of the gospel, old man Ramsay, who lived next door to Stanley and sometimes chased him down the street with a horsewhip.

No, we were not taught to admire, much less venerate, such simple souls as Johnny Paul. How interesting that a mere boy should discover what constitutes the sterling qualities in an individual when his parents and teachers recognize only the counterfeit. I cannot resist dwelling on this theme because I have believed all my life that children have more to teach adults than the other way round. The person who has never dealt with children is a spiritual cripple. It is children who not only open our hearts but our minds as well. It is only through them, only in seeing the world through their eyes, that we know what beauty and innocence are. How quickly we destroy their vision of the world! How quickly we transform them into the image of us shortsighted, miserable, faithless adults! To me the root of all evil is our parents, our elders. And I don't mean simply bad parents, ignorant parents: I mean parents as such, all parents. Johnny Paul opened my eyes; not Jesus, not Socrates, not the Buddha. Needless to say, I didn't realize the gift he had made us until many years later, when it was too late to thank him.

Since Stanley's parents couldn't afford to give him the spending money he required to purchase his little luxuries, Stanley found himself a job running errands for Mrs. O'Meilo, the little old lady who loved cats. She was regarded as soft in the head or eccentric by the neighbors because she kept from thirty-five to forty cats on the flat tin roof over the veterinary's stable. From my window on the third floor I could look down on her feeding this motley assortment of felines twice a day. I didn't share the opinion of my parents who called her a nut; I considered her a good soul. I was the more convinced of this when she asked Stanley if he would run her errands, for which she would give him a dollar a week. I knew she did it because she wanted to help Stanley. I wished that someone would offer me a job like that; I longed to do something useful. I didn't need the extra money, because my parents saw to it that I had everything I needed. I was embarrassed and ashamed that I should have everything I wanted while my companions lacked all but the bare necessities. One by one I gave my toys away to those who craved them. When I finally gave away the beautiful drum my parents had given me for my birthday I was severly punished. More than that, I was deeply humiliated. My mother had taken it into her head to recover some of the beautiful toys I had given away. So what did she do? She took me by the ear and dragged me to my friends' homes and made me ask for my toys back. She said that would teach me not to give away my presents. When I was old enough to buy my own things I could then give away whatever I chose. Presents cost money, I was to remember that. I did indeed remember her words, but not in the way she intended.

I made a few feeble efforts to find work but with no success. Why did I want work, my prospective employers would ask. Your parents are well-off, aren't they? Whereupon I would hang my head and slink off. In truth I didn't want work, I only wanted to imitate Stanley. To be honest, I hated work. All I wanted was to play. If I had had the means I believe I could have been a playboy all my life. I never had the desire to make an honest living, which everyone is supposed to have. I was born with a silver spoon in my mouth and I wanted to keep it there. I didn't think then that I was a spoiled brat, nor did I think, as I did later, that the world owed me a living. When I realized that it didn't, it was a rude awakening.

Playing in the street had a more sinister aspect at times than one might think with regard to children's pastimes. One of our chief delights was to go on marauding expeditions, dealing death and destruction, so to speak. Stanley was the leader fortunately, because only he, it seemed, knew when to call a halt to our depredations. Stanley could influence and control the wildest ones among us, and I must say it was no mean job since some of the gang had truly murderous instincts.

One of these was a snot-nosed lad named Alfie Melta whose old man was a cop. There was something of the fiend about his youngster. He had no brains at all, and no language.He was a low-grade moron with a touch of evil in his makeup. He wasn't crazy, like Willie Payne, nor a half-wit like Louis Pirossa. He was an out-and-out dope who opened his mouth only to emit bloody oaths and filthy objurgations. He could lie like a trooper, throw fake epileptic fits when necessary, have tantrums at will, and was an absolute dare devil and a sneak, a rat, a coward to boot.

When he wished to express something, anything, the muscles of his face would twitch and his eyeballs would roll like dice in a box. He could turn anything into a weapon, even a toothpick. He had the ingenuity and the inventiveness of a good second-story man. He loved the sight of blood; even if it was his own blood it made him gleeful.

His counterpart, and a wonderful asset to our raids, was Sylvester, the son of a hod-carrier who seemed to be on a perpetual spree. His name fitted him superbly—it had an angelic sound. It was a name you caressed in pronouncing. He had the look of innocence itself, the look of a cherub by Fra Angelico, a cherub just sprung from the arms of Jesus, or the Virgin Mary. Such beautiful violet eyes? Such lovely golden locks? Such a fair complexion with just a tinge of pink in his cheeks! The women in the neighborhood adored him, would pat him on the head, offer him candy and sweets of all kinds. He talked like a little angel too, devil that he was. When he accepted a compliment or a gift he would lower his big, violet eyes with their long, curly lashes, and blush. Little did these adoring mothers know what a monster they were dealing with.

Sylvester had "cool," as we say today. He was never ruffled, never disturbed, never rueful, never touched by regret or remorse. It was Sylvester who was entrusted with the dangerous jobs; it was Sylvester who robbed the church; it was Sylvester who gave false alarms; Sylvester who upset baby carriages for kicks; Sylvester who stole from the blind; Sylvester who set fires to stores. There wasn't anything Sylvester would not do, if he had a mind to. The difference between him and Alfie Melta was that Sylvester played it like an artist. His deviltries were all *actes gratuits.* Clever as he was, however, he was to end up in the penitentiary before coming of age.

Sylvester's doings were born of pure, ice-cold malice. Alfie Melta, on the other hand, was hot-blooded, impetuous and reckless. He hadn't brains enough to figure things in advance. He wanted action, spectacular action, no matter what the risk. He ended up in a reformatory before he reached his teens.

How it was that Stanley could influence and control these little monsters I never could figure out. Perhaps it was because they feared him, perhaps because they admired him. For Stanley too had some of their baser qualities. Some of that brutality his uncle had shown toward him had to be worked off on others. Some of that daily humiliation he suffered at home had to be inflicted on others. No, Stanley was far from being an angel. He was a good kid who was always getting the dirty end of the stick. He needed to rub some of that shit under other people's noses. His young, tender heart was already becoming rancorous.

Stanley was at his best when leading us to invade enemy territory. In every poor neighborhood there are feuds between one side and another. In our case it was perpetual war between the North side and the South side. We were of the North, which was like being on the wrong side of the railroad tracks. Our pleasure was to invade the swanky South side, beat up a few helpless sissies and return with a few captives whom we tortured to the best of our ability. I don't mean by torture that we pulled their nails out or cut them to ribbons; we were content to steal the clothes off their back and rip them to shreds, or swipe their pocketknives and watches, if they had any, douse them under the fire hydrant, give them a bloody nose or a black eye, and so on. Alfie Melta always had to be restrained because he liked to see blood. A great coup would be to rob a South side boy of his bike. The greatest enjoyment we got from these escapades was to send the other side home in tatters bawling like two-year-olds.

Most of the boys in our gang were Catholics and were sent to a Catholic church on the North side. My parents, though they practiced no religion, insisted on sending me to a Presbyterian church, run by a wealthy English minister, on the South side. I often had to run the gauntlet going to and from church. Because

21

I was bright, well-dressed and came of a good family the church brethren regarded me as a little angel. For reciting the 23rd Psalm by heart I was given a little gilt-edged Bible, or New Testament rather, with my name embossed in gold letters on the cover. I never dared show this testimonial to any of the gang except Stanley. Stanley was puzzled over the award of such a gift. In his church, he said, no one but the priest was allowed to read the Bible. Nor did Catholics go to Sunday school, only to mass, and that at an ungodly hour. What was Sunday school like, he wondered. I tried to explain it to him but he only shook his yead. "Your's ain't no church," he said, "it's more like a kindergarten."

One day I told him I had seen a moving picture in the basement of the church. "What's that?" he asked. I explained just what I had seen on the screen. "A Chink walking across the Brooklyn bridge." "And anything else?" said Stanley. I confessed there was nothing much else. Stanley was silent a moment, then said: "I don't believe it." To tell the truth, I hardly believed it myself, though I had seen it with my own eyes. The superintendent, another Englishman who always wore a cutaway with striped trousers, had explained to us that a man named Thomas Edison had invented this miraculous moving picture machine, and that we were very fortunate to have had the privilege of seeing one of the first films ever released. He spoke of the "silent screen," a phrase which impressed me greatly for some unknown reason. At any rate, for Stanley that was one of the differences between his church and mine—in mine you could see moving pictures for nothing in the basement.

Perhaps we would never have discussed religion, Stanley and I, had it not been for this Chink walking across the Brooklyn Bridge. Now, among other profound subjects we would discuss on his doorstep of an evening, was this business of religion. Did we go to confession, he wanted to know. What did I know about the Virgin Mary? Did I believe in devils and angels? Who wrote

22

the Bible and why wasn't he allowed to read it? Was I afraid of going to Hell some day? Did I take Communion? I confessed I didn't know what Communion was. He was taken aback by this. I asked him to explain it, but all he could say was that it was like eating Christ alive and drinking his blood. The thought of drinking blood made me queasy. But Stanley quickly assured me that it was only imitation blood—just some kind of red wine which the priest blessed first. I got the impression that Catholics were an outlandish sort of breed, something like refined savages.

He told me he had an uncle living in New Jersey somewhere who was a priest. "He can't marry," said Stanley. "Why?" I asked. "Because he's a priest. It's a sin for a priest to marry." "Our minister is married," I said, "and has children." "He's no priest, that's why," said Stanley. I couldn't understand why it was such a sin for priests to marry. Stanley volunteered an explanation. "You see, a priest can't go near a woman," he began. He meant "sleep with her." "A priest belongs to God; he's married to the church. Women are temptation to a priest." "Even good women?" I asked naïvely. "All women," said Stanley emphatically. "Women lead us into temptation." I didn't quite understand what this word temptation implied. "You see," said Stanley, "if a priest went to bed with a woman she would have a child, and the child would be a bastard." I knew the word bastard, I had often used it in calling a fellow names. But this bastard was a new kind of bastard to me. I didn't press him further on this because I didn't want to appear to be totally ignorant. I began to realize that Stanley knew a lot more about religion than I did, even if I could recite the 23rd Psalm by heart.

Stanley was not only more sophisticated than yours truly but he was a born skeptic. It was he who opened my eyes, and nearly broke my little heart, by informing me that there ain't no Santa Claus. It took quite a bit of explanation to convince me of this. I was the sort who believed in anything: the more impossible it was, the quicker I believed it. I was an apt pupil for St. Thomas

Aquinas. However, in the Protestant churches they didn't talk much about saints. (Was it because the saints were such sinful guys at bottom?) As I remarked earlier, Stanley hadn't much use for fairy tales; he preferred reality. I doted on fairy tales, especially the grim, terrorizing ones, which gave me nightmares. Later in life I see myself marching to the public library on Fifth Avenue, reading day after day the fairy tales from every country in the world.

There was another myth which Stanley almost knocked out of my head a year or so later, and that was that storks deliver babies. I had never thought much about this subject, since babies aren't particularly interesting to little boys. When I asked Stanley where they did come from he said, "from the mother's belly." This sounded absolutely incredible to me. "How do they get out then?" I jeered. That Stanley couldn't answer. It didn't occur to him that babies came out of that little crack between the legs which we saw on Jenny Payne. Nor was he sure how they were made. All he could say was that it had to do with parents sleeping together. It's not so surprising, when you think of it, that his little brain couldn't make the connection between babies and sleeping together. Many primitive peoples didn't make the connection either. In any case, for once I was the one who was skeptical. I thought of asking my mother, but then I knew in advance she would never answer a question like that. She could never answer anything which profoundly interested me. I soon learned not to ask questions at home...I had a hunch Johnny Paul might know the answer, or even Jenny Payne, but I was too shy to put such a question to them.

Jenny Payne...Jenny had a brother who was off his noodle. Everybody called him "Crazy Willie." He was a big, gawky, gangling idiot about fifteen years of age whose speech was limited to a dozen words or so but who wore a perpetual Steeplechase smile. He was quite a problem to his family, naturally, since they couldn't always keep an eye on him. When he wandered into the street he was mercilessly tormented; it was considered good sport to take advantage of a helpless lubber like Crazy Willie. Stanley always defended the poor bugger. Why, no one could understand. Stanley could calm him down when he threatened to run amok; he was even able to hold communication with him. Sometimes he would bring Willie a slice of rye bread with butter and jam on it, which Willie would gobble down in two mouthfuls. Willie often imagined that he was a horse, and he would act like a horse, to our great amusement. He would put his head down and snort and whinny, exactly like a real horse, or he would gallop and frisk his imaginary tail. Occasionally he would let out a tremendous fart, at which he would do a pirouette, then stand on his hind legs and paw the air with his front ones. His parents were kind folk who didn't have the heart to put him away. In those days the insane asylums weren't filled to overflowing as they are now. Many who should have been there were walking the streets or kept prisoners at home. In our own respectable family we had several crazy specimens, including my mother's mother.

One of the serious problems Willie's parents had to face was how to prevent Willie from masturbating in public. It seemed that Willie usually had the urge to give an exhibition around six o'clock in the afternoon. Willie would usually take his stand outside his window on a narrow ledge one story above the street level. Suddenly he would open his trousers and pull out his prick, which was of no mean size, and with an ecstatic grin and a few unintelligible exclamations, would jerk away for dear life. At this hour the trolley car which ran through our street would be jammed with workers returning home. If it were summertime the trolley would be an open one with a running board on either side. Seeing Willie performing his antics the motorman would stop the car and the passengers would shout and wave to Willie in hilarious fashion. Soon a crowd would gather and the police would be summoned. Willie wasn't afraid of the police, but his

25

parents were. After an incident of that sort Jenny Payne would blush and lower her head as she passed by. As for Willie himself, the worst that would happen to him would be a good strapping from his old man. Until the next time...

Soon now I will be moving to another neighborhood. Stanley will drop out of my life for a while—but he will return, and in a different guise.

The ninth year of my life is approaching and with it the end of my first Paradise on earth. No, the second Paradise. My first was in my mother's womb, where I fought to remain forever, but the forceps finally prevailed. It was a marvelous period in the womb and I shall never forget it. I had *almost* everything one could ask for—*except friends*. And a life without friends is no life, however snug and secure it may be. When I say friends I mean *friends*. Not anybody and everybody can be your friend. It must be someone as close to you as your skin, someone who imparts color, drama, meaning to your life. Something the other side of love, yet including love.

That's why I write this, to tell about those friendships which meant so much to me. I realize that I have touched on some of these relationship before, in other books of mine. I relate them again now in a different way—not as the solipsist I am often accused of being but *as a friend*. The difference between the Paradise of the womb and this other Paradise of friendship is that in the womb you are blind. A friend furnishes you with a thousand eyes, like the god Indra. Through your friends you live untold lives. You see in other dimensions. You live upside down and inside out. You are never alone, never will be alone, even if every last one of your friends should disappear from the face of the earth.

The German physicist Fechner said that we live three lives: one in the womb, one in the world, and another in the beyond. He overlooked the multiple lives we live in and through others, because of others. Even in prison we do not live a solitary existence. Was it Socrates who said: "He who would live alone must be either a god or a wild beast"?

Once I wrote that I was born in the street and raised in the street. I was speaking then of the glorious 14th Ward which I am soon to leave for "the street of early sorrows." Today I prefer to think that we who lived in the street, we for whom the street was everything, created these streets, created these homes, created the very atmosphere we breathed. We did not come into a world ready-made: we invented our world. I cannot leave it without paying homage to it once again.

Until I went to France I never realized why I was so attached to this little world of my childhood. In Paris I discovered a replica of that microcosm called the 14th Ward. In the poor quarters of Paris where I wandered penniless and unknown for many a day and month I saw all about me the sights of my childhood days when I was a spoiled brat. Again I saw cripples, drunks, beggars, idiots roaming the streets. Again I made friends of poor and humble origin, real friends who saved my life time after time. Again I felt that I was in a man-sized world, a human microcosm suited to my taste. There in Paris, in its shabby, squalid streets teeming with life, I relived the sparkling scenes of my childhood.

It is so hard to believe that poverty too can have its glamorous side. I don't recall anyone in that old neighborhood whom I thought of as well-off except the family doctor and the minister of our Presbyterian church. The shopkeepers probably made a decent living, but they were certainly not rich. No one owned an automobile because there were no such animals in existence then, or if they did exist they belonged to some other planet.

When I think of those streets now they are usually in full sunshine. Everywhere bright awnings, parasols, flies and perspiration. No one is running or pushing and shoving. The streets are becalmed, swimming in heat, and slightly perfumed with rotting fruit. At the veterinary's a stallion is pinned to the earth and his balls are being cut off. I can smell the scorched, seared

27

flesh. The shanties, which are already caving in, seem to be melting. From them issue dwarves and giants, or little monsters on roller skates who will grow up to become politicians or criminals, whichever way the dice roll. The brewery wagon with its huge kegs of beer looks gigantic. There are no skyscrapers, no high rise buildings. The candy shop just a few doors from our home is out of Charles Dickens, and so are the spinsters who run it. Mrs. O'Melio is moving amidst her thirty-eight cats of all stripes and denominations with a big bowl of food in her hand. There are two toilets in our house; one is in the garden and is just a plain old-fashioned shithouse. The other is upstairs on our floor and has running water and a wick floating in a little cut of sweet oil to light when it is dark. My bedroom is just a cell with one window giving on the hallway. There are iron bars protecting it, and through the iron bars come most of my nightmares in the form of a huge bear or a fearsom monster out of Grimm's fairy tales. After dinner in the evening my father would dry the dishes which my mother washed at the sink. One evening he must have said something to offend her for suddenly she gave him a ringing slap in the face with her wet hands. Then I remember distinctly hearing him say to her: "If you ever do that again I'll leave you." I was impressed by the quiet, firm way in which he said it. His son, I must confess, never had the courage to talk that way to a woman.

I mentioned my proclivity for reading. One of my favorite books, one I read over and over again, was *Stories from the Bible*. They were Old Testament stories largely, with unforgettable characters such as King David, Daniel, Jonathan, Esther, Ruth, Rachel and so on. I wondered sometimes why I never met any people like that in the street. I sensed that there were two worlds, the world of heroes and heroines which I found in books and the world of ordinary people like my parents and all the other parents in the neighborhood. There were no flaming prophets, no kings, no young heroes with slingshots among us.

There was that crazy preacher with the horsewhip, old man Ramsay, but he was no Ezekiel. I tried to tell Stanley about these wonderful people who inhabited the Bible but he dismissed them as being fictions of the Protestant religion. "The priest never speaks about such people," he said, and that was the end of that.

Just as there are frontiers which separate nations so there were boundaries which marked off our world from neighboring ones. Those who lived beyond these boundary lines were potential enemies. We were always wary, always on guard, when we stepped into their precincts. In our own little world everything was understandable, including cruelty, thievery and eiplepsy. We were one big family composed of micks, wops, kikes, heinies, Polaks and an occasional Chink. The important thing was to keep alive. The next important thing was not to get caught. The world is an abstract term for something which exists only in the mind. The earth is real, and the sky and the birds of the air. For us there were no "airs," as in Greek philosophy. There was only ozone which, taken in deep draughts, was good for the lungs.

As I say, Stanley had moved to New Jersey or Staten Island. His aunt had divorced her husband, the barber, and married an undertaker. I wouldn't have known it had not Stanley waved to me from the driver's seat of the hearse which happened to pass through our street one day. I could hardly believe my eyes.

We too had moved to a new neighborhood which at first had little appear for me. The boys of this new neighborhood lacked the charm and the character of the boys of the old neighborhood. They seemed to be replicas of their parents who were dull, strict and extremely bourgeois. However, I soon made friends—I have a gift for that, it seems. In school I became friends with one boy who was to remain a life-long friend and to play quite a part in my life. He was a born artist. I saw him only at school, unfortunately.

Now and then I had a letter from Stanley and now and then we met, to undertake one of those shady operations Stanley now let himself in for. We would take the ferry to Staten Island and during the course of the journey Stanley would discreetly drop over the side of the boat a little box. In the box was an abortion. Perhaps he received some extra spending money for doing his new uncle this favor—he never said. A little later he was to do even shadier things. Somehow he managed to get himself a job as an interpreter at Ellis Island. Instead of helping his compatriots, Stanley robbed them. He had no sense of shame about it either, which really surprised me. His attitude was—if I don't do it, someone else will.

During these few years in which we were growing up we saw very little of one another. Stanley never spoke of girls, I noticed, whereas I was deeply involved and would continue to be so for many years to come.

Finally the day came when Stanley joined the Army—the cavalry, to be more precise. All the Army ever taught Stanley was how to drink and how to gamble. The day he got his release from the Army we met—in Coney Island. He must have had his full pay with him for he spent money like a trooper. He drank beer, nothing but beer, steadily from the time we met. Naturally he tried everything—from the rides to the shooting galleries. We were loaded down with prizes he won—he was a sharpshooter in the Army. About three in the morning, we checked in at a shabby hotel somewhere in Brooklyn Heights. He went to bed drunk as a pope and cleared his head next morning by drinking stale beer. He was a different Stanley alright. Tough now and ready for trouble at a moment's notice. Despite his condition, he still had a mind for literature. His two favorites, of whom I was to hear a lot later, were Joseph Conrad and Anatole France. He wanted to write like them, either one, it didn't matter.

Some more time elapses, during which he learns to become a printer. And the next thing is marriage—to a rather dulllooking Polish girl about whom he had never breathed a word.

By this time I too had married. As chance would have it, we

30

found ourselves living only a few blocks apart, he on the wrong side of the tracks, as they say.

Now we saw one another more frequently. Nights after dinner, Stanley often dropped around to chew the fat with me. Both of us were trying to write, and each was critical of the other. We were terribly serious about it all too. I was still working as employment manager for the telegraph company.

To prove to myself that I was indeed a writer I wrote a book about twelve messengers during a three week vacation. I don't think I even mentioned it to Stanley; why I don't know. Possibly I didn't want to embarrass him. Of course I never dreamed of showing it to him for he would have picked it to death.

What I remember vividly about this period are Stanley's two boys. They were scarcely a year apart in age. Always well-dressed, polite, immaculate and painfully well-behaved. They were always deathly pale, as if made of alabaster. Stanley often brought them along of a late afternoon. What they did during these visits was a mystery to me. They remained out of sight until called for, as children should. They never quarreled, soiled their clothes or complained about anything.

When I think of their behavior now I wonder that they did not arouse my wife's admiration. They behaved exactly according to her principles. But for whatever reason, she paid them little attention. Nor did she ever inquire after Stanley's wife, who, though a good person, was definitely not very interesting.

It was when I got to know June that Stanley pricked up his ears. Though he didn't approve of my doings he sympathized with me. And, he was extremely discreet. Little by little he watched the whole drama unroll.

One day, out of the blue, he said to me: "Do you want to get rid of her?" Meaning my wife. I probably nodded yes. "O.K. Leave it to me," he added. And that was that. Not another word.

I don't believe I gave it serious thought. It was just a whim of his, I supposed. But it wasn't.

31

What role he played with my wife I don't know. I can only imagine that he said something similar to her. At any rate, one fine morning, when June and I are sleeping together—in my own home, to be sure—suddenly the rolling doors are pulled open and there stands my wife, her girl friend from upstairs, and the girl's father. Caught in *flagrante delicto* as they say. A few days later my wife's lawyer serves me with court papers—for divorce.

Now how had I been caught like that? Stanley was very clever. He had suggested to my wife that she and the child take a vacation—and then return unexpectedly. To make sure that my wife *was taking a vacation* I had accompanied her to the little town she was stopping at. I had returned on the next train and, happy as a lark, had called June to give her the good news. That's how we happened to be caught in bed.

What I remember about this scene of the three witnesses is that, despite her embarrassment and her desire to leave the house as soon as possible, I managed to persuade June to stay. I fixed us an excellent breakfast—just as if nothing had happened. June thought this rather strange on my part. Said something about lacking feeling.

I never understood how Stanley could be sure I would bring June to the house that night. "My instincts told me so," he replied when I questioned him about it. To him it was a simple, cut and dried affair. All he demanded of me was that I would have no regrets later. I never did.

Of course I had to quit living with my wife. I have related elsewhere the many places June and I lived at and the people we were beholden to.

It must have been soon after the divorce that June began to press me to give up the job with the telegraph company and start writing. The idea was that she would provide the necessities in one way or another. And so, one day, I did just that. I quit the telegraph company and swore that henceforth I would be a writer and nothing else.

I won't attempt to recount my struggles here. Suffice it to say, they were Gargantuan and never-ending. Finally came the day when, alone and penniless, we faced the grim reality that we had failed. What was worse, we were hungry. We were kicked out of the place we lived in. To this day I don't know what impelled me to do so but I thought of Stanley as my last resort. I had never borrowed a cent from him nor he from me. I knew I couldn't ask him for money—but perhaps he could put us up for a week or so until one of us found something to do. With that in mind I dragged June along to see Stanley. They had never met and, strangely enough, Stanley had never expressed the least desire to meet this woman with whom I had become so infatuated. I was a little uneasy about their meeting—they were at opposite poles.

Fortunately June seemed to appeal to Stanley's chivalrous side. He was overgenerous. He decided to give us the mattress off his bed so that we could lie on the floor in the parlor. His wife and he would sleep in the springs.

It was understood, to be sure, that June and I would diligently look for work and leave as soon as possible. Though it was a bit awkward, a bit uncomfortable, things went all right for the first few days.

Usually June and I left in the morning together—to look for work. Shameless though it sounds, I must confess neither of us ever did look for work. She sought out her friends and I mine. We were lazy and inconsiderate, and what is worse—ungrateful. It's this I feel bad about, even today, some fifty years later.

Fortunately, things didn't last long at this rate.

In some unknown way Stanley discovered that we were doing nothing. One evening, when we both arrived together, Stanley simply said: "The game's up. Pack your things and I'll take you to the subway." That was all. No display of temper, no histrionics. He had found us out and he was through with us.

Shamefacedly we packed our things, said good-bye to his wife

33

and kids, and followed him down the stairs. (It seemed to me that I detected a grin on his wife's face during these proceedings.)

At the subway station Stanley handed me a dime, shook hands and said good-bye. We scuttled down the steps, took the first train that came along and then looked at one another blankly. Where would we go now? At what station would we get off? I let June decide.

That was the last of Stanley. I never saw or heard from him since. The last episode has left a nasty scar in my memory. I was guilty of doing something one ought never do, especially to a friend. And Stanley was my first friend. No, I have never forgiven myself for my shameless behavior, for my betrayal of a friend. What became of Stanley I don't really know. I heard in a roundabout way that he had gone blind, and that he had put his sons through college—and that's all.

His life must have been a very dreary, lonely one. I'm sure he hadn't much interest in his wife. I know he hated his job of printer. And I am sure he never had the least luck with his writings. What I might have done for Stanley is a question, since I was never able to help myself. But I had Fortune on my side. Time and again, when all seemed hopeless, I was rescued, most often by a perfect stranger. Stanley had no one working for him, least of all the gods.

Joey and Tony

Just to say their names makes me think
of the Golden Age. Unfortunate the man who has never known
a Golden Age. I am still in that period between seven and twelve.
Living now in a new neighborhood, on Decatur Street in the
Bushwick Section. "The Street of Early Sorrows" I dubbed it
later. But at this time I am not too unhappy. To go to Glendale, a
suburb of Brooklyn, with my mother and sister, was an event-a
joyous one. We could walk to their home in an hour's time. For
us it meant walking into the country. For me it was my first
contact with nature—and with art.

John Imhof, the father of Joey and Tony, was an artist. He
made watercolors (usually at night when every one had gone to
bed) and he also made stained glass windows for the little
churches in the vicinity. How my parents became acquainted

with the Imhofs I don't know. Probably through the "Saenger-bund" (Singing Society) where they made so many friends.

When I think of these two little friends now they scarcely seem real to me. They were more like something out of a child's book. They had qualities none of us city boys possessed. For one thing, they were always bright and gay, always full of enthusiasm, always discovering things. They talked a different language than we others. They talked birds, flowers, frogs, snakes, pigeon eggs. They knew where to look for birds' nests. They raised chickens, ducks, pigeons, and they were at home with them.

They always had something new, something interesting, to show me on my arrival. Perhaps they had acquired a peacock, or else another puppy, or an old billy goat. Always something live and warm.

The moment I arrived I had to accompany them—either to see some new nest eggs or the new stained glass window theirfather had just made. I was at that time totally uninterested in stained glass windows and watercolors. I never dreamed that one day I too would be sitting up until all hours of the night making watercolors. Anyway, John Imhof was the first artist to appear in my life. I can rcall hearing my father pronounce the word artist. He was very proud of his friend John Imhof. And every time I heard the word a commotion took place inside me. I hadn't the slightest conception of what it meant. I only know that the word "art" did something to me. By contrast, Tony and Joey were already familiar with the names of the great religious painters and they had big, heavy books in which the works of these painters were shown. Thus from an early age I knew such names as Giotto, Cimabue, Fra Angelico and such like. Sometimes, to tease Stanley, I would reel off these names.

The Imhofs were Catholics. And so I became familiar with the names of the saints as well as the great painters. I often accompanied Tony and Joey to church. I must confess I didn't like the atmosphere of the Catholic Church. Nor was I able to believe any of the doctrine which they tried to impart. I particularly disliked the portraits they kept at home of the Virgin Mary, of John The Baptist, and of Jesus who died for us hanging on the cross. All this was terribly morbid to me.

Even as a youngster the Christian religion never meant a thing to me. It reeked of the grave. It spoke of evil, sin, punishment. It was morbid and death-like. I never derived peace or joy from it. On the contrary, it often filled me with terror, especially the Catholic faith. The confessional was a huge joke to me. A hoax, a fraud. No, everything about the church seemed made for nitwits.

However, I soon noticed that my little friends didn't take these things to heart. They weren't born Catholics, so to speak, such as you would find in Spain, Sicily or Ireland. They could just as well have been Turks.

This Glendale was just a tiny village, bordered on one side by a golf links and on the other by two Catholic cemeteries. Between these lay a valley which we never penetrated. It was more like a No Man's Land. The streets were wide and flanked by huge shade trees. Every house was fenced. At the corner of their street lived the Rogers family, consisting of an ailing aunt and a young man in his late teens who was to my friends what Lester Reardon and Eddie Carney were to me. This Rogers lad was on his way to becoming a golf champion. My little friends were only too honored to caddy for him. Myself, even to this day I have never had the least interest in golf. I don't understand the game any more than I do football.

There were so many things I didn't understand, it seems to me. By comparison, Tony and Joey were extremely sophisticated. They took a delight in opening my eyes.

I have always envied those born in the country. They learn the essentials of life so much more quickly. If life is hard for them it is also healthier. From the city boy's point they may seem retarded but they are not. Their interests are different, that's all.

37

Until I met Joey and Tony I had never held a bird in my two hands, never knew what it was to feel the warmth and the trembling of a tiny live creature. With my friends I soon learned to handle mice and snakes. Nor was I afraid when a goose would go after me.

Just doing nothing was such a wonderful treat. To lie in the sweet smelling grass on warm earth and watch the clouds drift or the birds wheel overhead. The days were mapped out for us, to be sure, but there was always plenty of time between chores to laze around.

There were bizarre characters in this community. One man, named Fuchs, I believe, was what my friends called a "hundski" picker. That meant he went about all day with a shortened broomstick on the end of which was fastened a spike with which he gathered dog turds. He carried these turds in a sack on his back and when he had a sufficient supply he brought them to a perfume factory where he was well paid for his efforts. He spoke a strange language, this Mr. Fuchs. Of course he was a bit light in the head. He knew it too. That's what made his antics more droll. He was a devout Catholic and was forever blessing himself or muttering a "Hail Mary." He tried to get us to work for him but we couldn't see it. As for work, there were plenty of odd jobs my friends could take. They were never at a loss for pin money. Usually they gave half their earnings to their mother.

It wasn't long before I detected something amiss between father and mother. Mrs. Imhof, it was obvious to all, had begun to hit the bottle. Her breath was always boozy, her steps uncertain. She would do silly things too, which one could not help but notice. The conversation between her and her husband was indeed limited. Usually he was complaining that things were going to hell. And they were. Fortunately, there were two other members of the family who did their best to help—Minnie, the elder daughter and Gertrude, who was about my age.

Why the sudden rift between these two who had been married a good twenty years was uncertain. The boys maintained their father was in love with an old sweetheart in Germany who had begun writing him letters. They said he had even threatened to leave them and go to Germany to live with his sweetheart. (Which is exactly what he did do a few years later.)

Usually the father retired fairly early. He did not go to sleep immediately. He made watercolors by the light of a student lamp. We had to pass through his room (on tip toe) to go to our bedroom. It always gave me a holy feeling to see Mr. Imhof bent over a pad of paper with a brush or two in his hand. He seemed not to be aware of our presence.

Evenings after dinner we usually played chess. Joey and Tony were quite good at the game; they had been taught by their father. More than the game I liked the chess pieces themselves. They were elaborate and expensive—from China, I believe. I have played the game at intervals all my life but never succeeded in becoming a good player. For one thing I lacked the necessary patience. For another I was too reckless. It didn't matter to me whether I won or lost. I enjoyed the beauty of the moves— aesthetics rather than strategy.

Sometimes my friends permitted me to read to them from my books. I hadn't lost the habit. Generally they fell asleep before I had gone very far. Next morning they would ask me innocently to tell them what I was trying to read to them the night before.

Near the city limits of Glendale, near the German-American section of Brooklyn called Ridgewood, was a place called Laubscher's. It was a huge beer hall, with pool tables and bowling alleys, and plenty of parking space for horses and buggies. There was always an arresting aroma of stale beer, horse piss, horse manure and other pungent odors. This is where the elders congregated once a week—to sing, to dance, to guzzle it. We were always taken along and once there left to our own resources. I must say they were jolly evenings, unlike anything we know of today. They loved to sing—in chorus. And to dance. At that time

39

the waltz was the favorite dance. But they danced all the other dances too—the polka, the schottische. And the square dances. These were something to behold.

While all this activity was going on we were raising hell on our own. Many was the half-empty glass of beer we polished off. It was an excellent place to play cops and robbers, for instance. And with all the running and sweating, it did us no harm to consume as much beer as we did. Sometimes we would set up the pins in the bowling alley—for free—because we felt good. That usually earned us some change and some good turkey sandwiches. All in all these were marvelous weekends, with the entire family walking home (or reeling) and singing at the top of our lungs.

I often wondered as we passed the Rogers' house (which was by no means a mansion) if we were not in danger of waking old Mrs. Rogers. About the singing—the songs they sang on these occasions—I mean the coming-away songs—were familiar to everyone.

I suppose the one most frequently sung was *"Wien, Wien, mur du alleinn..."* Even today, if I am in the right mood, that is mildly intoxicated, grossly sentimental, thoroughly mellow and in love with the world, tears fill my eyes. I become what my friend Alf always nicknamed me—*"un pleurnicheur."*

There are certain American folk tunes which have the same effect on me—notably Stephen Foster's songs. No one, it seems to me, can sing "Way Down Upon the Swanee River" or "My Old Kentucky Home" with dry eyes. I should add another, one composed by Theodore Dreiser's brother—"On the Banks of the Wabash Far Away." Paul Dressler was the name his brother adopted, and a most lovable character he was.

For some reason the mention of these songs reminds me of the music class in the high school I attended. The teacher, Barney O'Donnell, was a jovial Irishman in his sixties, who made no attempt to teach us music. He simply sat down at the piano, ran through a few keys in his own inimitable way, looked up and said—"What'll it be this morning?" This meant we could choose whatever we liked to sing. And sing we did—with heart and lungs. It was the best day of the week for us. We were always grateful we had Barney O'Donnell with us. Between songs he taught us a few Irish (Gaelic) phrases, such as *"Faugh a balla!"* (Clear the way) or *"Erin go bragh!"* (Ireland Forever). If only the other subjects could have been taught us in this light-hearted fashion! Perhaps then we would have retained some of that deadly knowledge they were trying to teach us and which most of us were unable to swallow.

In those days nearly every home seemed to sport a guitar. Even my mother, who had little music or poetry in her veins, had learned to play the guitar. At an early age I was taught to play the zither. On these weekends I can still recall the strange old woman, gypsy-like, who sat in a corner of the big beer parlor, strumming the guitar or zither. And always a glass of beer beside her. The songs she sang were anything but gay. But she seemed to be appreciated. Her voice was dark and throaty and the expression on her face as she sang was one of utmost sadness. People would stop and listen, shake their heads, and offer her another drink. Years later, in Vienna, I saw her double. She was seated in a little cafe', scantily clad, shivering with the cold. And looking fit for the grave. But when she played the zither it was unforgettable. All this to say that at the Imhofs they had both a guitar and a zither, which no one played.

Joey and Tony were almost the same age, Tony being the younger. Tony, even at that early age, had something of the priest about him. (Later in life he was to become one.) He was forever telling us not to do this, not to do that, or that he would tell the Father (meaning the priest) of our immoral conduct. We all three slept in one big bed. Joey and I had acquired the habit of buggering one another. We thought nothing of it, but to "Turk," as we had nicknamed Tony, we were committing a grievous sin. Sometimes we tried to bugger him, but it was useless—he was incorruptible.

41

There was another thing I was guilty of at bedtime. Next to our bed slept their elder sister Minnie, who was several years older than any of us. When we thought she had fallen asleep I would sneak out of bed, pull the covers off her, and raise her nightgown so that we could have a good look at her quim. She always threatened to tell my mother the next day but never did. This too, of course, was an unholy deed in Tony's eyes. No matter how much we twitted and teased him about his Puritanical attitude we could never shake him. If there is such a thing as a born priest then Tony was one.

Finally Mr. Imhof did up and leave for Germany, to the dismay and complete puzzlement of my mother. "He was such a good man, such a fine man," she kept repeating. "How could he do such a thing? How could he leave his children like that?" Obviously it never occurred to her that there was a powerful force in live called love and that in the name of it people did strange and unpredictable things.

At any rate, it wasn't long after their father had flown the coop that the family moved to Bensonhurst where they occupied a much larger house with ample grounds about it. How this happened, how they were able to make such a change, I never found out. Perhaps Mr. Imhof hadn't been such a bad one as people imagined. Perhaps he had left some money behind so that they would not be in want.

The new place was a delight. Now they could really fend for themselves. They had chickens, geese, ducks, pigs and more pigeons of course. Also dogs and cats. In the yard was a big skup. There was room for a tennis court as well, but no one knew anything about tennis. They had plenty of vegetables and beautiful flower beds. In a way Mr. Imhof's going was a windfall. The two daughters were bitter about their father's behavior and absolutely unforgiving. But not Tony and Joey. They took his departure as a matter of course. Joey even said he would have done the same thing had he been in his father's shoes. Minnie, the elder daughter, was as I said before, a few years older than us. She was a rather homely girl, and none too bright. It wasn't long before she fell for the wiles of a young Polish fellow who soon made her pregnant. This was another calamity. I remember the day the boys told me about it. They made no recriminations against her Polish boy friend. He was a decent sort, they said, but not serious. He had refused to marry Minnie. He said she had no proof that it was his kid she was carrying under her belt. Anyone who knew Minnie knew this was untrue, that Minnie couldn't possibly carry on with more than one man at a time. So eventually the child was born—out of wedlock—and accepted as a member of the family.

The younger daughter, Gertrude, was totally different from any of the family. She was very good-looking, healthy, alive to the fingertips and extremely respectable. As soon as she was able she went to work and became the main support of the family. As I grew older I became more and more attracted to her. I mistook her curiosity for intelligence, her liveliness for full-bloodedness. I had only to go out with her once or twice—to the theatre or a dance—to realize that she was not all the creature I had believed her to be. As a matter of fact, I quarreled violently with her and eventually grew to despise her. If her brother Tony had the makings of a priest, she had the makings of a nun, or rather a Mother Superior. Beneath the glamour she was cold as ice, unforgiving, uncharitable, and downright stupid. What became of her I don't remember, but I assume she married and had children.

But in those early days when we visited the Imhofs in Bensonhurst all went relatively smoothly. The boys had part-time jobs, the family lacked for nothing, and we did pretty much as we wanted to. A short distance away, by trolley, was an unforgetable place called Ulmer Park, where there was an outdoor theatre; the audience sat at little tables in the sunshine and ate and drank during the performances. My mother had begun

43

taking me to this wonderful spot when I was still quite young. It made a tremendous and lasting impression on me. For here, in this out of the way corner of the world, came the famous stars of Europe—clowns, trick cyclists, slack wire men, trapeze artists, opera singers, magicians, acrobats, comedians, tightrope walkers and so on. Later in life I wondered how it was that my mother had the sense to take me to such a place. Here I heard Irene Franklin sing "Redhead."

And not far from this place was another equally unforgettable place—Sheepshead Bay. Here in a cove many boats of all kinds were anchored. But the principal attraction of the place was the wonderful fish restaurants. Here one could always get oysters on the half shell, raw clams, clam chowder, soft shell crabs, and every variety of fresh water and sea fish imaginable. Not so many years later, when I was miserably in love and seemed abandoned by all my friends, I would take to my bike first thing in the morning and ride and ride until I was exhausted. I called my bike my only friend. If it were possible I suppose I would have slept with it. But the point is that there were only a few years between the happy, carefree days with Joey and Tony and these present miserable, almost unbearable ones. All because of a girl. All because she didn't return my love. And so, setting forth on the bike I would often find myself in Bensonhurst, Ulmer Park or Coney Island. Only now all was different. I was alone, forlorn, of no use to the world or myself.

In Bensonhurst I could no longer find the place where the Imhofs once lived. Where had they gone? Meanwhile Mr. Imhof had died—in Germany. I am sure his sons took it with their usual equanimity. It was my mother who made a fuss over his death, weeping crocodile tears and muttering to herself what a good man he was, that it never should have happened to him, and so on. After a time, I learned in a roundabout way that both boys had become letter carriers. After a few years Tony quit to become a priest in some distant parish but Joey remained to become superintendent of the post office he worked in. He also married a school teacher, much to my surprise.

The last time I saw him was some ten or fifteen years later. It was during those desperate days with June. I visited him to borrow what I could. He was the same old Joey, the same good friend. He gave me ten dollars and said I could forget about paying it back. I had expected to receive more but was thankful for this much. Hadn't one of my good friends handed me a nickel when I asked him for subway fare? I was getting to the point where pennies counted. Soon I would become an out and out panhandler. I had lost all pride. It was solely a matter of survival.

Cousin Henry

He was like the King of 85th Street
(Manhattan) and I was like the Prince of the 14th Ward (Brooklyn). Every summer our parents arranged that we stay two or three weeks at one home or the other.

My cousin Henry was anything but a king by nature, yet he commanded respect and the obedience of the boys in his neighborhood. It was through him that I first realized I must be different from the other boys, perhaps even a genius, though I showed no aptitude for creativeness as a writer, painter, actor. But I *was different*. Something about me, even at that early age, elicited the admiration and the loyalty of other boys my age.

When Cousin Henry announced to his cronies that Henry Miller would be arriving next week it took on the importance of a State visit. I was an emissary from another world. I had something different to offer. Besides, we were blood cousins, and that carried weight.

I can see myself arriving of a summer's day and being gradually introduced to all the members of the gang, each one a unique character, in my estimation. I wondered what was so different about myself as to win their instant favor. One thing I noticed almost immediately was the way they hung on my words. It was as if I spoke another language which they could only dimly understand but which enchanted them. Aware of this, I was fearful lest they take me for a little gentleman. Nothing was more unthinkable in this neighborhood than a "gentleman." There were simply no such animals about. (Suddenly I thought of one of my boyhood idols, Lester Reardon, who had the air of a young lion—an *aristocratic* young lion. I wondered how he would fare with these young hoodlums.)

My Cousin Henry, as I started to say, had nothing of the king about him. Already, at that early age, a melancholy aura hung about him. He was very quiet, withdrawn and introspective. In my presence he seemed to come alive—he even looked happy at times.

It was through Counsin Henry that I first became aware of the other sex. I had hardly arrived when he introduced me to a charming young creature whom they all called "Weesie" (after Louise, I suppose). She was presented to me as if to say—"Here, here's something nice for you. Have a good time together." It was all done so naturally, so matter of factly, that I failed to be embarrassed. I immediately assumed the role I was supposed to play. There were other girls besides Weesie, of course, but Weesie was like the Queen of the harem.

In those days summertime was different than today. For one thing, I believe it was actually hotter then now. One sought the shade, whether a cool room or the cellar of a building. One made ice-cold drinks of all kinds. And, willy nilly, one became more sensual, more passionate, more eager to explore. And the girls were not averse to such explorations. I had difficulty at first suppressing my reactions. Everything here happened too easily, too naturally. Of course, I didn't know what moral and immoral meant—I never heard those words at home or on the street—but I could recognize the difference between one kind of behavior and another. However, when in Rome do as the Romans. Which I did, to everyone's delight. The situation was rendered more strange—*and* more delightful—by reason of the fact that where I came from the two sexes occupied separate worlds. No one thought of girls as something different. Except for those little intermissions in the cellar—as with Jenny Payne—no one seemed the least concerned about sex. We might enjoy watching the monkeys hump one another in the zoo, but there it ended. Sex was more of a healthy, pleasurable sport. As for love, it was something utterly unknown to us.

Summertime. A glorious time, despite the flies, the mosquitoes, the cockroaches. The street seemed wide open, like a corpse just dissected. It was a perfect setting, what with the relatives and friends hanging out of their windows, usually only half dressed. Take my father's sister, for example—Aunt Carrie. A good-natured slut who was a little too fond of her beer. She was a most easygoing creature, loose with her tongue, and content to gossip from morning till night. My mother looked upon her with open disgust. Indeed, my mother looked upon the whole neighborhood as a bed of sin—and what was worse, as unclean. Idlers were something new to her. And women who drank. No, she did know one or two who drank, but their drinking was done in secret. You might well imagine my mother saying to herself—"If one has to go to the dogs one should do it in as refined a way as possible."

But 85th Street was neither refined nor secretive. Everythng was out in the open. That's why it appealed to me. Add to this that there was an air of sophistication which was unknown in the 14th Ward.

I should have explained that my father had three married sisters living in this street—he himself came from one of those houses.

It was only in this vacation time that he ever saw his sisters. My mother wouldn't dream of inviting them to our house. Later on I got to thinking of his sisters as belonging to Tchekov's gallery of characters. They were kind, gentle, sympathetic, but poorly equipped educationally. Their husbands were not much better. One of them, Uncle Dave, to whom I later became greatly attached, could not even sign his own name. Yet he was a born American, a baker by trade. His wife, Aunt Amelia, another sister, was most lovable. Unfortunately, she was to die of cancer at an early age. They all seemed to be afflicted with incurable diseases, yet they maintained a joyous air, were fond of coarse jokes and loved the little things of life. Beer cost practically nothing in those days and was consumed in great quantities—without anyone seeming to be too drunk. They drank because they were thirsty and because the beer tasted good. They never drank just to get drunk, nor to drown their sorrows.

My Uncle Henry was my cousin Henry's father. A big, hulk of a man, with a thick Germanic accent, he sat around most of the time in his fireman's wool undershirt. With the "growler" in front of him, to be sure. My mother found him too absolutely disgusting. It's true he had no manners, but then what use was there for manners in such a place? He had been my father's boon companion when they were young men. That's how he happened to marry one of my father's sisters, I guess. To see these two men side by side now one wondered how there had ever been anything between them. Strangely enough, it was the theatre which had enchanted them both. They had seen the greatest actors and actresses from abroad in their time. They even enjoyed Shakespeare when played by renowned artists. It was in the evenings, seated about the table, that I caught snatches of their adventurous lives. To me it opened up a New

49

York which was glamorous and romantic. A filthy street like 14th Street now became an avenue of importance, full of color and of great names. One felt the affinity which then existed between Europe and America. Immigrants were still pouring in in great numbers and many were becoming rich or famous. All the names which we look back upon nostalgically were then living idols. One could encounter them in the flesh in any bar or saloon or in the lobby of a hotel such as the Waldorf.

Because of his size, his hairiness, his usually unshaved condition, Uncle Henry looked comically fierce. He was, of course, tender as a lamb, and the way he spoke to his son was a revelation to me. The impression I got was that Cousin Henry was something very precious and one could not do enough for him. In some ways Cousin Henry resembled me. At any rate, we understood one another thoroughly. Nothing he said or proposed ever surprised me. He was a strange boy for his age. I mean, he behaved like a man and always seemed to act reasonably. He seldom laughed or told jokes. To him I was something of a phenomenon. He could not get over the fact that I was a great reader. I always brought my favorite books along and, at the first favorable opportunity, I would read aloud for them. The results were usually disastrous. One by one my listeners fell asleep. Some snored heavily. But I did not seem to mind. I continued reading, probably for myself now.

In those days I could reread a book a dozen times if it interested me. I was familiar with stories from the Bible, Aesop's Fables, Aladdin's Lamp, Homer's Illiad and Odyssey, and such like literature. It was very familiar stuff to me, required no effort to read. Why others didn't instantly like it always mystified me. Robin Hood and Helen of Troy were like intimate friends. I found I had to do a lot of explaining when reading these things to my little friends. They always wanted to know why or why not. Very vexing questions.

The girls who listened, on the other hand, seemed to be

enchanted. I rose a few inches in their estimation because of this predilection of mine. The other boys, apparently, fed on the cheap magazines for boys, such as Nick Carter, Buffalo Bill and so on. Myself, I was never able to read one of these magazines. They had nothing to offer me.

Among all his peculiar friends there was one fat fellow whom I will call Louie and who, for some strange reason, reminds me now of one of Herman Hesse's unforgettable characters. Louie, however unprepossessing in appearance, somehow exerted a charm to which no one was immune. His talk was suave and smooth, rather above people's heads, his manner absolutely bland, his curiosity about even the most trifling things, absolutely enormous. He seemed to know about everything and to be happy in dispensing his knowledge. With it all he was extremely modest and humble. One regarded him as a walking encyclopedia. Like babes, we fed at his breast. He was also somewhat psychic, this Louie. For example, after stunning us with his account of life on the lost Atlantis, he might suddenly turn to one of the boys, point a finger at him, and warn him to take good care of himself because he felt there was a good likelihood of the boy getting pneumonia a few days hence. Or he would predict a great fire somewhere, which later events would prove true.

Despite these abilities Louie was very much a child still. To offer him a piece of candy or a piece of cake made him very happy. All that was needed to round out the picture was to put a balloon in his hand. But that may also have changed his character, for Louie was many-sided. With a balloon in one hand and a stick of candy in the other Louie might easily have been transformed into a child murderer. It should also be remembered that Louie was one thing with us and quite another with grown-ups. Like so many angelic types, there was something sinister about Louie, about his ability to please and to deceive his elders. The worst I ever heard about him, to be sure, was his obsession for strangling cats.

51

One night Cousin Henry asked me if the noise kept me awake. "What noise?" I said.

"There's a crazy man in the next street who comes home drunk every night and beats his wife up. You can hear her for blocks around."

"I've never heard anything," I said. "Good." Pause. "O, Henry," he began, "I wanted to tell you something. Weesie told me to tell you that she leaves the door of her room unlocked. She's hoping you'll pay her a visit some night."

"I didn't think it was as serious as all that," I said, not knowing what to do or say.

Cousin Henry now proceeded to tell me how to reach her room, which was a rather elaborate affair. I said I would visit her immediately.

Just as he had said, her door was ajar. A faint light came from the interior. I opened the door and walked in on tip toes. Weesie greeted me from a dark corner where her bed was. She spoke in a natural tone of voice, as if to assure me that there was nothing to fear.

I advanced slowly and timidly to her bedside. She put on a soft light and sat up in bed.

"You wanted me to come?" I said.

"Of course," she replied. "I've been waiting to see you for days. I want to talk to you—about many things."

These last words reassured me. If it was only talk she wanted I could provide plenty of that.

"Henry," she began, "you're so different from the others. I fell in love with you before I ever met you. Your cousin Henry has told me a great deal about you. He worships you, you know."

I didn't know, but I nodded affirmatively.

Weesie continued. "I'm a little older than you, that's what makes it easy for me to talk to you freely. I feel you could teach me things. Some of the books you mention, I would love to read them. No one around here reads such stuff."

I was embarrassed, yet not too much so. I had never been placed in such an exalted position before. The strange thing was it was a girl I was talking to. A few years later, after I had been studying the piano, I would astound her with my ability. Now it was words—only words I had at my disposal. I must have told her a lot of rubbish, but it pleased her. She said if I felt like it, I could get in bed with her and talk all night. I didn't know how to interpret this. I thought it better to remain outside the bed. She didn't seem to care which way it went. That made me still more comfortable—and loquacious. I was waxing strong when all of a sudden there came a loud noise from an adjoining room. It was her mother. We decided I had better go. I gave her a quick kiss and found my way back to my room.

I didn't wonder much about the event, strangely enough. Living with Cousin Henry nothing ever totally surprised me. I knew, of course, that from now on there was a secret bond between Weesie and me. I thought vaguely that maybe I would marry her one day.

The following day was a blistering one. We awoke in an atmosphere as if all the ovens were turned on. One by one we instinctively assembled in Cousin Henry's cellar, the coolest spot in the house. We came equipped with marbles and tops and dice. We also had greasy packs of playing cards. Anything to pass the time. It was the girl's task to make cool, delectable drinks. And to keep out of sight as much as possible.

This morning Weesie greeted me with an extra warm smile and a hug. I was aware for the first time that the dress she wore clung to her figure. It was made of a very soft material, very feminine, which women seldom wear. To my genuine surprise, she said, as she pulled away from me—"I don't want you to answer me immediately. Tomorrow or the next day will do. What I would like to know is what you think about God. Do you believe there is one? Do you like him? Don't tell me what they told you in church—I know all that crap. Tell me what you yourself honestly think. Do that for me, won't you?"

The hot sultry air, the way her dress clung to her body, the taste of her lips, all combined to give her words another connotation. It was a most unusual question, in any event, and especially from a girl her age. It was the first time the subject had come up since those days with Stanley and I talked on his doorstep in the evenings.

What I started to say was that in posing this million dollar question Weesie seemed to be really saying—"It's so damned hot today, why don't we take our clothes off and make love? I've been wanting you to fuck me ever since you arrived. But you always seem to have more important things on your mind."

How can I explain this seeming indifference on my part? Was it simply that I was too young or was it an aspect of that quality of being "different"? Or was it just a natural purity? I am baffled to explain it, as I look back on it. It wasn't that Weesie was unattractive or lacking in seduction. She wore very few clothes, no panties, and was forever exposing herself. Maybe she should have been another two or three years older than she was. There was no question but that the difference in age counted. Had she been twenty or twenty-one the whole picture might be different. But she wasn't. Besides, had she been that much older she wouldn't have been playing with us in the cellar.

I make no mention of the other girls. Each of the gang seemed to have a girl of his own. To me they were dull and decidedly uninteresting.

At that time the neighborhood was definitely Germanic, with a scattered Bohemian contingency living on the margin. There were plenty of saloons, restaurants, pool parlors and dance halls. I doubt there were any brothels. It was an eminently respectable neighborhood, coarse and vulgar in many ways, but respectable nevertheless.

One difference between Henry's life and mine was that he attended no church. His parents had no use for religion and

Cousin Henry was left to decide for himself. When he came to visit me I took him with me to Sunday School. He was extremely interested, surprised how free and easy it was. What also pleased him was the burlesque house, which of course neither of us attended. But we did go to the Vaudeville Theatre Saturday matinees. The theatre was something unknown to him and he was at home in it immediately. What he also liked was to roam the streets with me. They were quite different from those in his own neighborhood and they had a strange fascination for him.

I forgot to mention a little incident at the Presbyterian Church I took him to. The minister of this church was English and well off. Rather aristocratic and definitely condescending. As we were leaving that afternoon he suddenly came up to us and asked who our friend was. I told him. "And what denomination does he belong to?" he asked genially. "To none," I promptly replied. "He's an atheist."

"An atheist, is he," repeated the minister. "Well, we'll have to do something about that," and laughing to himself he strode off.

Cousin Henry was furious. First, he thanked me for being honest with the minister. But then he let loose his venom because of the off-hand way in which the minister had received the news of his being an atheist. To Cousin Henry being an atheist was almost the same as being an anarchist. You didn't take anarchists lightly, nor atheists either. This was a side of my cousin I had never seen before and it raised him in my esteem. As for myself, there was nothing I cared deeply about.

What pleased Cousin Henry most was Mrs. O'Melio and her cats. Like Stanley, he had a great respect for a woman who would give so much of her time and attention to these creatures. He was equally fascinated by the veterinarian below Mrs. O'Melio. He could stand for hours watching the doctor castrate a stallion. These were things which simply did not exist in his neighborhood. He said it was a pity Louie wasn't along. Louie would appreciate such things.

It seems as if there were more shops, more fruit stands, more bakeries in my neighborhood. And I was on speaking terms with all of them, including Mr. Daly who owned the fish market. Now and then he would throw me a few heads of fish he was cleaning, saying—"Here, give them to that Mrs. O'Melio women for her cats."

Gradually it dawned on me that there was one thing I didn't have to worry about—work. Already, they were talking of fixing up Cousin Henry in the pipe-case factory where his father worked. One would never suspect that this big, gross man, his father, could turn out such beautiful and delicate pipe cases. Of course it was a period when pipes were in vogue, not cigarettes. The meerschaum pipe especially, which improved in color from smoking. (I remember receiving one, and prizing it, for my 21st birthday.)

I had another Uncle Henry who also worked in a factory, was also a big, heavy man, and did delicate work. This uncle made tooth-picks which were carried on one's watch chain. They were either of gold or pearl-handled, and rather expensive.

Both businesses reflected the manners of the day—the solid bourgeois, cheap in his tastes, flashy, ultra-respectable.

There were things about my Cousin Henry I found difficult to understand. His attachment for, or affection, if you like, for Alfie Melta. Alfie, as I have said before, was a born liar, a sneak, a sadist and a coward. Henry seemed fascinated by his ability to become a gang leader. He was right. A little later Alfie would become a gangster, a rather notorious one, and remain in the limelight until cut down, stabbed to death by another gang leader, who in turn would be shot to death in some dark alley. It's curious, this gang business. As simple as North and South. A kid has no choice. He's either for or against. He either does or he doesn't. *He's got to belong,* that's the imperative thing. Nor does he do the choosing. He has to choose the side he's born on, whether good or bad. Why there must be a North and a South is a matter

56

of climate and different ways of life. Inevitable, you might say. And so, from early on, a guy is taught to love and hate, to kill what he doesn't like.

If Alfie was nothing to brag about neither were many of the others. My idols were exceptions, rare birds indeed in a corrupt world. And what saddened me a bit, though I never showed it, was that Cousin Henry never seemed to notice these idols of mine, never questioned me about them. How could he overlook Johnny Paul?

In both neighborhoods we had the same sort of material—dumbbells, morons, idiots, lunatics, incipient gangsters, and here and there a potential leader. It wasn't so much the differences between us as the similarities which attracted.

There's where the girls proved better than us. They looked for individuals, not sheep of the same stripe. But it was almost impossible for a boy to achieve the freedom of a country, say, like Sweden or Switzerland, or even achieve the neutral attitude of a Luxembourg or a Lichtenstein. We were committed from birth. Political pawns, you might say, from which we developed into political monstrosities, accepting war, accepting corruption and buggery of every sort.

Every time I returned to visit Cousin Henry I was more conscious of the warmth with which I was received. There was no difference in the way his parents treated me from the way they treated him. All warmth and tenderness. Far different from the atmosphere in my home.

And then there were those wonderful slices of rye bread with rich sweet butter and sugar which his mother handed us when we came home from play. She did it as if we were two little angels. Never did she suspect, sweet innocent creature, what her two "good little boys" were capable of. Never would she have believed that we two had killed a boy in a gang rock fight. No, we looked just the same as ever that day, or perhaps a little paler, for we were conscious of the crime we had committed. For days we

57

trembled if there was an unexpected knock at the door. The police were constantly on our minds. Fortunately none of the gang knew we were responsible for the killing. We were intelligent enough to keep our mouths shut. Besides, it was an accident and not a deliberate killing. As soon as it happened we had sneaked away. We didn't feel very heroic about it either.

But when I think of my Aunt Anna, her good homely face, all pock-marked from the small-pox, I realize that she was indeed what one calls a "pure" human being. I am sure that if we had told her what had happened she would have forgiven us immediately and shielded and protected us.

Now with my own mother it was quite different. I could never fool her, though I tried many times. I think from an early age she recognized that her son had a touch of evil in him, that he was capable of doing unthinkable things, things which she preferred not to bring to the forefront of her mind. She was a "respectable" woman. Everybody conceded that. Respectability! How I hated that word! Not that it was mentioned much. But it was there, in the atmosphere, poisoning all my thoughts and deeds.

As I look back I wonder—did those respectable elders of ours really believe that we swallowed all that shit they crammed down our throats? Did they really think we were so stupid, so naive, so unobservant? Even in short pants I could read their minds. I didn't have to grow up to become a psychologist to realize that they were handing us nothing but bullshit and that they, being stronger and in power, bullied us into accepting their lies. Some were such obvious liars, such obvious hypocrites! One had to blush for them. And then the pious ones—who only punished you for your own good! What shit that was!

Yes, each time I returned the reception was warmer. Weesie was developing into a real woman. She was filling out. Her breasts were just right. And she had hair under her arms as well as between her legs.

Occasionally we would go to the Carl Schurz Park nearby, sit on a bench or on the grass, and discuss some of those fundamental questions she loved to put to me. I could answer them better in her room, with one hand between her legs. She was lascivious, Weesie, and loved to be fondled. And she always wore such tempting garments, especially that tulle dress I mentioned earlier which clung to her body like a drape.

Weesie wasn't preparing for any higher education any more than my Cousin Henry. It would not be long before she became a sales girl at the Five-and-Ten. She had a good mind, Weesie. It was a joy to discuss things with her. How she put up with the louts who formed Cousin Henry's circle of friends I don't know. Like so many of the denizens of this neighborhood she was blessed or cursed with an easygoing disposition. Things didn't matter too much one way or the other. Had it not been that I was very shortly to meet my first love I think I might have fallen deeply in love with Weesie. But with the advent of Cora Seward it was impossible for me to look at another girl.

I doubt that I visited my Cousin Henry any longer after entering high school. As I said, his parents were not concerned about higher education. What they needed was an extra breadwinner. And by the time he graduated from elementary school, Henry was just that. There was no trouble finding him a job in his father's factory. Business was good momentarily. And so, like his father, Henry got himself a lunch box and a thermos bottle. They traveled to work together and came home together. I never heard Henry complain that the job was dull or boring or the hours too long. To me the situation was almost incomprehensible. It was as if he had chosen to go to prison voluntarily. But they were all doing it, in my neighborhood as well as chez Cousin Henry. It was like joining the Army. When the time comes you sign up. No questions.

I must have seen Henry now only at rare intervals—it's all very dim in my memory. I heard about him through a mutual cousin who lived in the same house.

After a few years he married, had two children and moved to the suburbs on Long Island. It was a miserable, God-forsaken place, depressing, morbid, ugly. Here misfortune began to assail him. I did not know how bad it was until I visited him one day. My visit was an act of desperation. We were broke again, June and I. And I had exhausted all the friends I could think of. Then one morning Henry's image came to mind. He had a job, he must have a little dough to spare, thought I. But I was wrong. He was out of work, the factory had closed down. Add to that, that only a few months before, his wife had died. He himself seemed to be in very poor condition.

I sat and listened to his tale of woe. Tears poured down my cheeks as I listened. He was so abjectly helpless. There was no one he could appeal to for help. His friends seemed to have evaporated. There were no more pipe-case factories in operation. People had given up pipe cases along with beautiful pipes.

I had come to borrow a few cents. A quarter would have helped. But he was penniless and I felt guilty for thinking of begging from him. I should have gone home and borrowed money for him, hook or crook. But I too was up against a stone wall.

We left his house together, to walk to the train station. It was a dark, dreary lane, an utterly miserable place. We shook hands, pretended to smile, and said good-bye. And that was the last I saw of Cousin Henry.

Jimmy Pasta

In grammar school he was my only rival.
He was athletic-minded like myself, a serious student, and filled
with ambition. (He aimed to be President of the United States
one day—nothing less). The fact that his father was a cobbler
and an immigrant, from Sicily, I believe, only strengthened his
ambition. Besides, his old man loved him and would have made
any sacrifice for him.

We got along all right, Jimmy and I, but we were not what one
would call great friends. The one great friend I had during that
school period was Jack Lawton. But he died very early—at
twelve or thirteen—of rheumatism of the heart.

The reason our relationship was on the cool side was twofold.
Jimmy was a wop and a Catholic and I was a product of that one
hundred percent American white collar Protestant tribe which

seems to dominate America. Jimmy's friends were all of the lower or lowest class. They were all good fighters—some were already getting to be well-known in amateur boxing circles. But perhaps the thing I could least stand in Jimmy was his pride and ambition. He wanted to lead in everything. What's worse, he *believed* those myths and legends about our heroes. One could never convince him that George Washington was a real pain in the ass or that Thomas Jefferson had several children by his Negro slaves.

The teachers, of course, adored him and helped him in every way. No one ever dared make fun of him. His skin was very dark, he squinted out of one eye—and he had an Italian accent.

Jimmy made it a point to be friends with everybody. That was his "political" side. I had not known anyone before Jimmy who was filled with ambition. To me his antics were like those of a freak.

He was always organizing, or raising funds for this or that. At twelve or thirteen he behaved like an adult. It was unnatural. I refused his invitation to join the club he had formed. I never told him about *our* club. He wouldn't have understood the spirit animating us. We weren't going anywhere or getting anywhere, in Jimmy's mind. Everything he did had to have a purpose, be meaningful. Needless to say, that was not the dominating spirit of the Deep Thinkers or the Xerxes Society.

Jimmy also managed to get his name frequently in the local papers. He was always being praised, admired or envied.

Once he ran the marathon. A heart-breaking experience, and rather foolish to undertake—but Jimmy had to prove that he had what it takes.

He was hardly out of school—I think he was going to night school—when there would be pieces in the paper about him giving lectures to Boy Scout groups and others. Headlines reading—*James Pasta lectures tonight on "Loyality and Obedience"* or *James Pasta lectures on "What makes great men."* Stuff like that. My old man used to read these squibs in the papers and tell me in a meaningful way how much he admired Jimmy. "He's going to go far," my father would say. "Not like you" was implicitly understood. He couldn't see any future for me at all.

About the time Jimmy is building a reputation for himself I am training to become a lieutenant or a captain in a boy's brigade called "Battery A" which belonged to a Presbyterian Church I attended. I attended church only because I wanted to be in the brigade. I had good times drilling in the basement of that church. I soon became top sergeant and was very proud of my red chevrons. Red, because we were a part of the Artillery—Coast Guard Artillery.

The man who organized this brigade, Major ——, was a queer. He loved boys—and all the parents referred to him as a "lovely man." He loved us a little too much for his own good. Every night, when we reported for duty, he ushered us into his little office, made us sit on his lap, then hugged, squeezed and kissed us as much as he could. We all dreaded these sessions but none of us had the courage to tell on him. No one would have believed us anyway, because he didn't look the part. He was probably bisexual and he probably did love us. One day, however, someone did tell on him, and he was expelled from the church in disgrace. To tell the truth, we felt sorry for him. There were worse buggers in the church than poor Major —— but they never got caught.

Anyway, this was the sort of activity Jimmy did not take part in. He was probably too busy with school anyway. He had made up his mind to become a lawyer, and he did become one, after a long, hard struggle.

We met rarely now—usually by accident on the street. At each meeting we would exchange views—about God, about politics, about books and about the state of the world. Somehow even at that early stage Jimmy secretly admired me because he sensed the writer in me. About most everything we disagreed, but in a friendly way. I usually ended up telling him that though I didn't believe in politics, if he were to run for office I would vote for him. And I really meant it, though to be honest I never voted once in my whole life. Yes, if Jimmy had run for President of the United States I would definitely have voted for him. He was honest, truthful, serious and loyal.

The school we attended was P.S. 85—on the corner of Covert Street and Evergreen Avenue. We had a school song which began—"Dear 85 . . ."—very sentimental, sloppily so. Even to this day I get a card now and then from Jimmy, reminding me of dear old 85. He is, of course, one of its honored alumni.

But this street, Evergreen Avenue—another one of those Brooklyn Streets which had no character. Not exactly slummy, but poor, run-down, and nondescript. Jimmy's father had his shoe repair shop on it, almost opposite the school. I remember the bakery and the delicatessen store vividly. They were both run by Germans. (Only the druggist was non-German. He was Jewish—and a man I could talk to.) The rest were walking vegetables—turnips, kohlrabi, cauliflower, artichokes. What are called "solid citizens." Somewhere along this avenue was a Baptist Church painted all white. Aside from that I remember nothing. Just sameness, dreariness, shopkeepers, vegetables.

The school I shall always remember, especially for several unusual teachers. Number one was Miss Cordes. "Miss," I say— she may have been fifty or sixty. Whatever she taught—arithmetic, English or what—was only secondary, relatively unimportant. What she really taught us, and that's why we all loved her, was brotherly love—how to look at the world, one's neighbor, and oneself. She emanated joy, peace, confidence—and faith. Not religious faith but faith in life itself. She made one feel that it was good to be alive, that we were *lucky* to be alive. How wonderful! When I think of all the sour pusses we had to put up with, or the sadists, Miss Cordes stands out like a Joan of Arc. I often say I learned nothing at school. But to have been in Miss

Cordes' class was a great privilege and worth more than all the knowledge in the world.

Number two was Jack ——, teacher of the graduating class. He was what you might call "a card." I imagine he was either a homosexual or a bisexual. The female teachers adored him. He had a glib tongue, could tell risque stores, and was always in good humor. Unlike Major —— he made no advances to any of us. At the worst he told us dirty stories. If anything, he seemed to like women. He was very free with them, both in speech and with his hands—and they adored this. I can still see him patting Miss ——'s rump and she giggling like a schoolgirl.

I used to watch him leave school on his way home. He was very dapper, always well dressed, always sporting a bowler and sometimes an ivory-handled cane. We didn't learn very much from him. We enjoyed ourselves in his class—he made us feel as if we were already young men, not fourteen and fifteen-year-old kids.

There were other teachers, also important in my life. Miss M, whom I just mentioned, made me aware that even school teachers have sex. With M it wasn't just sex, but cunt. You felt that hers was forever itching, that the thing she craved most was a good lay by Jack wearing a carnation in his buttonhole. You could very easily imagine her cornering him in some dark corner and opening his fly. She had a premanently fixed expression of lust on her face, her lips always slightly parted as if waiting to take it in her mouth. Her laugh was a dirty laugh. She was thoroughly impure, you might say. But attractive. She made the other teachers look sick. She always wore tight-fitting skirts, low-cut blouses which revealed her beautiful boobies, and she used strong perfume, the musky kind which tends to give one a hard-on whether horny or not.

Last but not least was the good, honest Scot, Mr. McDonald. I was quite young when I was in his class, and quite shy and innocent. I remember one day especially when he singled me out as an example to the class. He had been explaining to us via the blackboard some difficult arithmetical problem. When he finished he turned to the class and asked if we all understood now. Everyone nodded in agreement. Excepet me. I stood up and told him that I didn't understand anything. Whereupon the whole class burst into laughter. What a dummy I was! And to stand up and admit it—no, that was too good a joke.

But Mr. McDonald took a different view of it. Holding up his hand he ordered the class to be silent. Then he beckoned me to stand up again. And then he told the class to take a good look at me and try to behave like me. "This Henry Miller has courage," he said. "He's not ashamed to admit he doesn't know. He's genuine, he's sincere. I want you to take an example from him."

Naturally I was flabbergasted. I hadn't given any thought to my behavior—it was just a natural reaction. But I was rather proud of myself nevertheless.

The one person I detested and despised was the principal—Dr. Peewee. To me he was a fop, a show-off and a hypocrite. To begin with he was not my idea of a man. He was frail, flat-chested, and haughty. He gave the illusion of being a great scholar, a know-it-all, but I never understood what he was a doctor in. Every now and then he would invite a Dr. Brown to visit the school and give us students a chance. Evidently Dr. Brown had at one time been a pupil at "dear old 85." Soon as he appeared on the platform the whole auditorium broke into song—"Dear 85, we'll ever strive, to honor thy fair name…" Then Dr. Brown, always freshly returned from his travels abroad, would launch into a speech that might last an hour or two. Always very interesting, I must say. Somewhere along the line he would turn to Dr. Peewee and in his most melting tone of voice tell how he missed dear old 85. Perhaps it was in Singapore or Sierra Leone, or the Engadine—some far-off place none of us knew anything about. Anyhow it all came off perfect—like a good cheese cake. One never asked Dr. Brown what the hell he was doing in these far away places.

Certainly Dr. Peewee and George Wright were two utterly different types of principals. Dr. Peewee never seemed to look at a woman in the eyes. Nor did he size up her bottom or her teats. He would pop in and out of a classroom like a lost owl.

He was a frequent visitor at my friend Jack Lawton's home, as was Major ——, and distinguished guests like Dr. Brown or some cock-eyed Senator or Congressman. The Lawtons were from the old country—England—and very social-minded. My friend Jack at eleven or twelve was already highly sophisticated and very well mannered too. I used to like to hear him say— "Sir." "Sir, may I pour you another cup of tea"? or some such shit. Which made him a little suspect with the other students. Was he a queer? Was he putting on airs? Where did he think he was getting off? And such like. He proved himself by becoming a first lieutenant in the boy's brigade. He was a great reader for his age. At fourteen he had swallowed all of Dickens and Kipling, and most of Joseph Conrad and Thomas Hardy. He didn't have to work, I mean, study diligently, like most of us. Everything came easy to him, it seemed. He also was lucky to have a loving, devoted mother. He didn't think much of Jimmy Pasta. Referred to him as a climber and a peasant at heart. Naturally one could not possibly think of Dr. Peewee visiting Jimmy's home, in the back of the cobbler's shop. Mrs. Pasta wouldn't have understood a word Dr. Peewee said. Nor would Mr. Pasta, it goes without saying.

Only a short distance up the street, or avenue, was the German delicatessen shop. I can see myself dropping in there every Sunday evening to buy the same things for our Sunday meal. Pot cheese with rich cream on it, salami, liverwurst, head cheese, potato salad, blutwurst, and a variety of bolognas that were very tasty. Then a dash to the bakery across the street whether I either got an apple cake or *streusel kuchen.* This was our Sunday meal come rain or shine. And I never tired of it.

But what I could never get over were the proprietors of these shops. Both places run by women, fat, bloated, ignorant, illiterate, narrow-minded, money mad. Never once did I hear an intelligent conversation between them and any of their customers. I used to be furious. Just looking at them gave me the creeps. Long before the rise of Hitler I was anti-German. Later I discovered that these GermanAmericans were worse than the Germans themselves, that is to say, more stupid, more swinish, more mean and money grubbing. More vegetable-like.

The years passed and Jimmy still had his nose to the grindstone and one eye always open to publicity. While Jimmy was busy studying to get his degree in law and from there work his way up to being a Congressman, I was busy living my chaotic get-nowhere life. During this period I went from one job to another, never lasting very long in any of them. One of the better jobs I got was through a customer of my father's. Grant was his name. He was a vice-president, I believe, of the Federal Reserve Bank in the Wall Street district. I was given a job, along with about thirty other men and women, checking the adding machines for errors. A boring job, but the pay was good and my fellow workers a jolly bunch. I was on the job about two months, everything going well when one day I was asked to go see the personnel manager. To my great surprise he told me he was discharging me. Why? I wanted to know. Wasn't my work satisfactory?

Oh, there was nothing wrong with my work, he hastened to assure me. It was my character.

"My character?" I exclaimed.

"Yes," he said. "We have been investigating your life, interrogating your friends and neighbors—we know quite a bit about you."

And then he told me how they hd discovered about me and the widow.

"We are not questioning your morals," he went on, "but we feel we can't trust you."

He then went on to tell me to my face that because of this obvious infatuation for an older woman, there was no telling what I might do.

I was enraged. "What is it I might do that would hurt the bank?" I wanted to know.

"Rob it!" he said blandly.

"No, you don't mean that," I said. "Why it's preposterous."

He didn't think so. There was no way of talking him out of it. I was finished, no question about it.

And so it went from job to job. Until finally I managed to put in four years as employment manager of the messenger department in the telegraph company. It was toward the end of this period I met June at the dance hall. A few months later I quit my job in the Western Union, having decided to risk all in becoming a writer. It was now my real misery began. What I had been through before was only a preparation for what was to follow.

In quitting the Western Union I had promised June I would not take another job. I was to stay home and write and she would take care of things. It didn't work out as planned, not that we were not diligent, but luck was against us. I did a lot of writing which never appeared in print. Finally I wrote under *her* name—June Mansfield—and thus had a bit of success. But it was short-lived.

Then came Jean—a strange beautiful creature whom June took a fancy to. They behaved like a pair of lesbians. After a couple of months they began talking of going to Europe together. Jean was a painter, a poet and sculptress. She also made puppets. She made one they christened "Count Bruga," which caused a sensation wherever they appeared.

It was about this time that I took to panhandling at night on Broadway. Even that was a failure. Night after night I came home empty-handed. We were living like savages now in the basement of an apartment house. The rooms we occupied had once been a laundry. It was a cold winter and I had chopped all

69

the furniture to pieces to make firewood. To me it seemed like the dead end. How much lower could we sink?

One day toward dinner hour, I am wandering slowly back to the house. I am not merely depressed, I am dejected. Besides, I am starved. I don't recall when we last had a good meal.

All of a sudden whom do I run into but Jimmy Pasta. He is now an Assemblyman from his district. Looks keen and prosperous. Cordial greetings.

"Well, Hen, old boy, how are you doing?" says Jimmy, giving me a slap on the back.

For answer I say—"Rotten." Immediately a genuine look of concern came over his countenance.

"What do you mean?" says Jimmy.

"I mean I'm broke. I have no job, and I'm hungry."

The moment I said hungry his face lit up. "If that's all it is we can fix that right away," he said, and taking me by the arm he led me to a plush bar where he was known and ordered a meal for me.

"Tell me all about it," he says, as we sat down. "What's happened to you? The last time I heard about you you were the editor of some magazine.

I gave him a wry smile. "I was the assistant editor of a catalog for the Charles Williams Mail Order House. No literature connected with that job," I added. Well, we sat and talked. I had a few beers, we spoke of "dear old 85" and so on. Finally I said—"I need a job, Jimmy. I need it bad. Could you help me?"

I knew he was secretary to the Park Commissioner—a cushy job that probably paid well.

To my surprise Jimmy replied that he could fix me up with a job in his own office.

"I may have to put you on the payroll as a grave digger first," said Jimmy. "Do you mind?"

"Hell, no," I said. "I've been a ditch digger, a garbage collector and what not. Just so long as I get a salary."

When I left Jimmy I went home sailing. I had agreed to be at his office at nine in the morning next day. He would introduce me to the Commissioner himself—a big-wig now in the political world.

June and Jean took the good news rather unenthusiastically, I thought. They were curious to know what my salary would be.

Next day I went, met the Commissioner, and was immediately put on the payroll. For the first week or so I might be obliged to dig graves but after that I would be made Jimmy's assistant. It sounded wonderful to me.

The next morning I was up bright and early to tackle my new job. It didn't take me long to catch on. The other workers were friendly and helpful. Two of them were from the old 14th Ward. That made things still nicer.

On the way home that evening I stopped off at a florist to buy some flowers.

"A nice touch for a change," I thought. I rang my door bell. No answer. No lights either. In order to get in I had to ring the landlady's bell.

I entered our joint in the dark, lit a candle or two—the electricity had long been shut off. On the floor, in a corner, were a few pieces of discarded clothing. I roamed up and down several times before I noticed a note on my desk. I picked it up and read— "Dear Val, we left for Paris on the *Rochambeau* this morning. Love. June."

In another book I have described the emotion that overcame me and my feeling of desolation.

"No wonder," I thought to myself that they showed such little enthusiasm when I told them of the job. What they really felt was a feeling of relief, that someone was looking after me. It made them less guilty.

Next day I told Jimmy what had happened. He could read the sad news on my face.

"You say you love her?" he asked.

I nodded.

"Maybe I'm lucky then," he said. "I haven't met anyone so far who could play such tricks on me."

It was true. Jimmy had little time for women. He was completely involved now in politics. He aimed to go to Washington in a year or two.

Sometimes he invited me to have lunch with him—usually at a bar in the back room where the local politicians met, played cards, drank like fish and so on. More and more he was becoming disillusioned with the racket. He even went so far as to say there were no honest politicians—impossible.

When I inquired what kept him from behaving like the others he replied very simply—"Because I'm different. Because I have ideals. Lincoln was no crook. Neither was Thomas Jefferson. I wouldn't bring disgrace on my mother and father's name... Remember, Hen, old 85? Remember Miss Cordes? Maybe she's helped a lot to keep me straight."

To his credit I must say that Jimmy never did waver. That's why perhaps he never got very far. But everyone respected him. He was still written up in the local papers—as something of "a white hope." He still gave lectures to Boy Scouts and other groups of youngsters. He talked as if he actually *were* President.

It was only three or four days after the two of them had sailed that I received a radiogram from the ship. It said, "Please cable fifty dollars before we dock. Desperate. June."

Once again I had to face Jimmy. I felt terribly ashamed and humiliated. He lent me the money, not without a little sermon and a monologue about what fools men can be.

Myself, I couldn't understand why they needed this sum. Could they be in debt already? I knew that once they reached Paris they would be o.k. June had the faculty of making people believe in her and trust in her.

Meanwhile I would pay Jimmy back so much a week out of my salary. I had gone back to the folks' house to live—it was cheaper. Almost every day I sat at a little desk they had given me as a child and I wrote to June.

Every Saturday afternoon found me at a dance hall on Broadway. In one afternoon I would spend a week's pin money. But I enjoyed it. Besides I needed to relax and to get a good fuck, even if it were only a dry fuck. Most of these taxi dance girls were very good looking and hot in the pants. They enjoyed these blind fucks on the dance floor—their only concern was not to have their dress soiled by the man's sperm. I think I have already mentioned how I would take them to another kind of dance hall on their day off. And give them a stand-up fuck in the hallway when I took them home. One girl used to take me to her home and squat over me while I sat on a chair in the kitchen in the dark. Sometimes her mother passed through the room while we were at it but she was unaware of our doings because she was stone deaf and almost totally blind. This particular bitch seemed to enjoy it all the more when her mother passed through the room. She could come easily and it always seemed to me that she came during these critical moments.

Meanwhile I was getting letters from June. They weren't finding it easy to get along in Paris, but fortunately she had made a great friend of the famous sculptor Ossip Zadkine. She might just as well have said Picasso. Zadkine was world famous. Some years later when I myself went to Paris he asked me what had become of the paintings and pieces of sculpture he had given June to sell in America. June must have disposed of them without telling me. From the brief conversation I had with him and from a few slips June made herself it wasn't difficult to deduce that they had a merry time of it together, punctuated by occasional trips to the Bois de Boulogne where, like in Hyde Park, London, any and everyone lay on the grass and fucked whomever they pleased.

Working as Jimmy's assistant I grew more and more familiar with Jimmy's life. Part of his job was to write the political speeches his boss, the Commissioner, had to make. Now and then he would ask my aid in phrasing a sentence. He seemed to regard me as a full-fledged writer. I was in fear he would one day ask *me* to write the speeches for him.

Best time was lunch time at the bar, when he would pour out his heart to me. He really hated the life his brother politicians lived and some of which he had to share. There was never any mention of women. Only card playing, gambling, pool and guzzling. He was with them but not of them.

Somehow it was only now that I began to warm up to him, to discover that a good, loyal friend he was. He had all the sterling qualities which a politician seldom has. As I said before, this was probably his handicap. He never got to Washington. He remained a local Congressman. I never heard much from him or about him once I quit the Park Department job. Occasionally, I would receive a postcard from him. I still do. And I always answer immediately. For I regard Jimmy as one of the few genuine friends in my life, one of the several men who saved my life.

But perhaps what I am most indebted to Jimmy for is this. One afternoon, thinking about Jean and June in Paris, and all the ups and downs in my life, I decided to outline the events in my life from the beginning. I sat down to type out this outline, which in fact became the synopsis for all my autobiographical romances. I sat down at closing time one afternoon and I remained there typing till about five o'clock next morning. In the space of about thirty pages I managed to recall most everything of importance in my life to date. And all without effort. It was as if I had turned on some tap in my memory and the images just flowed out. It was with this outline that I began writing my autobiography in Paris. Not immediately, to be sure. I first wrote a couple of novels in which I used the third person.

As I say, about five in the morning I was pooped. I lay down on the rug in the Commissioner's office and fell asleep. Around eight A.M. the first worker arrived. He saw me lying on the rug and thought I was dead, thought I had committed suicide.

Now that I have told the story of our friendship I must send Jimmy a card to wish him well. He has read my books but I never told him that they were really born in his office.

Joe O'Reagan

Joe came into my life out of nowhere.
All his life he was dropping in on me—from nowhere, it seemed.
He was a born wanderer, of a buoyant, optimistic disposition and
possessed of great (Irish) charm. He was attractive to women,
with his blarney, his black, curly locks, his violet eyes and long
eye lashes, plus his way of throwing himself on their mercy.

As a boy of five he and his older brother had been put in an
orphan asylum, a Catholic one, by his Irish mother and her
second husband, a Russian Jew. Joe had never forgiven either of
them for this. At the age of ten he and his brother managed to
escape from the asylum. The brother later became a sheriff
somewhere in Texas.

Evidently Joe hadn't received much of an education at the
orphan asylum. He had a perpetual itch for knowledge and

culture. On the other hand he was rather precocious. For example, he had diddled the Mother Superior, who apparently was very fond of him. He did it cunningly and cold-bloodedly.

I said that women found him attractive—perhaps because he had a perpetual hard-on. As for men, no, they were not taken in by his Irish charm, his cunning and his boasting. At first blush he seemed to inspire distrust. As my friends often remarked— "There's something fishy about him." What Joe was looking for was a mother's love, or at least confidence in his good faith. He needed people to believe in him, trust him.

When he ran away from the asylum he joined a circus and shortly thereafter met a man, a zoologist, I believe, who took a great interest in him. Through this man he learned to love all God's creatures, including snakes. Animals belonged to his world—he understood them.

When I say he came from nowhere I mean he lacked the usual, ordinary background most of us possessed. He knew a little about everything and nothing much of anything. He read a great deal and was very responsive to books and authors. He had his idols, as did Stanley and I. He could talk well—the gift of gab, as we say.

I came across Joe, oddly enough, about ten o'clock at night in a New Jersey village where my folks were spending their summer vacation. They had chosen the place because of the lake—Swartswood Lake—which offered swimming, boating and fishing.

I had taken with me, for a few days, a friend of our neighborhood, a fellow my own age, named Bill Woodruff. Joe and he worked together in a maintenance and repair shop run by an eccentric bachelor who was interested in young men. Bill Woodruff was somewhat of a sissy or "molly-coddle" as we called it them, a spoiled brat, a weakling, and in no sense of the word manly or robust. Anyway, he kept telling me about this O'Reagan chap and thought I should meet him. And so, one night, as we were standing on the road, along comes a horse and carriage, and who jumps out to greet us but Joe O'Reagan. I liked Joe immediately. I liked his voice and his handshake. He struck me as not only handsome but very manly.

In a few minutes we were on the lake in a rowboat. It was pitch dark. Suddenly I hear a splash and it is O'Reagan who has dived into the middle of the lake. He takes an eternity to surface. "I was caught in the bullrushes," he explained, laughing it off as if it were nothing. Woodruff was terrified. He didn't know how to swim and was frightened of the water. But Joe was like a water snake. Then and there we sealed a pact of friendship. It lasted till Joe's death a few years ago.

As I said earlier, Joe was always coming and going—destination unknown. He followed his hunches. Just before we met he had been released from the Army, where he had worked his way up from private to top-sergeant. It was a treat to hear him talk about the abilities needed to be a good top-sergeant. To hear him talk, a top-sergeant, a good one, that is, was more important than a general.

In a way the Army furnished him with some sort of education. He had gone to the Far East—to China, Indo-China, Java and Japan. In Japan he discovered the Japanese woman. He never ceased admiring her. One of the things he liked to swell on was the cleanliness of the Japanese—even in their whorehouses. To hear him, the whorehouse procedure was a ceremony of the highest order. The girl not only bathed herself scrupulously, but the man too. Then came the exquisite kimonos, the cup of tea, the samisen, flowers, birds in their cages. Not even Count Keyserling, who devoted some of his best pages on Japan to the Japanese woman, told it better than Joe. It was then and there I really began dreaming of the Orient, and of Japan especially. (Of course Joe had greatly exaggerated and improvised, as I learned later, but what matter?)

Wherever he had been he could discourse on it like a poet. I often wondered that he had never tried to write. I could listen to

78

him, rapt, for hours at a time. What a treat to hear about such little-known parts of the world, to learn of the delicacy, the finesse of these people.

It took me some time before I discovered that people didn't think as highly as I did of Joe. As I remarked before, most of my friends were distrustful and suspicious of him. Joe was always promoting somebody or something. (For a good part of his life it was me and my work.) He went about it, unfortunately, as if he were stalking big game.

Women regarded him quite differently from men. They usually adored him and melted under his blandishments. With them he acted the abandoned child, the misunderstood and unappreciated young man of the world. He didn't have to sell women—they took to him immediately. Being sly with his hands, Joe usually made his women fast. Often he let them keep him. Not that he was a sponger. No, Joe was generous at heart. But he was often broke. When things got too bad he would up and leave—it didn't matter where to—he simply had to find other air to breathe.

Every time he came home to roost it was *chez moi*. Joe liked the way I lived and the women I was in love with. He would often implore me to share a woman with him. He saw nothing wrong with that. He would tell me that I was "lucky."

At the same time he would take it upon himself to defend me, protect me. He couldn't understand how a "great writer" such as myself could go unnoticed. He read everything I wrote, not once, but several times. He talked of my pieces as if he had written them himself.

Evenings, when he returned from his self-imposed campaigns, he would relate in detail what had happened in the course of his interviews with editors, publishers and critics. He was always promising me quick results, great results. But somehow everything always fell through at the last minute. This hurt Joe more than me. I was getting habituated to rejection slips. Perhaps I

79

bolstered my courage by pretending to myself that I was America's greatest writer, the logical descendant of Walt Whitman. Certainly everything I wrote seemed like pure gold to me. I compared my work only to the foremost writers—Petronius, Rabelais, Emerson, Whitman. I considered myself superior to such as Sinclair Lewis, Theodore Dreiser, Sherwood Anderson, Ben Hecht, *et alia*. I was unique—in a class by myself.

And so, when Joe was deflated, I would comfort *him*.

I don't remember ever quarreling with him. Discussion and argument we had aplenty. We spend interminable hours bandying words about every subject under the sun. For Joe, if uneducated, was highly intelligent. Moreover, he questioned everything. He had been raised a Catholic in the orphan asylum but had ceased to believe in it long before leaving the asylum. The only thing he liked about the nuns, for example, was that they were so naïve. To Joe they were all pushovers, including the Mother Superior, who wore a truss. It was like listening to the "Decameron" to hear Joe tell about the nuns and their craving for a bit of nooky.

When I became employment manager of the telegraph company I made Joe my assistant. He thoroughly enjoyed the work. It gave him pleasure, for example, to spot a crook or an epileptic. Frequently he would slip me a note while I was interviewing an applicant, warning me that the guy I was talking to was a bad egg or urging me to observe the scars on the man's hand or arm. (A sign that he was an epileptic and had suffered many falls.)

We sat opposite each other at the same desk. It amused me to see how seriously he took the job. What a thing he made of it! As if he were the president of the company. In the office we had two beautiful young women; he took one and I took the other. The two girls lived together, which made it easier for us. At this time I was still married.

It often happened that I repaired to the couch for a snooze after dinner. I was usually pooped because during all the time I served the telegraph company I never got enough sleep. It was always two or three A.M. before I got to bed. And I was supposed to be at my office at eight o'clock A.M. (Naturally I was always late, often unshaved, often appearing in a blue denim shirt frayed at the collar and sleeves.)

When I lay down to take my nap my wife would first sit down in a rocker near the couch, waiting for me to invite her to lie beside me. But most of the time I would fall sound asleep. Then my good friend Joe got in some good licks. Pretending to feel sorry for my wife he would soon have her on his lap, and no doubt massaging her cunt while I snored blissfully away. But things always worked out to my advantage somehow. After Joe had warmed her up she would slip over to the couch, and, without waking me, would put her hand in my fly and play with my prick and balls. Naturally, I would soon open my eyes. Then I would commence to give her a going over. She was a very passionate, if inhibited creature. (She too had been brought up as a Catholic, in a convent.) Later, when I knew her better, I suspected that some of her "dear friends," as she called them, were out and out lesbians. But this did not prevent her from being a good lay. And so, as a reward, Joe was allowed to sit in the rocking chair and watch us make love. I can still see him putting his hands to his ears to shut out the groans and grunts we made.

Joe had lived with me during the period I was with the widow. We were all frightfully poor then, kept alive, you might say, by our boarder, a streetcar motorman. On the pittance he doled out to us from his weekly salary, we managed to eat round steak and boiled potatoes at least three times a week. Never a dessert. Never a good drink—of wine, gin or whiskey. We lived like hermits and fucked like rabbits. There was nothing else to do. The money Joe put on the table when he arrived was soon gone. Perhaps we managed to see a movie a few times—Clara Bow, Charlie Chaplin, Charles Ray—or Alice Joyce. As there seemed no hope of getting a job, we slept late. Joe would sometimes crawl into bed with us and try his best to get his end in. He always pleaded like a man who had been terribly deprived. How could we let him suffer like that, was his attitude.

If I were absent of an afternoon he would be sure to make advances to her. I would sometimes come home to find her in tears. What was the matter? *Joe.* She liked Joe, but she deeply resented his making advances to her. (We regarded ourselves as good as married then.) Later I was actually going to get married to her, but my mother had come at me with a cleaver, threatening to kill me if I ever said another word about marriage!

The motorman, Tex was his name, was a *"gentleman."* He would never dream of doing anything behind my back. (He was from Texas.)

This business of Joe coming to live with me (or us) continued into my next marriage. But with June he didn't dare make any overtures. June impressed him from the first. The two had something in common—extreme generosity and a flair for exaggeration. I used to listen to them as if I were observing a stage performance. Both were wonderful liars and both believed their own lies.

What hurt Joe, what he found difficult to believe, was that even by this time I was still in the soup. I had not as yet sold a thing. (I had had a short article—my first!—accepted and published in a magazine for Negroes, but had received no money for it.) Joe wanted to rectify all this. How could the world ignore his great friend and great writer, Henry Miller? But the world did, and not even a Joe O'Reagan, with all his charm, bluster and blarney, could prevail. The time was not ripe. Somehow I understood it and accepted it patiently and impatiently.

I cursed not only editors and publishers but the public too. I scorned their heroes, their idols. I cursed every mother's son for the stupid, insensitive bastard that he was. (I still do in my better moments.)The picture has not changed since those days. I was lucky, that's all. I have a wonderful Jupiter.

One of the things I never told Joe was that I was fucking his girl friend on the side. I didn't do it out of revenge or to teach him a lesson. It just happened. She had been married to one of my very best friends, a young man I admired and regarded as a genius.

Anyway, the two of them never got along very well, and I soon got to know his wife intimately. I made the mistake of introducing her to O'Reagan, who was quick to nibble at the bait. For a while we were both screwing her. But then there was the other girl in the office—funny, I can't remember her name anymore—and I was content to leave Elsa to Joe.

We did a lot of fucking in those days, especially after the telegraph company decided to hire women as messengers. Now Joe could no longer complain. He was swamped with lays. Everything ended in cunt, it seemed. I often tend to forget this glorious period, being so pissed off by my failure to make it as a writer.

Though cunt was in the air and we were getting our fill, I was madly in love with my second wife. It sounds crazy, but I never felt that I betrayed her. To fuck someone else was not necessarily an act of betrayal. It was a sign of life, the celebration of life.

When I left for Europe in 1930 I didn't see O'Reagan again until some time after my return. I don't recall now what he was doing for a living then, but it must certainly have been promotional work or public relations. He hadn't changed a bit—the same bluster, same blarney, same empty rhetoric. The only good thing about him was his taste in literature. We would sit up till all hours of the night talking of our favorite writers and favorite characters. By now he had read most of Dostoyevsky and the other great Russians. I introduced him to Berdyaev. He had also digested Thomas Mann, Gide, Proust and much of Balzac. He spoke with authority. I didn't dare contradict him. As for me, my work, well he had faithfully followed my career, had read everything I wrote, and knew what the critics thought of me.

It must have been after the *Air-Conditioned Nightmare* trip that I ran into Joe—at some bar on Third Avenue. I was happy to tell him about the old friends I had looked up during that trip. I was particularly eager to tell him about the colonel and the general I had met. They had grown up with me—lived only a few doors away from us. One was about seven years older than I, the other (the general) about four years older. They still treated me as if I were a little boy. Naturally, they had never cracked a book of mine. They simply didn't read. Mostly they played cards, swapped stories with fellow officers and guzzled tons of beer. Thoroughly uninteresting characters, both of them. I reminded Joe of what he had told me about top-sergeants. Though I have never had any traffic with them I could believe what Joe had said, that without them the Army couldn't get along.

The thing about the general was that as a boy or young man I had thought him effeminate. Now that he was a general he was still effeminate-looking to me. His brother, the colonel, on the other hand, was a whore monger. Every other word he uttered was a curse word.

Later in life I had occasion to meet other officers of the Army, Navy and Marines. Of them all I can say that they seemed to have only two things on their mind—cunt and booze.

Yes, later in life I had occasion to meet what might be considered the cream of our society. I must confess I never met one officer for whom I had the least respect; I met only two college professors for whom I had any respect; I never met a great business executive for whom I had the least respect. I did meet now and then a priest or a monk with him I could converse intelligently, laugh heartily and discuss spiritual matters with enjoyment. I say a priest or a monk. Never once a Protestant minister, a Rabbi.

On this trip I had also stopped off to see a buddy from high school days. He was now a professor of music in a girl's college somewhere in South Carolina. Another disappointment. He might just as well have been a professor of zoology or paleontology. Yet at fifteen he was a marvelous pianist, someone obviously destined for the concert stage.

This time Joe didn't ask me to put him up. I was on the go myself—and besides, he now had a job and a woman (not his wife) who was devoted to him. He had become quite a respectable citizen. Still a great boozer, still a bamboozler, but toned down now, two feet on the ground. I inquired about his sister. Apparently she had married. He said it mournfully. I recalled the look on his face when he first introduced her to me. She was indeed a beauty—an Irish beauty—and it seemed obvious that he not only loved her as a sister but that he was in love with her.

Knowing what a disreputable bastard he was, I often wondered why he didn't fuck his own sister. *I* would have, had I been in his place. But Joe did have certain scruples after all. Though he always referred to his mother as a dirty Irish bitch it was obvious that he loved her dearly. His hatred for her husband was based not only on the fact that he was a stepfather and a Russian Jew to boot but that he had robbed Joe of his rightful place—as her lover.

When we talked of these things Joe would come out with some rather surprising reminiscences. One was about his attempt to screw a cow. He had screwed sheep a number of times and maybe mares (Shetland ponies) too, for all I know. He was capable of screwing a snake, if it could be managed. I wondered why he had never fallen in love with a Japanese or Filipino girl. "Lack of money," he always replied. By that he meant that were he to find one such he would feel obliged to treat her like a queen. American girls were to him just cunts, at the best "broads." He despised the Average American Girl. The English, of course, were beneath attention.

It never occurred to either of us in those days that I would one day marry a Japanese woman. As for Chinese women, one never encountered one anywhere. The only Chinese we knew were the laundry man and the waiters in chop suey joints.

85

Joe was not much of a correspondent, nor did he telephone often. Usually he just dropped in—from God knows where. He *could* write, however. Only his letters were all alike. He wrote the same sort of letter whether telling me about Dostoievsky, deep-sea fishing, golf, a new sales campaign, or the art and elegance of the Japanese woman. To me, knowing him as I did, it was incredible. It was as if he had been put through some correspondence school as a kid, been thoroughly brainwashed, and given 100 percent on his exams. It's been my great misfortune that for most my life I had to be the letter writer. Whether I wrote to a man friend or a woman I was deeply in love with, the responses were usually tardy and never what I expected. Which only led me to write more letters. The true letter writer seems to be a thing of the past. To be honest, those famous letter writers are not my favorites.

But as regards Joe—if he wasn't much of a letter writer he was, on the other hand, a great storyteller. And here is another thing which baffles me—the natural born storyteller may be totally unable to write a simple tale, or a decent letter, for that matter. He may not know how to spell, his grammar may be nil, his imagination paralyzed, but he can hold you spell-bound once he starts to spout. Whereas I have often noticed that good writers may not have the ability to tell a good story at all. Well, Joe was a natural born storyteller. He told fantastic yarns. He worked in all the details, just as do certain classic composers who bore the shit out of me. For some strange reason, in a story these details are exciting, heighten one's interest, and so on. Also, should you happen to question a certain detail, let us say, that leads the storyteller off on a detour which can be utterly fascinating. Of course the ideal storyteller demands the ideal listener. I regard myself as an ideal listener. I am a sucker for anyone who has something to get off his chest. That endears me to many people. They think I am sincerely interested in what they are telling me. Often I am not, but I listen attentively just the same.

Sometimes, while listening to such people, I am thinking what *I* might do with such a story, or I interpolate silently where there are gaps in the tale. Or I get lost, thinking of the corrections in grammar I am making. Or again, his story may remind me of one I had intended to write long ago, and I am feverishly making mental notes—brief, telegraphic messages—which will help me to remember when he's through.

With Joe it was possible to play games. I could interrupt him at any time, I could question his veracity. I could tell him what his story reminded me of—frequently, even an untalented individual like Joe could hit on a theme already exploited by, say a de Maupassant, a Flaubert, a Gogol, or to come down a bit, by a Jack London or an O'Henry. In a way, this storytelling of his took his mind off cunt. He never told dirty stories. He would like to have talked, he told me, like Joseph Conrad wrote. The strange thing is, Irish that he was, he had never read Shaw nor O'Casey. He liked Oscar Wilde and the man who translated *Tristan und Yseult*. He adored Lewis Carroll but couldn't abide Shakespeare. (He preferred Marlowe.)

All in all, he was a strange mixture of things. Very much like myself. Perhaps that's why we got along so well. I don't recall ever quarreling with him. Nor did it bother him that I never introduced him to my other friends. (I told him in the begining that my friends didn't take to him very kindly.) It didn't seem to bother him. He simply shrugged his shoulders and put them down as fools and imbeciles. Sometimes he would say—"I don't see what you see in so-and-so." "Don't try," I would reply. Or, now and then, if we happened to run into a nut in the street or in a coffee shop, he would say—"I hope you'll put him in your next book. He's pure gold." And usually he was right. Writers don't get much nourishment from other contemporary writers or professors, or intellectuals; their material usually comes from the gutter, from the potentially insane or criminal.

Up to the end, which was only a few years ago, O'Reagan's

letters always ended with his telling me in what bully condition he was. (He died in his early seventies.) Yes, his bowels moved perfectly, he had no trouble pissing, could fuck like a stallion, drink all the booze he wanted, and so on. And, so, when I got the news of his death, I was surprised rather than shocked. I had expected him to live to be a hundred at least. Like millions of other poor bastards in this fucking land of "the free and the brave," he died of a heart attack—in a bar on Third Avenue.

Considering the efforts he put forth to survive, to find his place in the sun, he should have died twenty years earlier.

I don't know what it takes to survive in this bloody country. One must have the morals of a stoat, the aggressiveness of a pug, the ruthlessness of an assassin, and the heartlessness of a big magnate—*plus* a barrel of luck! Joe was an ornery bugger, but he was a cavalier compared to the guys in the swim today. Though he had no use for the Pope or the Church, he might, under different circumstances, have made a good Irish priest. All he lacked was their stupidity and bigotry.

Max Winthrop

Why there was ever a strong bond between us is a mystery to me now. In many ways we resembled one another, so much so that we were often taken for brothers. In a way, we were both clowns, both ham actors. And, of all those with whom we associated we two possessed the most verve, the most vitality.

We met in high school. Out of nostalgia I had chosen to go to a school in the old neighborhood. And Max was from Greenpoint, not far from my old home in the 14th Ward.

One thing we had in common was our ability to play the piano. He was more adept than I, but I was more serious about it. In the famous Xerxes Society which we formed all the members could play *some* instrument.

In school he and I, together with perhaps a dozen other gentiles, were an enclave in the midst of a completely Jewish population. The teachers, all gentiles and all rather eccentric, naturally favored us with good marks. There was no open conflict between the Jews and the gentiles, but we definitely did not mix. And it very obviously rankled us when the Jewish boys showed their superiority in athletics. At handball they were wizards. It seemed as if the game was meant for them. We who were gentile never visited the homes of any of the Jewish boys. Naturally, the boy who carried off scholastic honors was a Jewish boy, a very shy, introverted type, whom we did everything possible to embarrass and humiliate. I said "naturally" he came off first, because we gentiles took our studies lightly whereas the Jewish boys studied like fiends.

It was in the third year of high school that I fell madly in love with Cora Seward who, alas for me, lived nearer to Max than to me. Max saw her frequently and treated her rather nonchalantly, I thought. Which meant to me that he was not in love with her. Max was not in love with any girl. All he had on his mind was cunt, and it was a failing, if you like, which was to last his whole lifetime. All my friends, both in and out of school, knew that I was infatuated with Cora. They all felt sorry for me for being so deeply in love with her. How ironic! As if the supreme gift were not love. Statistically all my friends were "in love," if one could call it that. They all had girl friends whom they called on regularly or brought to the parties we held. Most of them (my friends, I mean) were still virgins. Whereas they saw their girls at regular intervals, I saw Cora rarely, only at parties. To dance with her was a great privilege. I trembled all over when I held her in my arms. At these parties we played innocent games like "Kiss the Pillow" and "Post Office." Somehow we had a good time without much drinking. Perhaps a bowl of punch served to take care of all our needs.

As I have related elsewhere at length it was my custom on finishing the evening meal to put on my hat and coat and go for a walk. It was the same walk night after night—a long, long walk to Cora's house on Devoe Street and then home. I never stopped to ring her door bell and have a chat with her. I was content to merely walk slowly past her home in the hope of seeing her shadow in the parlor window. I never did, not once in the three or four years during which I performed this crazy ritual. It finally came to an end when I met the widow and began fucking my head off. Not that I ceased to love Cora. Oh no! I thought of her even when in the midst of fucking the widow. She was on my mind night and day without let. This is what is called "first love" and in the eyes of most people is a sort of puppy love. How woefully ignorant people are, how envious of true love. I have often said, and I repeat it now, that on my dying bed, Cora will probably be the last one I shall think of. I may die with her name on my lips. (On the other hand, if she is still alive and I should chance to run into her one day, what a calamity!)

Max made it his business to keep me informed of Cora's doings. His wife had become friends with Cora, it seems, though what these two had in common, I could never understand. Of course to Max my love for Cora was like a sickness. To him I was an uncurable romantic. As I said before, all he had on his mind was cunt. No wonder he later became a gynecologist. Though to tell the truth, he soon found it a disillusioning profession. As he would say to me confidentially now and then—"There's nothing more disgusting than to be examining cunts all day." Even so, it did not prevent him from fucking everything in sight. Sometimes he thought he would switch to becoming a psychologist or a psychiatrist. He declared that women's ailments were a simple problem—all they needed was to be properly fucked. In the course of time he attracted quite a few well-known figures from the theatrical world. He would give me intimate details about their love life or sex life or and about the kind of cunt they had. It was no trouble giving them a lay. They all seemed to be grateful to him for his attentions. Clever as he was, he now and then got into trouble, but somehow always managed to squirm out of it. I find it interesting to observe that what was then regarded as malpractice is now advocated as excellent therapy by some analysts. The question of therapy aside, there is no denying the fact that a woman who is screwed often and expertly is a happy creature. The woman who hums or sings under her breath as she goes about her chores has more than likely been well fucked that day.

At twenty-one Max fell violently ill with pneumonia and probably would have died had it not been for his mother's loving care. When he was well out of danger his parents decided to send him to the farm of a relative where he couldfully recuperate. I got permission from my father, for whom I was then working, to spend a week or ten days with Max. I have described this episode in full in *Plexus* and so will not repeat it here. The point is that it is almost impossible to believe that two grown-up men such as we two, could behave like children. Rarely have I enjoyed myself as much as during that week at his uncle's farm somewhere in New Jersey. Even there, a total stranger, he soon discovered a young girl whom he used to meet under the bridge after dark and screw.

He wasn't a mime, Max, but he was definitely some kind of actor. He knew how to keep a straight face. Also, he gave the impression that he spoke with authority. At the same time he was an out and out sentimentalist. We who were so often taken for brothers were so very, very, different. Even then, when we were close friends, I despised some of the things he believed in or championed. He always predicted a hard life for me, and of course he was right. But that was one of the things I heartily disliked about Max—that he could be right so often, and so utterly conventional in his thinking at the same time.

Naturally all the parents of all the club members admired and approved of him. To them he was a model young man. As for the rest of us—we were just trash. But what they could not deny was that we knew how to enjoy ourselves. They loved to hear us sing and play. As musicians, none of us became any-thing, by the way. We weren't anything of any account, any of us. These were the few bright years allotted us. After the club broke up we just became the usualy run of the mill-workers, parents, nobodies.

Why am I writing this book, I ask myself. Most of the events narrated I have dwelt on at length in other books of mine. Yet I feel compelled to relate everything over again, even for the twentieth time. Is it that I am bedazzled by my own life? Do I think my life was so very different from that of most men? I'm afraid I do. And the strange thing is that now, in writing about it again, I can see myself as a person objectively. I am not blind to my own faults or vain about my accomplishments. What I see more and more is the miraculous element of my life. It was a "charmed" life, as they say. I wriggled out of situations which would have killed or ruined other men. I think immediately of one little example.

During the time I was giving piano lessons—for thirty-five cents an hour!—I met, as I said before, the widow at the home of her friend Louise. I was teaching Louise's daughter. After the lessons her mother would send the girl to her room, then try to seduce me. One night I came dangerously close to letting myself be seduced. I didn't know that she had syphilis or that she was being kept by a Negro, the bicycle repairman who took care of me when my bike needed fixing. Ed was his name. Anyway, one night I am standing by the door, saying goodnight to Louise, when we hear a key being put in the lock. Before Ed could open the door she had pushed me behind the curtain. I heard her say, with a quiver in her voice, "Oh Ed, is that you? I didn't expect you so early." He touched me in brushing by, never suspecting that it was me or anyone else. Had he known I think he would have killed me. I shall always remember how caressingly she said, "Oh Ed, is that *you*?"

"Meet me Tonight in Dreamland" and "Shine on, Harvest

Moon, for me and My Gal." Today they refer nostalgically to the '50s and '60s. When these two songs were the rage—and they were indeed the rage, like no hits we know of today—you might say the world, *our* world was in flower. No one who ever sang these songs has ever forgotten them, I am sure. It was the time of the open trolley car, of Trixie Friganza and Elsie Janis, of George M. Cohan and Charles Chaplin, of the great dance halls, the marathon and little bunches of violets for your sweetheart. Then New York did seem to have a glamorous side. There were so many celebrities dear to the public's heart. There were great wrestlers, like Jim Londos, for example, or Earl Caddock, the man of a thousand holds, not phonies like today. There were great fighters, like Fitzsimmons, Corbett, Jim Jeffries, Jack Johnson. There were the six-day bike riders and polo players. Football and basketball were virtually out of the picture. An Elvis Presley was unthinkable, as was a crazy loon like Moon Dog Main, who eats glass and swallows live gold fish. I can still see myself at the piano, pulling out of my music roll a song Cora would like. My favorite was "Meet me Tonight in Dreamland." That's where I spent most of my time—in Dreamland. Strange that I never thought of fucking her. Not that she was too sacred, too holy to be fucked. No, it was Love I felt for Cora, love with a capital L that reached to the skies. And I never mixed the two—love and sex, which shows what an imbecile I must have been.

How wonderful to be sitting beside her in the open trolley, on our way to Rockaway or Sheepshead Bay, and singing at the top of our lungs—"Shine on, Harvest Moon, for me and My Gal." Or, "I don't want to set the world on fire..." How many ditties there were like that in those days! All from Tin Pan Alley, from "little ole Broadway," as we used to say. And what a shit-hole it is today! The glamour has been converted to smut, the celebrities have disappeared, a cunt like Linda Lovelace, who is able to swallow the biggest cock imaginable, is a big name. Just for her ability to do that! Imagine it!

That's why, perhaps, at twenty-one, Max Winthrop and I could play like little boys on that farm in New Jersey where he was convalescing. It was early Spring and the nights and early mornings were bitter cold. We slept under eiderdown quilts, as there was no heat whatever in the bedrooms. Maury, Max's nephew, who was mentally retarded or a bit nuts, perhaps both, slept in the same room with us. We would lie awake for hours telling stories or exchanging jokes. Maury looked upon his Uncle Max as Jesus Christ himself. He would have done anything for him. Max, on the other hand, treated his nephew like the imbecile he was, cuffed him, called him names, made him do all manner of things his parents would have disapproved of. The worse he treated the boy, the more the boy revered him. He even, out of gratitude seemingly, dug up some nice young fresh cunt for Max. Served them to him on a silver platter, with a sprig of parsley to give it additional savour. All this horseplay was right up Max's alley. As I said before, he knew how to keep a straight face. Evenings, he would sit at the organ and play hymns for Maury's parents. They hadn't the least suspicion what a jolly monster they were harboring in Max.

In bed Max would keep Maury in stitches, imitating the pious look of his parents. Max could even make them look thoroughly imbecilic without danger of hurting Maury's feelings. Maury laughed easily, laughed at anything Max said. I had to laugh myself. I laughed, knowing well just who and what Max was. At home a good husband, a good father; in his office, a good doctor. In the poolroom a shark. On the dance floor a satyr. With his pants down, Priapus himself. And all these characters were combined in the one person known to the world as Max Winthrop, Henry Miller's friend. It was assumed by most everyone that we were such great friends that nothing could ever separate us. No matter how gregarious I was, I was also a loner, very much of a loner. In everything but sociability and camaraderie, I was exceedingly different from the other club members. It was the same thing in the street; everyone considered me to be his friend, his special friend, whereas I was highly indifferent to the face of my friends. Now and then, to be sure, I did a dramatic thing for one of these friends, such as selling my bicycle or pawning my watch to prevent a friend from going to jail for some petty theft.

One has to be truly adolescent, I suppose, to attach the importance we did to our secret handshake, our passwords, and so on. Or to be so genuinely moved at meeting one another again after the lapse of only a week or two. Myself, I was probably the most emotional of all. When I saw Georgie Alford take his violin out of the case and tune up, I was almost in tears. I adored the way he played the instrument. He loved everything in a minor key and was marvelous as a second fiddle. He was also killing himself, with women, liquor and tobacco. He had the consumptive look of a Chopin and when he played it was always with a wholeheart. At the same time he was an absolute good-for-nothing—not a redeeming quality in him except for his lovable nature.

In the early days of the Xerxes Society, I was holding a miserable job in a famous cement company. I was a file clerk and evidently not very capable, though an idiot could have filled the job capably. I was too wrapped up in my bicycle, staying up too late with the widow, and of course thoroughly disinterested in my job. The boss who was over me, an irascible Canadian, would fly into a range over the mistakes I made. I am sure he thought I was mentally deficient. The salary I received was ridiculous. In those days grown men, married, perhaps with children, were paid as little as fifty dollars a month. I think my salary was fifteen or twenty dollars a month.

The only one of us who ever had any money in his pcoket was Max Winthrop. He was careful with his money, and thrifty. The rest of us had no sense of the value of money whatever. My lunch money for the week, for example, I could piss away in one night. So the rest of the week I starved or I would borrow a nickel from a fellow worker to buy a chocolate candy bar. I had a sweet tooth. The thirty-five cents I earned for a piano lesson was gone before I got home. I would buy myself two banana splits, which cost me thirty cents. Sometimes I was so disgusted with myself, with the lack of cash, that I would throw the remaining nickel in the gutter. Later, I would be bending over in the rain, to pick up the pennies someone had thrown me out of pity.

I could never imagine Max doing such things. But then I could never imagine him writing a *Tropic of Cancer* or even a Mickey Spillane thriller. One could see his life well in advance—it was as if someone had tattooed a blueprint of it over his body. No surprises, unless for the ability he showed to dig up fresh cunt. I could never imagine him showing a girl much affection—or writing her a love letter. With Max it had to be quick work or nothing. The funny part of it is that Max did not give the impression of a guy who was always on the prowl. The girl herself wouldn't know sometimes that he had his eye on her until she felt his prick inside her. Max would devour her like a sandwich. Then a friendly pat on the rump and ta-ta! That was it. Bye bye, baby! Usually these fucks didn't cost him a penny either. Max's philosophy was simple—if they like you, you can fuck them; if they don't, money won't get you anywhere. In the main he was right. But what sort of trollops were these conquests of his? Some he liked because they had big teats, some because of a cute ass, whatever that might mean, and others because they not only know how to fuck, but because they *loved* to fuck. Those were number-one gals for Max. He never spoke of a girl's beauty. He spoke of separate parts of the body. He could go into dithyrambs for example, about the hair on a certain girl's cunt. Once he raved about a fifteen-year-old who he said loved to do it standing up. In addition she never stopped coming once she started. He was afraid to let her suck him off for fear she would bite his prick off in sheer ecstasy.

There was another member of the club who was as much of a wolf as Max. But I will devote a chapter to him shortly. Anyway, never again have I met two men who were so hungry for cunt, who made it their business, you might say. Neither of them ever spoke of being in love. It was just cunt they were after, or, as they put it, "another piece of tail."

In a way, then, it was easy "to get one's nookie" in those days as it is today. Men haven't changed much, nor women either. The big difference between those times and this era is that now love is dying out. The songs may be full of love but not men's hearts. To be madly in love with someone is to be old-fashioned. Supposedly. That's not true either. The big difference between now and yesterday is that today you don't have to ask anyone's permission. All that matters is that she likes it and wants it. No danger of her becoming an old main if she has the necessary. Even marriage is no longer important. In my time even if it was only a prostitute you were taking to a hotel room you had to have a suitcase with you and you had to sign the register Mr. and Mrs. So and So.

Today a good whore—a call girl let's say—can make a couple of hundred dollars a day and not break her back. In my day you could sometimes buy a piece of ass for fifty cents. Today these gals ride around in cars, have cute apartments of their own, are not diseased and are not out to make a quick buck. You needn't be ashamed to take them to dinner or play a round of golf with them. Some of them are so sportive, and so well read, it's hard to make them keep their mind on the business at hand. They'd just as likely talk about Hemingway or Tolstoy or give you the low-down on Muhammed Ali and Joe Frazier. They're not whores any more. They're bright, educated young women who make a good, clean living fucking—and they only fuck those they like— what they call "gentlemen."

Today a girl who is eighteen and who hasn't been fucked yet is looked upon as lacking something. Most kids begin at twelve or fourteen. By twenty-one a girl today could have had a hundred different men. Not that that makes her any happier than her counterpart of fifty years ago. Nor does one have to have a great pair of teats today or a cute ass. Just being ready at any time is the essential. One should be able to count up to one hundred, of course. No need to know calculus or higher mathematics. No need to know Shakespeare, Homer or Dante. Think of the movie stars who came up from the gutter. Who cares? Can she still turn you on, that's all that matters. There was one woman, an entertainer, who had only to sing one song a night to have the whole country at her feet. She didn't have to show her belly button or wiggle her ass, or let her teats fall out like a "For Sale" sign; she simply had to sing in her own inimitable way, the song she had made so popular—"Red Head." Irene Franklin was her name. Not a great star, nor a great personality either, for that matter. But she had found that people wanted—a catchy tune. And because of it she could have anything she wanted. There were a number of men and women like that in the old days. Everybody loved them. Who does not remember Jack Norworth and Nora Bayes? They didn't have to be great actors or actresses, they didn't have to be too intelligent either. Nor was their sex life common knowledge. None of them was anything like a Garbo or a Duse. Americans simply took them to their hearts. Lucky creatures. A type that is growing rarer and rarer. Today it is more apt to be a football star than a stage or movie personality. What I am trying to say perhaps is that there was a light touch to things in the old days, more affection, more warmth, more devotion and loyalty. Advertising was only in its infancy. The public relations man was unknown. Champagne was more in vogue than cocaine.

In the beginning of my life there were books—plenty of them. Everyone who knew me wanted to contribute to my thirst for books. Today I am swamped with books—in many languages. Many I throw in the trash can. I have no respect for books per se. I am almost being buried alive under the avalanche of reading matter. And the more I read the more I realize that there were only a few great ones. I wanted to be one of those, one who would be remembered. And here again was a disturbing difference between Max and myself. He had a reverence for books and little ability, if any, to distinguish between a great author and a mediocre one. He was always baffled by the diversity of authors I pretended to read and admire. For I did not read *all* the books I could talk about so eloquently. Some authors make me drunk before I ever read them. Some were like gods to me, though I never read a line of theirs. I could *sniff* a good book or good author like a dog sniffs a good piece of tail. I didn't have to be in rut to tell the diference between a genius and a mere scribbler. I always despised the books we were given to read in school. Max, on the other hand, thought these books were "real literature."

Most people are born blind, deaf and mute. They think that acquiring what is called "Culture" will restore these missing faculties. They learn to recite names—of authors, composers, actors, and so on. They pass these off for the real thing. Lectures, for example, are most important to them: the easy way to imbibe culture. I have always been leery of Culture. Born imitator that he was, Max oozed Culture. If, as he once said, "the sun rose and set in his mother's ass," then Culture might be said to have done the same in *his* ass. Strange, how the ass was such an all important part of the body to him. To hear him rave about so and so's beautiful ass was like listening to Vergil reading from his own "Aeneid."

Like his father—who resembled a French peasant—Max was big, heavy and without subtlety. One would think his thick fingers unwieldy for the piano, but not so. They knew how to "tickle the ivories," as we say. They also knew how to get to the mouth of the womb without wasting time. He could play the "Maple Leaf Rag" like a drunken coon.

100

As I have said, it was through Max that I kept track of Cora's doings. His wife knew someone who was very intimate with Cora. Thus I learned that she was planning to become a school-teacher, something which truly saddened me. Through the same source I learned that she was getting thinner, paler, more serious, which was also depressing news. In short, I counted on Max to keep me posted as to Cora's doings. Sometimes I would inquire timidly if Cora ever asked about me. Evidently she didn't.

However, from another source I learned that she did inquire about me from time to time. By a curious coincidence, her brother-in-law, who was rather wealthy, was one of my father's customers. He knew about Cora and me and would volunteer information about her whenever he visited my father's shop. Usually he would tease me for not being more aggressive. He would warn me to wake up or she might fall in love with some-one else. (Strangely enough, I never gave this possibility much thought. I always saw Cora as being there, waiting for me—until eternity.) Yet we never telephoned one another, nor did we exchange more than three or four letters a year. Her letters were thoroughly conventional—her handwriting inflamed me more than her words. We just were not made to be together in this life. In some other time—past or future, maybe, but not this one. To think of her in bed with another man, a husband per-haps, was impossible for me. She did not belong to that race of women who took out a license and then permitted themselves to be raped night after night. And yet . . .

We are coming to it. In one night all my illusions are shattered. In one night all my hopes are dashed, all my feelings smashed. A pure accident. We are on the farm in New Jersey. It is night time and we are telling one another stories while snuggling under the cosy eiderdown. Suddenly, out of the blue, I ask Max if he's heard anything about Cora lately. I hadn't any news about her for over a year.

"I think she's O.K.," Max replied.

"You *think*," I repeated. "Don't you *know*? Doesn't your wife see their mutual friend any more?"

"Sure, Myrtle still sees her, only now that Cora's married—"

I sat bolt upright in bed. "*Married*," I roared. "*Since when!* You never told me she was married."

"I did too, Hen, only you weren't paying attention, I guess."

"When was this?" I asked

"Oh, a year or so ago. You had just left home to live with the widow."

I shook my head in disbelief. Cora married—impossible.

"What sort of guy did she marry?" I asked.

"A nice guy," says Max. "A chemist or a physicist, I think."

"How long had they been going together?"

"Oh, a year or so...You see, Hen, when Cora found out about the widow that finished it."

"How did she find out?"

"Ask me. News travels, you know. Besides, she ran into you two at the beach once, remember? That was quite a blow to her. Then, when she heard you were living together, well you can put two and two together."

I was only half-listening to his words. I was furious, furious at him, for not telling me sooner, and more furious because he was taking it so matter of factly.

"You know what I ought to do to you?" I yelled. "I ought to beat the living shit out of you."

This time *he* sat straight up in bed. Maury urged us to moderate our voices or we would wake the old folks.

"Listen, Hen," Max begins. "You've been acting strangely ever since you took up with the widow. You're jumpy, edgy-you're not yourself any more. We've all urged you to give her up but you turn a deaf ear. You don't see—"He broke off abruptly.

"Don't see what?" I asked.

"You don't see how incongruous it looks to see you going with a woman old enough to be your mother."

102

"No, I don't," I replied. "She doesn't look old. Besides, thirty-seven or eight isn't old."

"No," said Max, "It's just the difference between you. It ain't natural."

"But I—" I cut it short, I was just about to say—"But I love her." In my strange way I suppose I did love her, though I told myself it was pity which kept me tied to her. That was a lie, of course. A man doesn't fuck a woman night after night, in bed, on a chair, under the table—out of pity. The truth of the matter was every day I was thinking how to disengage myself. She knew I loved Cora, though we seldom spoke of her. Now, as I found out the next day, the house Cora and her husband lived in was on the next street to ours. Her house, in fact, was directly opposite ours. We both occupied top floors. With a spyglass I could look through my back window directly into hers—into her bedroom no less, that room which I didn't want to know existed. And this had been going on for over a year. Somehow I couldn't bring myself to believe it. And I hated, despised and loathed Max for telling me. I had rather he lied to me. I could not and never would, never did, forgive him.

Alec Considine

I'm not sure if it was from Galway or County Cork that his parents hailed but they were as Irish as Paddy's pig. His old man was a hod carrier and looked the part. His mother was more like a blue-nosed Nova Scotian than an Irish biddy. The old man threw tantrums now and then. He was crabby and cantankerous. He could get hopping mad and actually dance with rage. If I thought my home life was difficult, Alec's was a hundred times worse. His old man was a constant source of humiliation to him. The old man was that ignorant he had never heard of Robert Burns. Add to this that he was a prejudiced, narrow-minded Catholic, stubborn and obstinate as they make 'em.

Alec was from the old neighborhood though not attending the same school as I. He was going to a business school, learning stenography and typewriting. He intended to become a public stenographer while putting himself through college. It was through Max Winthrop that I met Alec. They lived in the same neighborhood. The fact that Alec's father and mother came from Ireland meant they might just as well have come from another planet. Alec's ways were incomprehensible to them and theirs to him. There was no possibility of understanding one another.

Like my friend Jimmy Pasta, Alec too nourished ambitions though he had not definitely made up his mind what he intended to be. First of all he wanted a good education.

It was with Alec that I had the greatest rapport, as far as intellectual matters were concerned. Whereas Max Winthrop was thoroughly conventional in his thinking—if not in his behavior—Alec Considine was a rebel and a radical right down to the bone. We were always arguing and discussing things, chiefly about books and world events. Many a night it was four or five in the morning before we would separate.

If we happened to see a good play, say by Shaw, Galsworthy or O'Neill, we could mull it over for weeks. Of course we had both read the great European dramatists, such as Ibsen, Ernst Toller, Strindberg, the German Expressionists and so on. We were both voracious readers and we rather looked down upon the other members of the Club for their ignorance.

Alec's chief obsession was—as with Max Winthrop—*cunt*. It didn't matter what she looked like, how ignorant she might be—was she fuckable? That was all he was interested in. Ever so often he got the clap which didn't bother him too much: he treated it like a cold in the head. Also, it seemed to make him even hornier.

What he liked was to find a good-natured whore, fuck her in her own room, then bolt without paying her.

Of course he liked the dance halls. Not the ones with taxi girls but the dives where girls went to pick up men and vice versa. He drank heavily, but that was a natural part of his Irish background. His old man hailed from the slums. It was amusing how well I got along with his parents. They thought me to be quite a gentleman; they liked the respectful way in which I addressed them and my behavior in general. Why couldn't their Alec be like me? In their eyes he was nothing more than a bum, he would never be anybody or get anywhere. (I should add that my own parents thought pretty much the same about me.)

However, he fooled them all. He made his way through business school, then college with a Master's degree. What now? he asked himself. What was he going to do for a living? All this did not improve him. He was incorrigible. It was through a strange coincidence that he happened to decide on the career of architect. Someone had lent him a book about the famous Sullivan of Chicago, forerunner of Frank Lloyd Wright. That decided him. He would give New York some buildings to remember. And, strange to say, he did just that eventually.

But I'm getting ahead of myself.

One of the things that irritated him about me was that I was always broke. Wherever we went he paid the bill, but not without a lot of grumbling and cursing. He used to lecture me about my lack of ambition. What was I going to become eventually? He knew, to be sure, that I was writing, or trying to write, but this never impressed him much.

My first wife hated him. She knew that Alec was like and would always try to hold me back when he asked me to go out with him. Alec had watched me go through my ordeals with Cora and the widow and knew I wouldn't last long with the wife. "I didn't suggest you marry her," he said to me once. "I only said she would make a good lay."

Incredible as it may seem, I fought with her every day. There wasn't a single thing we ever agreed about. She had been reared in a Catholic school, later a Catholic conservatory of music in Canada, and was naturally filled with all sorts of wrong ideas. In

106

spite of their rigid moral codes and stupid beliefs some of her Catholic friends were good sex pots. I remember one who used to finger her rosary and, while fucking away for dear life, would exclaim, "O mother of God, O blessed Virgin, forgive me for what I am doing!" And so saying, she would grab my cock and hold it in her hand a while, caress it, kiss it, then shove it back in her cunt and whisper—"Do it some more, Henry, it feels so good. Fuck me, fuck me! And may the holy Virgin forgive and protect me!"

What Alec liked was nurses. They knew how to protect themselves, they were free in their ideas, and easy to manipulate. Many was the nurse he fucked in the park, her back up against a tree. Like another bosom pal of ours, he didn't believe in spending money unnecessarily on women. On the other hand, he *would* tell them he loved them. He would say anything, even promise to marry, so long as he could get his end in.

The exciting thing was our conversations and discussions. Being Irish he had a flair for argument and dispute. But he was a logician too. Anything and everything was food for argument. He also enjoyed giving advice but was seldom able to take any himself. Our best talks occurred in his room. Unlike my hall bedroom, which was more like a prisoner's cell, his room was spacious, boasted a sink with running water, a couch, a couple of comfortable old chairs and a huge bed. He got up when he damn well pleased. Sometimes there was a girl in bed with him. He would introduce her in a casual way, pretending to have known her a long time. "This is the kid I've been telling you about, Hen," he would say, pulling the covers off her to expose her charms. Patting her belly or her rump he would add—"Not bad, eh?"

One of the things about our relationship was the intimacy we indulged in. We were more like two Russians out of Dostoievsky than natives of Broooklyn.

If he had the clap, for instance, he would get out of bed, ask me to approach the sink, then take out his cock—a dreadful

107

sight—and ask me in all seriousness if I thought he should see a doctor about it. While holding it in his hand—it looked like a bloody sausage—he would begin a long story about some girl he had met and her relations with the parish priest. (He hated the Catholic church like poison.) "Listen, Hen, get this," he would begin. "She goes to confession and this time she has to confess that she has just had her first experience with a man."

Here's how the dialogue went . . . He imitates the pious, honey-tongued hypocrite, Father O'Reilly.

Father: "You say you let him touch you. Just *where* did he touch you, my child?"

The girl is too embarrassed to reply immediately. The father tries to help her out.

Father: "Did he touch your breast, my child?"

"Yes, Father."

Father: "Tell me, where else did he put his hand?"

"Between my legs," she replies.

"Did he leave it there long? I mean—ten minutes, twenty-five minutes or an hour?"

"Nearer to an hour, I guess, Father."

"And what did *you* do all that time?"

"I got very excited, Father. I lost my head completely, I fear."

"What do you mean by that, child?"

(Mind you, this "child" is about eighteen, built like a race horse.)

"I mean, Father, that then he unbuttoned his trousers, took out his thing and put it where he had his hand before."

"Did he put it inside you?"

"Yes, Father, he did."

"Did it feel good or were you very ashamed of yourself?"

"It felt terribly good, Father. I'm afraid I may let him do it again—that is, if it isn't too great a sin."

"We'll see about that later," says Father O'Reilly. "Now I want you to step into my office for a few minutes."

"You can imagine the rest, Hen. He gets her into his office, asks her to lift her dress so that he can fiddle with her vagina, and then, in the twinkling of an eye, he's got his prick out and fucking the BJesus out of her.

"That's an everyday occurrence. That's nothing compared to what took place a few centuries ago. The Popes, some of them, were not only thieves and murders, they committed incest too." He went to his bookcase and pulled out a book on the lives of the Popes. "Here, read this sometime when you have nothing better to do."

Then, with a strange smile on his face, he quickly adds—"What do you do with yourself all day, may I ask? don't tell me you're sitting in the library reading all day. I suppose you're still looking for a job. By the way, how much dough have you on you now? Can you return that dollar I lent you last week?"

I made a wry grimace and pretended to laugh it off.

I pulled my empty pockets out to show him I was telling the truth.

"I can't get over it," he says. "Always stone broke. Tell me, Hen, how do you manage to get around? Do you scrounge from everyone you meet? Don't you have any pride? I won't speak of ambition. I know that would be inconsistent with your philosophy." This was intended sarcastically, because I was always telling him of the philosophers I was reading.

"I suppose," he went on, "your Prince Kropotkin never used money. And what about that German philosopher who ended up in the nut house?"

"You mean Nietzche?" I said. "Yeah, that's the guy. Didn't he think he was another Jesus?"

I pretended to be surprised.

"On the contrary," I said, "you forget that it was he who wrote *The Anti-Christ.*"

A pause, during which he applies some ointment to his sore, swollen prick, then sinks slowly, like a Pasha, back into the bed.

From the bed—"O, Hen, before I forget—open the top drawer of that dresser. In a tray you'll find some change. Help yourself! That'll save you the trouble of asking me later." An after-thought—"By the way, if I hadn't offered you a little money how would you have got home—tell me that, will you?"

I had to smile. "O, I always manage somehow," I said.

"*You* manage?" he repeated. "You mean someone always manages to rescue you at the last minute."

"Righto," I said. "It comes to the same thing, doesn't it?"

"It does to you, maybe, but not to me."

"Why do you worry yourself about these things?" I asked.

"Because I haven't anything better to do, I guess. Listen, Hen, don't take me seriously. I'm just as much of a bum as you, only I'm a little smarter. I like to poke my nose into everybody's business. By the way, would you write down the titles of those books you were talking about yesterday?"

"What's the use?" I replied. "You'll never read them. They're not the kind of books that get you anywhere."

"You don't have to tell me that," he said. "Sometimes I wonder what *you* see in them. That Dostoievsky of yours, for instance. Just the other day I picked up one of his novels, thinking to read it. But Jesus, he takes up twenty or thirty pages describing how someone bends over to pick up a toothpick. He may be great for the Russians—not for me. I know you dote on him. But then you have nothing better to do. Anyway, Hen, put the titles down for me, will you? Who knows, I *may* read them before I die."

I jotted down a few titles with the names of the authors.

"How do you come by such books?" he says. "Now this one, about Milarepa—is that how you pronounce it? What has he got to give *me*?"

"Why don't you read and find out for yourself?" I suggested.

"Because I'm too damned lazy, I guess," he answers bluntly.

As I'm getting ready to leave he suddenly remembers something. "Listen, Hen, I almost forgot. You know what? I think I'm falling in love. In fact, I may be in love already. It's someone I never spoke to you about. Someone who won't let me touch her. A school teacher *and* a Catholic. Can you beat that? Yeah, everytime I call on her I bring a box of candy or flowers. She thinks that's refined. In her eyes I'm pretty low in the scale. She says I'm intelligent but I have no principles. She's trying to make a gentleman of me, can you beat that? That's why I've got to get this dose of clap cured soon. I don't know what she'd say or do if she saw what it looks like now. That's why I asked you about the books. I can rattle off the titles—that will impress her. She says she reads a lot, but I don't think it's great literature. She likes to go to the opera and the ballet. The movies are too vulgar for her. Doesn't know much about art. I don't think she'd know a Gauguin from a Van Gogh. She'd like me to take piano lessons. I told her about you. She seemed impressed. Of course I didn't tell her what an unreliable irresponsible bastard you are."

I tried to find out her name but he wouldn't give it to me. "You won't like her, I think," he says. "Too damned refined, too conventional. She'd like your intellect though. And your smooth talk. By the way, how is it going with the widow? Still in love with her? Look out or she'll have you marrying her before long."

"She's already tried," I said. And I related how I had told my mother one day while sitting in the kitchen—told her I was going to marry the widow.

I had hardly got the words out of my mouth when my mother approaches me with a carving knife in her hand. "Another word of this," she exclaimed, "and I'll plunge this through your heart." By the look on her face I believe she would have.

"Your folks are almost as bad as mine," says Alec. "You should hear my old lady sometime. She sounds cracked to me, B'Jesus. And the old man is worse. Such moralistic monsters—from the Emerald Isle, no less."

111

At this juncture I thought it appropriate for him to let me dig into his coffer again.

"How much did you take the first time?" he wanted to know.

"About sixty cents," I told him. "O.K. Take another thirty-five cents, if you like, but no more. I have to work for my money," he added.

I agreed, but just the same I took fifty cents. I didn't mind cheating and robbing him. It made up for all the sermons he delivered. In a good mood he might lend me as much as five dollars, but it was like pulling teeth. Some days he had fifty or a hundred dollars on him. He bet on the horses frequently and won.

As I'm easing my way out he cries out—"Hen, what was that title of the Dostoievsky novel you mentioned the other day? I want to tell my girl."

"*The Idiot*," I yelled back.

"Thanks, Hen, I'll try her out with that one first. What a title! Is it really about an idiot?"

"Yes, Alec, but a most exceptional one. He'll put your girl in a trance."

It was always hard to take leave of him or to get rid of him if he came to see me. Sometimes, if I were reading an interesting book, for example, I would not answer a knock on the door. If it were Alec I would know it quickly, for he hated to be left standing in the hallway.

"It's me, Hen, it's Alec!" he would shout, rapping harder.

Then I would grow quiet as a mouse, hardly daring to breathe. After a time he would give up and descend the stairs. But sometimes he would try to fool me. (He always knew that I was in.) He would descend the steps noiselessly, in the expectation that I would believe he had gone and might open the door just to see. Sometimes we would carry on this game for an hour or more. It was always something urgent he had to see me about. At least, it seemed so to him. To me nothing was urgent,

112

nothing important, particularly if I were reading a good book. In those days I could read for hours at a stretch. Later on, when I began writing in earnest, I wouldn't dream of wasting my time reading in broad daylight. I almost regarded reading as sinful. Strange change of outlook. But in becoming a writer I had undergone many changes of viewpoint.

In any case, reading had now become a luxury with me. I permitted myself this luxury with only a few special writers, to wit — Dostoievsky, Oswald Spengler, Elie Fauré, Sherwood Anderson, Rimbaud, Giono, and such like. I never read a popular novel. Neither did I read the newspaper in those days. I was thoroughly disinterested in the news. If there were war or revolution, I always said, I would soon hear about it. The rest meant nothing to me. There was no television then, or radio either. I disliked the radio when it did come. The radio was for half-wits and simpletons, I told myself. Or housewives who had nothing better to do.

And so I read a great deal. My friend Alec absorbed my reading like a sponge. He always referred to my favorite writers as "queer birds" not meaning "homosexual" to be sure, but eccentric, slightly cracked, or downright mad. For a writer to be mad was o.k. in his opinion. An artist had to be a bit mad to survive in a world such as ours. Such opinions led him to say to me, when in the mood, "You know, Hen, I think you have it in you. At any rate, you're crazy enough to pass for an artist. *All you lack is talent.*"

I don't recall ever showing him anything I had written which he approved. "In the first place," he would say, "you use too many big words, you know that." Indeed I did. I knew that he was slowly reading the entire unabridged dictionary, which then contained about a half a million words. And how did he read this huge tome? By tearing out a fresh page every day and sticking it in his coat pocket. In the subway, on a bus, or while waiting to see someone in his office, he would pull out the page and study it. He took notice not only of the definition of the words, but of their pronunciation and derivation. So at times he would correct my usage of a word or its pronunciation.

Apotheosis was such a word. I pronounced it *apoth*eosis. The correct way was apoth*eosis*. He loved to trip me up occasionally. Sometimes he would call me up at some ungodly hour to ask if I knew such and such a word.

But it was not only that I used big words which bothered him—it was that my stories were dry and dull. I ought to read de Maupassant, he averred, or Somerset Maugham. They knew their craft! He was right, they were indeed good craftsmen, but then I didn't attach much importance to "craft." My favorites had gone far beyond mere craft. They were writing from their guts or perhaps some stranger part of the body. They didn't care about being understood by any and everybody. They addressed themselves to the elite, to their peers. Oddly enough, in doing so, they not only reached their peers but oddballs like me or simpletons who didn't read much. Actually, of course, they were writing to please themselves. They did not have to meet any requirements. They had no boss and no steady income. Most of them were recognized fifty years too late.

Alec couldn't understand anyone putting up with such delays. He wanted to see results—and quickly. A genius like Van Gogh, who never sold even one painting during his entire life was not only a genius, in Alec's opinion, but a fool. He could have painted signs or houses, in Alec's mind, instead of sponging on his brother. Nevertheless, he was intensely curious about such men. He raved about Maugham's book on Gauguin—*The Moon and Six Pence.* He even liked the idea that Gauguin had left a cushy job in a bank and a good-looking wife, in order to go to Tahiti and paint.

"That's what may happen to you one day," he said. "I can just see you picking up your rags and going to the Himalayas." What I found fascinating about Asia and Asiatics was hard for him to understand.

114

I pointed out that our own Lafcadio Hearn of New Orleans, whose stories he professed to like, had left America to go to Japan, where he married a Japanese woman and wrote most of his work. "Yes, Hen," he said, "but remember that Hearn himself was a cross between a Greek and an Irishman. He wasn't a typical one-hundred-percent American."

I didn't see that that mattered. I talked about Marco Polo and similar adventurers. He was unimpressed.

"You dote on crackpots and eccentrics," he said.

For all the criticism that he heaped on me, he had a strong affection for me. I think he secretly regretted being so "normal" and "conventional" himself. Though few people who knew him would have used those adjectives in referring to him.

Certainly there was nothing unusual in the way he dressed. Unless it was that he was unusually sloppy and dirty. (He used to pin notes on the mirror at the sink, reminding himself to wash his *whole* body, not just his hands and face.) Now and then he would ask me to come close and sniff him. "Tell me honestly," he would say, "do I smell bad? I'm so damned lazy I hate to bother to wipe my ass. That's the truth."

To tell the truth, he sometimes did smell bad. He always had a bad breath, for one thing. That was because of his drinking and smoking and his neglect in brushing his teeth. "Look at them," he would sometimes remark, "aren't they disgusting? They look more like fangs than teeth, don't they?" As you can see, he was not in the least ashamed of admitting his weaknesses and defects. In fact, he took pleasure in airing them—at least with me. His idea of a friend was one to whom you could tell anything about yourself. If it were incest, all the merrier.

He could smell like a horse *and* stable! Often he got into bed with his shoes on. Or he would get out of bed and shine his shoes with the bed sheet. Living like a pig and behaving like a bum, it sounded strange, coming from him, to advise his sister how to behave with men. She was not to trust *any* of them—

115

good advice!—not even the well-behaved ones. And especially the smooth talkers. (Well he might warn her of that type, for he was one of the smoothest talkers imaginable.)

The truth is, I guess, that we were both the confessor type. Yet to this day I have not read Jean Jacques Rousseau's *Confessions*. I have read most of the great confessions, such as the one by Saint Augustine. And the one by the celebrated young woman—Marie Bashkirtseff—and the *Diary of Amiel* (le Journal Intime). The one great confession (in thirteen volumes) which everyone seems to have read, I gave up on half-way through the first volume. I am referring to the great Don Juan—Casanova—to his *Memoirs*. These were the sort of books Alec loved to hear me talk about but, as he said, never had time to read.

He did find time, of course, to read *Fanny Hill's Diary*. But what a shrinking violet of a book compared to *My Secret Life*, written by an anonymous gentlemen in the Victorian era. I believe I communicated to him my passion for the works of Knut Hamsun, and to my surprise, he read two or three of his books, admitting for once, that my taste was good. But then, seldom in my life have I met anyone who did not share my love for Hamsun. Somewhere in his work Joseph Delteil writes that anyone who does not love his mother is a monster. I would say the same, only substituting for mother, Knut Hamsun. There were a few good authors, Alec adored aside from those I recommended. Oddly enough, two of them were Stasiu's favorites—Joseph Conrad and Anatole France. He also admired Jack London and Maxim Gorky, the Russian. They had much in common, to be sure. Both men were translated in over fifty languages, including Chinese and Japanese. Both men were trained in "The University of Life," which is the title of a film devoted to Gorky's life. I believe that both men were voracious readers, though neither had much schooling. Both men appealed to a wide audience; both were men of heart and wrote from the heart as well as the guts. With such men it matters little what language they choose to write in — they are understood everywhere by everybody.

There was nothing one could conceal from Alec. He was nosy, inquisitive and a gossiper. He fed on other people's disasters.

Even though he had "almost" fallen in love with his school teacher, he was still on intimate terms with a blonde called Lila and her older sister. It seems that he would go to bed with the two of them. Then, when one of the sisters had fallen asleep, he would quietly put the boots to the other one. As you can imagine, it was a very touchy situation. The more so since it was understood he was going to marry Lila, the younger sister—*i.e.*, when he could afford to marry. He always managed to leave himself a loophole. In one of his frank moods he told me one day that he preferred fucking the older sister—not because she was more experienced but because she was more neurotic. Indeed, she was always on the border of hysteria. That heightened the play, he affirmed. But he had to be very careful when fucking this one while her sister was in bed with them. When she got carried away she could squeal like a dog or bite or pinch.

But Alec loved these dangerous situations. If caught he always found a way to wriggle out. He was not only a first rate liar, he was a good actor too. I could very well imagine him in court defending a client. Criminals seemed to fascinate him. Yet Dostoievsky's *Crime and Punishment* left him cold. Sentimental, he called it. He wanted me to know that it wasn't *Crime and Punishment*, but *The Crime* and *The Punishment*. Whereupon, I told him that he was a living example of "the crime" and "the punishment." He was the crime and the punishment all in one. Instead of the prostitute—Sonia, was it?—he had his school teacher friend. He didn't think this at all funny.

If I dwell on his weaknesses it's because, as with Max Winthrop, I am unable to understand how a person can get away with so much right under one's nose.

My parents liked Alec Considine because he was "serious" (sic) and ambitious. They didn't know of or suspect his affairs with women, his doses of the clap, his gambling habits, his general filthiness and so on. But parents are not very good judges of other's children. Nor of their own, for that matter. "Don't give us any trouble," that's always their main concern.

Alec's mother resembled one of those blue-nosed Nova Scotians, as I said earlier. For some strange reason in that tiny corner of the world the Lord has turned out some of the most unprepossessing women in the world. Of course Mrs. Considine was Irish, but what matter? She carried with her that icy chill, that too correct deportment, that uncharitable look in the eye. She saw nothing good in anyone, friend or foe. She hated herself—and for no particular reason. She was all malice and venom. And her chief affliction, it goes without saying, was her son. When things became intolerable she would call *my* mother to discuss the situation with her. Fortunately, my mother was always eager to get Mrs. Considine off the hook. She said it was impossible to understand her because of her thick brogue. Besides, my mother was not the "simpatico" type. She had her own troubles, she would say. (And I was one of them.) Though he pretended, Alec, to look after me, it was really I who was looking after him. The only difference was that I did not relish the job, whereas he did. Every day he had to see me, for one reason or another. If I were home (in the evening) he would telephone and tell me where to meet him. I hated the phone—even then—but that didn't matter to him. One of the funny things he was doing was studying the piano. I say funny because he had no ear, no flair whatever for music. I took him to hear one or two Wagnerian operas, during which he fell asleep. He did not know one composer from another. Brahms he had never heard, nor Schumann, nor Ravel, nor Debussy. He liked only "light things," he said. It was the same with painting. He had no eye for painting. Only literature interested him—and the stage. It was about this time that David Belasco was all the rage—and his mistress, whom he had made famous. (Leonore Ulric.) The

American theatre was at a low point then—it only began to pick up in the twenties and thirties. The Jewish Theatre was much better than the American. With the Theatre Guild came some wonderful plays, such as Tchekov's and Tolstoy's—also Andreyev's and Gorky's. I think it was in his period that I saw "The Dybbuk," performed by the Habima Players. I saw it first in Hebrew, then in Yiddish and finally in English. Unforgettable. Exorcism. But utterly unlike the one now creating such a rage.

To come back to Alec...Yes, he thought he was teaching me—"wising me up" as he put it. In other words, teaching me sophistication. To me it was quite a joke of course. I never liked any of his companions, male or female. I never gambled, I didn't drink. And I was not a good storyteller. In short, I was dull company, which would lead him later, as we rode home, to expand on what a queer fellow I was. Snobbish, he thought. Choosy. Couldn't tolerate "ordinary" people. (To me his "ordinary" people belonged in the zoo.) Unhappy I was, he thought unless I could rave about Nietzche, Dostoievsky, André Gide, and such like.

Sometimes, when he wanted to show off in front of a girl, a new one, he would mention the name of some unusual author or the title of one of his books. He would pretend, of course, that he was also familiar with the author. One of these titles he liked to reel off was *Postprandial Conversations*. (Postprandial meaning nothing more than "after dinner.") Of course the girl, impressed by the unfamiliar word, would exclaim—"What is that about, in Heaven's name?" Then Alec would prod me to tell about the book. I usually invented something out of my head—it made no difference since neither of them had read the book. Which reminds me that, though I was not what is called a good storyteller, I could on occasion, especially with unenlightened people, make things up which were far better, far more exciting than mere storytelling. Sometimes I even ventured some psychic tricks, which never failed to stupefy my listeners. Later, Alec would ask quite seriously if there was anything to that yarn I had told at the table. He believed in my ability to read people. Whenever he was in doubt about someone he would invite me to go with them and look them over. He never took my advice, however. Himself, he was full of stories and jokes of all kinds. He usually began the conversation this way—"Listen, Hen, here's one I heard yesterday. You've got to listen to it . . ."

Max Winthrop was equally good at stories and especially at jokes. He had a better sense of humor than did Alec. Sitting in the back room of a saloon, drinking nothing stronger than beer, we could sit up for hours amusing one another. Now and then one of us would piss in his pants from laughing so hard.

As I said, I was getting an education, "getting wised up," as he put it. I learned many things I never put to use and hardly anything that was of any value to me. Except one thing: *people*. All my life I had this faculty of meeting people, of studying them, of being part of them. It matters little from what class they came, what education they had, and so on. Fundamentally all are alike. Yet each one is unique. Strange paradox. All are reachable —and redeemable. Those in prison are often better than those who put them there. Thieves and pimps are far more interesting than preachers and teachers—or most psychologists. Nobody should be wholly despised. Some should be murdered perhaps, in cold blood. But not all murderers are murderers at heart. I have often wondered how many people I have met in my long life. I know for certain that during the four and a half years I spent in the Western Union I met and talked to a good hundred thousand. And yet I regard myself as a loner. I don't mind being alone. As I said somewhere else—"At the worst I am with God!"

That was one thing Alec could not stand. Being alone. It didn't matter whom he chose—he had to have company. I must confess, most of my freedom to be alone developed after I became a writer. Before that I too was always in search of someone. One would think it would be the contrary, that after becoming

120

famous the world would be at one's feet. It happened to me also, but I soon learned how to get rid of these fawners and lick-spittles. No, most all the material in my books—people, places, events—happened *before* I began to write. What I enjoy now is to walk in a crowd and be unrecognized. Or perhaps recognized by some very unimportant person—a waitress, a chambermaid, such like. Or, as in France, to be recognized by a butcher or baker, asked to wait a moment till he or she fetches an armful of my books and humbly asks for my autograph. That only happens to me in foreign countries. In this country, people in such trades are usually illiterate, or at least *inculte* as the French say. As I have mentioned before, in Alec's eyes I was not yet a writer and probably never could be. Like Stanley, he seemed pleased to think of me as a failure. "I don't know what I find in you that makes me seek you out," he would say to my face. "Maybe it's because you're a good listener."

Anyone who knew us well could see in a minute what drew us together. It was the very difference between us that acted as an attraction. That and the fact that he liked complications. He also adored the same actresses that I did—Elsie Ferguson, Marie Doro, Nazimova, Elsie Janis, Olga Petrova and so on.

From an intense and prolonged discussion of the relative merits of Dostoievsky, Tolstoy, Tchekov, Andreyev, we could move to a poolroom and shoot pool the rest of the night. At midnight I would often go back to his room and discuss, or argue, the merits of other writers. We never tired of talking arguing, discussing.

We seemed to know every intimate detail of each other's life. We delighted in telling of the weaknesses and foibles of our parents. Which brings me back to Max Winthrop and the back-rooms of saloons. Especially that delicious phrase he let drop one night. About his mother—how the sun rose and set in her ass. When he said it Alec and I looked at each other with the same expression of disbelief, of stupor. But we said nothing. We left soon thereafter. It was only a few nights later that Alec brought up the subject.

"I didn't think he was quite that bad," he ventured. "What sentimental rot!"

I agreed—I had never heard worse.

Suddenly I said—"But Alec, maybe she thinks the same of Max, that he's her whole world."

"Then they're both stupid idiots," said Alec. "If they had said it, or felt that way, about Jesus or the Buddha, I could understand—but about one another! No, that's too much. You know, Hen, sometimes I think Max isn't very intelligent. He knows how to get good marks, pass tests, and that sort of thing, but when it comes to looking at the world he's just a baby. Have you ever noticed."

One day, in the course of our conversation, one of those conversations out of a book, he says to me—"You now, Hen, I'm really not such a bad guy as people like to think. It's true, I'm a bit of a lecher, I drink too much and all that, but I have a good heart. I don't take advantage of people. Now *you*, you bastard, you have a touch of evil in you. I may act like a character in a novel, but it's only acting, whereas you *are* a character in a book—a book that has yet to be written, of course. I *enjoy* making people dislike me. But *you*, you don't seem to care whether you're liked or disliked. You act as if you were a superior being. Where do you get that stuff, I wonder? What gives you such ideas? Probably the books you read. You don't read books the way other people do—you believe them! One day you are Glahn the hunter, the next day Alyosya and another day Martin Eden. The only difference between you and these book characters is that you have your eyes wide open. You know what you're doing and where you're going. You can let yourself be inflated by lofty ideas, yet not hesitate to steal a dime from a blind newspaperman.

"You never criticize me or preach to me, but you can make me feel like a worm. Sometimes I wonder why you bother to

122

associate with someone like me. It doesn't seem to matter much to you whom you associate with. All that matters is that they can give you a little change or a fat cigar. I can picture you getting along famously with a murderer, if he was taking good care of you. You seem to think the world owes you a living. You want everything your own way, don't you? The idea of working for a living never appealed to you—not because you're lazy but because you think you're above others. There's something perverse about you. You're not only against society, you're against human nature. You're not just an atheist—the very idea of a God seems absurd to you. You don't commit any crimes, but you're a criminal at heart. You talk about brotherly love yet you don't give a shit about your neighbor. As for being a friend, you don't know the meaning of the word. To you a friend is someone who helps you out. If he hasn't got what you need, to hell with him. You're one hundred percent selfish, one hundred percent ego.

"Look at you! You sit there listening to my tirade with a smile on your face. Nothing I say makes the least difference to you. You're not a utopist—you're a solipsist."

"O.K., Alec, so I'm a solipsist. But why all this? I haven't asked you for a cent so far today, have I?"

"No, but you will if I know you. You'd even borrow a pair of dirty socks, if you felt like it."

"I might borrow a clean handkerchief from you but never a pair of dirty socks."

Suddenly, with a wry smile, he says—"You would take a penny if I offered it to you, wouldn't you?" I replied smilingly that I certainly would.

"How come you don't ask for big sums anymore? You're so modest now—a quarter will do, or even a dime."

"That's because I've learned humility," I said with tongue in cheek.

"You mean half a loaf is better than none, don't you?"

123

"You could put it that way too," I said. "By the way, don't you ever steal from your mother's purse?" I added.

"I would if I knew where she kept it," he replied. "Why do you ask? Do *you?*"

I nodded. "Only small amounts," I said, "a dime, a quarter maybe, never a half dollar."

"And she doesn't notice it?"

"I suppose not. Or maybe she just can't believe I would stoop that low."

"She doesn't think you're an angel, does she?"

"I doubt it. Tell me, what exactly does your mother think of *you?*"

"I'll make it easy for you, Hen—*the* worst!"

"That's refreshing," I said. "It's good to live without illusions."

"Illusions!" he repeated. "That's exactly the world." He seemed awfully pleased with himself at this moment.

"I suppose you think that *I* live with illusions, don't you?"

"N-no, Hen," he replied soberly. "I don't say that. I say you live in a world of unreality. And very comfortably too. Perhaps that's what irritates me—the fact that you don't suffer. You have no remorse, no regrets, no sense of guilt. You have no conscience, damn you. You behave like an innocent babe. That's another thing I can't stand—this innocence of yours. Or are you only pretending?"

"I see that I'm not going to get much help from you today," I said. "But then I didn't expect any. I've come to give *you* some money—pay back what I owe you."

He began to laugh uproariously. "And how do you know how much you owe me?" he asked tauntingly.

"Because I've kept a record of it here in this little book." I opened the book, scanned the pages and said—"Exactly $52.75—that's what I owe you."

"And you're going to pay me back—now, today?"

"Of course. Why? Would you rather I paid you another day?"

He shook his head. "Don't tell me you *inherited* a sum of money," he began.

"No, Alec, I found it in the street. It was a wallet. I almost tripped over it. Naturally, I went through the wallet, wondering whom it may have belonged to. Would you believe it, I was almost on the verge of returning it to its owner, but then I came across his business card, with a good address, and I decided to keep the money. I had more need of it than he, I'm sure."

"Are you telling me the truth?" he asked, with a smile on his lips.

"Certainly I am. Why would I invent a story like that? Or did you think perhaps I had stolen it?"

"No, Hen, I didn't think anything. I was just curious. People don't pick up wallets in the street every day, you know."

"Especially not with several hundred dollars in it." I said.

That set him off for some reason. Now suddenly I was in the category of a thief. I should have made an effort to return it to its owner, or else surrendered it to the police.

"*The police!*" I exclaimed. "You must be out of your mind."

He had to admit that handing it over to the police was far-fetched. Now he was curious as to what I would do with the extra money.

"I'll buy some handsome gift for the widow," I said. "She'll appreciate it."

"Are you giving anything to charity?"

"Not this time," I said. "Maybe when I find another."

"Would you lend me any of it if I asked you?" he inquired.

"Why not? Of course! As much as you wish—you name it."

"Thanks, Hen, I don't want a cent. I was just testing you." I chatted another few minutes, then took leave of him. He seemed very pleased with himself for some reason.

As I was leaving he said—"You don't need to keep that note-book for my account," he said. "I trust you."

I don't know which of his moods I enjoyed most—probably

the cantankerous ones. Somehow, no matter how he berated me, no matter how farfetched his accusations, I remained untouched. He was a study to me, a most interesting one.

He had yet to be put to the test, of course. He was only a student now, a student full of theories and ideals. I had more confidence in my Italian friend, Jimmy Pasta.

But it was exciting to argue with him. And especially to pull his leg. He knew me inside out—and yet he didn't know me at all. He didn't *want* to know me, the real me. He wanted to preserve this image of me which he had created for himself. He wanted me to become a failure—to prove some vague point of his own. And he certainly did not, could not, believe that I might become a good writer one day.

One day, just like in a Russian novel, who should suddenly appear on the scene but Alec's older brother who had left home quite a few years ago when Alec was just a kid.

Bob, the brother, had apparently traveled all over the world during his absence. He had spent considerable time in Asia, in India more particularly. He had a lot to relate about the customs of the various peoples and their philosophy of life. To Alec's parents it sounded like so much Greek. But they were proud of their son who seemed indeed to be the very opposite of his younger brother.

At first Alec was impressed. In fact he never knew that he had an elder brother. The parents had said nothing about him, thinking he had become a worthless drifter. As for myself I took to him immediately. I was particularly interested in his spiritual and metaphysical ideas. India had become to him something like his true home. The elder Considines were naturally a bit bewildered by the discussions which now ensued between the two brothers and myself.

It took only a few weeks before Alec and his brother were at loggerheads. Alec simply couldn't swallow all the "spiritual nonsense," as he called it, which has brother dished out.

What I wondered was whatever induced his elder brother to return to the parental home. "Just plain homesick," he explained. Also he feared that he was losing his American heritage.

One of the good results of his brother's homecoming was the surprising change that came over Alec after reading a book of Swami Vivekananda's which his brother lent him. The effect was not only astounding but lasting. Alec changed his way of life overnight. He was now more than ever determined to be a great architect. If I was surprised by this about-face his parents were even more so. They attributed it to the brother's influence, which Alec stoutly denied. He maintained that he was capable of doing his own thinking and needed no help from anyone.

All this reminds me of a quotation which his brother dropped now and then. It was from Gautama the Buddha and ran thus: "I obtained not the least thing from complete, unexcelled awakening, and it is for this very reason that it is called complete, unexcelled awakening."

There was another line from the Buddha he was also fond of. It was the Buddha's rejoinder to a question put him by a passing stranger. Asked who he was and what he was, the Buddha replied: "I am a man who is awake."

Alec's brother professed to be puzzled that Alec and I could waste so much time discussing literature rather than philosophy of life itself. Names like Strindberg, Bergson, Boccaccio meant nothing to him. Whereas to us, these authors were the very breath of life. Perhaps this "literature" which we revelled in was our salvation. It helped us to realize that saint and sinner were alike, that holiness could be found in filth and crime as well as in a sacrosanct places and individuals. It made us accept the fact that the idiot of simpleton was not only the rival of the man of genius but often his superior. We were able to live on several planes at once. There was no right and wrong, no ugly and beautiful, no true and false—it was all one.

Sometimes, indeed, we must have seemed foolish to others.

some days we were characters out of Tchekkov, or Gorky or Gogol. Other days we were out of Thomas Mann. For a while year I signed my letters "Hans Castorp," from Mann's *Magic Mountain*. The pity is that we had limited ourselves to literature, that we hardly knew anything about the great painters and musicians.

We had great enthusiasm, but little reverence. We knew nothing of discipline. We were like wild animals, feeding on whatever was ready to hand. I consider it a wonderful period of my life. We were libertarians and libertines. We owed allegiance to no one. One day Alec's brother announced quietly that he was leaving for India in a few days. He showed us a photo of a stunning Indian woman whom he said he was going to marry. He had met her at the Aurobindo Ashram. They were going to live in that new planetary city of Auroville near the Ashram. He was going to work as a carpenter and she as a nurse. Everyone seemed to be relieved at the news, especially Alec.

It was as a result of Bob Considine's arrival that I finally broke with the widow for the first time. Bob had introduced me to a very unusual man, an ex-evangelist, named Benjamin Fay Mills. Mills lectured in Carnegie Hall, Town Hall, and such places, on all manner of subjects. It was through him that I first heard of Freud, for example. Anyway, after being admitted (free) to one of his special classes I discovered that he had a brother in California. I induced Mills to give me a letter of introduction to his brother. My thought was to go West and become a cowboy. It was only a month or so later that I left for the West, with what little savings my mother had put aside for me. I left without saying goodbye to the widow. Halfway to my destination I wrote her that I was on my way to Juneau, Alaska, which of course was a lie. I ended up, as one knows from my books, in Chula Vista, just outside San Diego. I never became a cowboy—I was simply another simple, ignorant ranchhand working in a lemon orchard eight or nine hours a day.

It was while working on this ranch that I sent one night to San Diego—ostensibly to visit a whore house—but, happening to notice a poster announcing lectures of Emma Goldman, I went to hear her instead and inadvertently thereby changed the whole course of my life. What a glorious feast it was to attend her lectures! Through her I became acquainted with Nietzche's works as well as those of other distinguished European writers. It was through reading these writers she lectured about that I gradually decided to become a writer myself.

I remember buying one of Nietzche's books at the end of one of her lectures. It was *The Anti-Christ*. I had quite a job convincing the man who was selling the books that I was capable of swallowing such strong medicine. I must have looked very immature indeed. Perhaps like a yokel as well, since I was still working on the ranch. At any rate, it was through attending her lectures that I got to know all the famous contemporary European dramatists, chief among them being Strindberg.

Was it she, I wonder, who introduced me to Hamsun's work? Strange that I cannot remember how, when and where I came across his work! Certainly the acquaintance with the Russian dramatists I owe to her—and certain German and Austrian ones as well. Even Rabindranath Tagore I owe to her! A few months later, back in New York, I had the good fortune to make the acquaintance of a swami and through him I got to know the work of Swami Vivekananda, for which I am eternally grateful.

As for Alec's romance with the school teacher, a word or two.

Naturally, Alec could not have an affair with her. For weeks she held him in utter contempt, despite the flowers, the chocolates, theatre tickets and so on which he sent her.

Little by little, however, she began to melt. He no longer had to stand outside the door and bid her good-night. Perhaps she felt sorry for him, perhaps she began to see that he had a better side than he first showed.

In all fairness I must say at this point that in addition to his pesky, crotchety, cantankerous side, he could also be a charmer. He could even charm my mother who was hardly susceptible to flattery. Never shall I forget my twenty-first birthday. Naturally all the members of the Club and their girlfriends were present. Even Cora, my beloved, came. I remember having one dance with her throughout the evening. My mother, having made a rather tame bowl of punch for us, was horrified to discover later in the evening that someone had spiked it with whisky and brandy. (This was the work of my friend Alec.) To our utter amazement, he brought with him that evening a stunning looking girl—quite a lady I might say—who was endowed with a remarkable voice. When she opened her mouth to sing "Kiss Me Again," it seemed as if we were listening to our idol Elsie Ferguson.

Toward the end of the evening I noticed that Alec and two or three other fellows had disappeared. Knowing that the punch had had its effect on everyone I thought that they had probably gone for a bit of fresh air. To my surprise, I heard them dropping a rather heavy load at the top of the stoop. What was it, but a huge bread box such as grocers used to leave outside their store at night. As I opened the front door to see what was going on, I noticed that my mother was right behind me. At this moment Alec and another fellow tipped the bread box on end and sent it flying down the stoop. My mother uttered an exclamation of horror and started calling them dirty loafers, all of them. To my amazement Alec went up to my mother, reached for her lifeless hand and almost with tears in his eyes said, "Dear Mrs. Miller, you must forgive us. You see Henry has only one twenty-first birthday in his whole life and I wanted to make sure that he would never forget it." My mother started to say something about the smashed steps of the stoop but he quickly stopped her words by saying, "Don't worry about the damage to the steps, Mrs. Miller, I will see to it myself that they are repaired. Thank you very much for the wonderful evening you have given us."

And with that he took off.

Vacation time was approaching. His girl made it known that she was going to spend her vacation in Europe. She would go to Paris first—abroad a French liner.

At first this threw Alec into panic. He could visualize her falling for some French Prince Charming. But then the thought occurred to him—why not go to Paris too? And why not (secretly, of course) on the same French boat? He would wait until they had put out to sea before he would surprise her by his presence. (He was fearful she might leave the boat if she knew he was also going to Paris.)

And so he bought his ticket and waited till the boat was well under way before he announced his presence.

She was indeed surprised, but also delighted. Flattered, no doubt, by such serious attention. And now, wonders to behold, she really did fall in love with him. It was agreed they would get married in Paris, soon as they arrived. And they did.

In March 1930, I arrived in Paris. It was in June of that same year that Alec and his Lydia got married in Paris, all unbeknown to me. One day as I am having a drink at the Café du Dôme, whom should I see approaching arm in arm, but Alec and his girl. Over a couple of Pernods, he recounted all that had happened since I had left for Paris.

We decided to have a marriage feast. I took them to the Coupole just down the street where we had a fabulous repast. They seemed like a very happy couple. I did not see Alec again until about forty years later, when he visited me at my home in Pacific Palisades. He was on his way to Reno to get married again—to the same woman. As she told me later, he was a rather difficult fellow to live with but she could not do without him. To my great surprise, when he was making ready to go he took me aside, held my hand, and embracing me warmly, said, "Hen, you have no idea how happy I am that you made it. I always knew you had it in you."

131

BOOK TWO
My Bike & Other Friends

Harolde Ross

It was the time of Freud and the swarm
of neuroses he let loose upon the world. Now we know what
was really in Pandora's box. The period I refer to was from 1910
to 1924. What an exciting, glamorous epoch it was. No drugs, no
hippies; at the worst only booze artists and con men.

It's the period of the glorious silent films with so many illustrious stars of all sorts. Chaplin and Greta Garbo are in the
vanguard. They are immortal, as perhaps some of the great
comedians also are. In addition to Garbo, there were such stars
as Nazinova, Olga Petrovna, Anna C. Nillson, Marie Doro, Alice
Brady, Clara Kimball Young, to name but a few. On stage there
were other stars, like Jeanne Eagels, Minnie Maddern Fiske,
Leonore Ulric, Mrs. Leslie Carter and a host of others. Things
were happening all the time. The first World War changed all
this. The world has never been the same since.

It was also the period of World War I, one of the most horrible
wars ever waged. One has only to mention the name Verdun to
relive it. Imagine a No Man's Land between the two sides piled
high with cadavers and that an assault by either side meant first
clambering over the dead bodies of one's comrades. (But in

ancient times there was the battle of Platea where between dawn and midnight one hundred thousand men were slaughtered in hand-to-hand combat.)

There was just time enough to catch glimpses of Eleanor Duse, Sarah Bernhardt and Mei lan Fang, the famous Chinese actor who played women's roles better than they could play them themselves.

In the midst of all this I became acquainted with a rare bird from Blue Earth, Minnesota. Harolde Ross, pianist, music teacher, later orchestra leader also. He knew my wife before me. He always brought a portfolio of music with him; on his way home he would read the scores of Brahms, Beethoven, Scriabin as one might read a book.

He always arrived looking fresh as a daisy, his face red from being scrubbed with soap and water. A bit of a corn still clinging to his ears. The picture of enthusiasm. Always something of interest up his sleeve—perhaps about Nijinsky, about Dreiser's latest novel, or the latest acquisition at the Met. Never about boxing matches or wrestling bouts or six-day bike races. To these events I went alone or with one of my "vulgar" cronies, as they wereusually referred to. He never once accompanied me to the opera either, that I can recall.

During the war period, while working in my father's tailor shop, I made the acquaintance of an elderly man who took a fancy to me. His name was Alfred Pach, and he was in the photographing business with his brothers. They boasted of having been photographers to every president of the U.S. from Lincoln on down. Alfred Pach was an eccentric. He refused to handle money. Thus for all his needs he bartered. He even exchanged photographs for the tailor-made suits and fancy vests he got from my father.

One day I happened to tell him I was going to the Met that evening to hear Caruso and Amato. I told him I would stand in line to get a ticket, something I did fairly frequently and usually on an empty stomach. This led to a vivid discussion about music. When I told him I had been playing the piano for ten years or so he was enchanted. It so happened that this dear old man could get seats free for the opera or piano recitals or nearly any musical event. It was thus I saw Nijinsky in his most famous ballet, not quite realizing then what an unusual opportunity I had been given. Needless to say, I took full advantage of the old man's kindness. What celebrities I saw and heard! Among them Paderewski, Toscannini, Pablo Casals, Jan Kubelik, Alfred Cortot, John McCormack, Schumann-Heink, Mary Garden, Geraldine Farrar, Tetrazzini, and dozens of others. The one great artist I failed to see but heard on recordings was Sirota, the Jewish cantor. What delicious moments I spent alone with him in our funeral parlor when I was madly and sadly in love with Cora Seward! To this day, when I hear his voice, I burst into tears. Perhaps the only vocal music I dare to put beside his is Tristan and Isolde, especially the Love Death.

For me the opera was the thing, though it was the Jazz Age, and the Roseland Dance Hall was doing a rollicking business, as was Small's up in Harlem. But to get back to Harolde Ross . . . For an opener it was always Percy Grainger's "Country Gardens." Despite all the great music I have heard it is this tune which lingers in my memory. Hearing him play it, which he did with gusto, was like saluting the flag.

During his visits to New York he always had to see his friend Ostergren who introduced me to the works of Knut Hamsun, whose name at that time was unknown to me. Being of Norwegian descent Ostergren would point out some of the grosser errors in the English translation . . . (or do I imagine all this?). I do recall with certainty that the first book of Hamsun's I read (Hunger) was put in my overcoat pocket by my wife as I was boarding a train to New York from Rochester.

When I look back upon this period New York seems like a very civilized place. It had everything—it also had electricity in the air.

Harolde Ross was particularly appreciative of it, coming as he did from Blue Earth. To me, on the other hand, Blue Earth seemed a fascinating place, maybe just because of the name.

It was the time of the silent screen—Laurel and Hardy, *and the Wurlitzer!* Political leaders are never leaders. For leaders we have to look to the Awakeners! Laotse, Buddha, Socrates, Jesus, Milarepa, Gurdjiev, Krishnamurti. Plus Marie Corelli who put down both men *and* women! 101 percent Christian—a fanatic. Beneath the archaic writing was a content of great import. What matter if she were of her time or not? She was beyond "the times." She wrote from the guts, which is always in vogue.

But to get back to music. I discovered a list of all the musicians I had heard in those days. It's a formidable one and somehow fits in with my days of hunger and nights of imaginary love. I notice I had overlooked Paderewski. What an oversight! And to think that later on, during my third marriage, my Polish wife would make a little speech to him in some New Jersey town because her old man was a great Polish patriot. Then there was the beloved John McCormack, the tenor who endeared himself to all who heard him. At my parents' silver wedding anniversary I put one of his records (*Mother Machree*) on the phonograph instead of playing something on the piano.

The fact that my then wife was a pianist and gave piano lessons (I was one of her pupils) had nothing to do with my craving for music, both good and bad. One night I am at the opera, the next night at the Roseland Dance Hall, swooning over Fletcher Henderson's band. One night I would be raving about Toscanini, and the next night watching a wrestling match (usually when my favorites were on the card-Jim Londos and Earl Caddock the man of a thousand holds). This very night (1977) I will sit before the television to watch the wrestling matches praying fervently that Mil Mascaras will be on hand to show his prowess.

At that time Harolde Ross was learning French, of which I

knew not a word. I was then employment manager of the messenger boys for the Western Union. One day I received in the mail a manuscript from Harolde Ross. He had translated for me a novel called *Batouala* by a René Maran. (I was then reading in translation such French authors as Anatole France, Pierre Loti, André Gide, and so on.) Did I perhaps already divine that I was soon to spend time in France?

The two actresses I cared for most at that time were Elsie Ferguson and Elsie Janus. Harolde often took my wife to the theatre or a concert. He had excellent taste and we would talk for hours on end about the authors, the plays, the musicians we adored. It was not like nowadays when one devours a book all by himself and throws it in the waste basket next day. No, men like Dostoievsky, Hamsun, Jack London, meant something to us. They were part of our daily thoughts—we lived by them. And so it was with certain actors, whether great or not. Who could ever forget Emil Jannings (especially in *The Last Laugh?*) or David Belasco, Sessue Hayakawa, Holbrook Blinn or, for that matter, Anna Held and Fritzi Scheff, and Pauline Frederick? Then there was the Theatre Guild, spawned from the Washington Square Players. What marvelous foreign plays which we so thirsted for. Andreyev, Tolstoi, Gogol, Georg Kaiser. "Gas I" and "Gas II," etc., etc.

And in the midst of it all comes the Russian Revolution. Lenin. Done with Prince Kropotkin and the Anarchists. Now it's Trotsky, whom I used to see in a tea room on Second Avenue, N.Y. Now everything is really topsy-turvy. The future is precarious, to say the least. Our good writers, like Theodore Dreiser, Sherwood Anderson, Eugene O'Neill seem suddenly to have dropped out of consciousness. We are reading Russian novelists— new ones created by the Communist revolution. In China, Sun Yat Sen has become the rage and my friend Bennie Bufano will visit him, come back and make a statue of him to be placed conspicuously somewhere in San Francisco. Bennie, the wonder boy from Sullivan St., New York. Never a cent in his pockets, but roaming the world.

About this time too the Six-Day Bike Races came to an end. Incidentally, I don't remember Harolde ever accompanying me to any sporting event. Harolde wasn't as crazy as I, who would go to Staten Island to watch the middle-weight fighter Stanley Ketchel train outdoors for his coming fight with Jack Johnson. It never occurred to me to ask him to go along with me. I accepted him just as he was and he did likewise with me. (A good basis for either marriage or friendship!)

Always after he returned to Blue Earth I would receive a slew of letters from him, always on the same yellow paper. (Which reminds me of the canvasses Stieglitz gave to John Marin and which lasted him all his life.)

In that period H.L. Mencken was something of a god to us. Mencken and Bernard Shaw. It was the fashion among us "intellectuals" to deride everything American. Mencken himself had coined a whole list of pejorative expressions to characterize the American yokel. But he had also written a great book called *The American Language*. Years later, on my return from France, I received a phone call at the Royalton Hotel. It was Mencken, asking if he could see me for a few minutes. He was most humble and most affable. He had protested the banning of my books, he told me. He was very flattering and left me in a state of confusion since I was not used to receiving praise from my American literary critics.

It was the period of the Hippodrome and the trial of Evelyn Nesbitt. Yes, and of *Pelléas and Mélisande*, of Mary Garden in *Thaïs*, Gadski as Brunhilde, Schumann-Heink, Frank Kramer, the champion bike rider. There were also such famous ones as Ben Ami, who came from the Bowery to play in the Theatre Guild. From Russia came not only Nijinsky, but Boris Godunov and Nastasya Filipovna, from Dostoievski's *Idiot*. There was also, besides Eleanora Duse, the immortal Pablo Casals. It was also

138

the time of the giant blimp, the Graf Zeppelin, which burst into flames at its hangar. Along with John Drew, a matinee idol, there were men such as Rudolf Valentino, Sir Thomas Lipton and the yacht races. Lillian Russell and her lover, the man with two stomachs—Diamond Jim Brady.

There were also women writers like Edna Ferber and Fanny Hurst. And still a handful of people who had read Marie Corelli. Not least of all there was the Houston Street Burlesk. (I can still recall the features of the orchestra leader with the red hair, who played the piano intoxicatingly.) Then too there was the famous Armory Show where Marcel Duchamp exhibited his "Nude Descending the Staircase."

My father had not yet begun bar hopping with the great Jack Barrymore. But they would shortly. And it would be from Barrymore himself that later I would learn what a wonderful companion my father was, though *un inculte*, as the French would say.

When I think of it, New York at this time was filled with incredible female beauties. They came from all over the earth. There is one grand figure I must not forget—Rabindranath Tagore, a man revered and talked about as much or more than Krishnamurti. I had to go to hear him speak at Carnegie Hall, soon after his arrival in America. This time Harolde accompanied me. For he too was a devotee of Tagore. What a deception was in store for us. The lecture consisted largely of a denunciation of America, but in a piping, whining voice which rendered his words into one long, continuous petty complaint. We were miserable, the two of us, to behold our idol turn to clay before our eyes. But with the years which passed since then, my reverence and admiration for the man has increased. What he wrote and accomplished in a lifetime are incontestably of a superior order.

And how can I ever forget the day Charles Lindbergh flew the Atlantic in his monoplane—with the whole wide world gasping with astonishment? A read red letter day in American history.

And what became of my good friend during all this time? For

139

one thing, he left Blue Earth and settled in Rochester, Minnesota, always teaching piano, always leading a small orchestra. And writing me on the same yellow stationery as always. Today he is in a nursing home there, but he has a piano in his room. He never says what ails him—I imagine it is just old age, as with yours truly.

Here was, or still is, a self-educated man cultured to the fingertips, yet living in the sticks all his life. What we shared is unforgettable. He enriched my life indelibly. I wonder sometimes if he still plays Percy Grainger's "Country Gardens."

Bezalel Schatz

I never heard any one call him Bezalel;
it was always Lilik. Somehow just as Picasso's name suited him,
so did Lilik suit Lilik. I use the past tense in referring to him
because it is long since I have seen him—somewhere in Southern France at a railroad junction was the last time—perhaps
twenty or more years ago. Actually Lilik lives in Jerusalem. He
was born there, and went to school there. But it was in Big Sur
where I first met him. He came to me on my birthday, beaming
all over, and full of a project which he was determined to interest
me in. It became the *Night Life* book which we did together. A
beautiful and most unusual piece of collaboration, if I may say so
myself. As with Lawrence Durrell, I was immediately taken by
Lilik. He radiated health, vitality, optimism. He was irresistible. It
took him no time to persuade me to do this book with him. (I still
have a few copies left of this limited silk screen edition.) It was
Lilik who did the major work. Not only did he do the illustrations
and the lay-out, but he did all the silk screen pages himself. I
think it took him almost two years to complete the job. Had it
required ten years it would have made little difference to Lilik.
His extraordinary good health enabled him to work twice as

hard as the ordinary man. Besides, he also had that rare gift—faith. He never undertook anything which he did not wholly believe in. Once launched upon a project, he was like an avalanche. Nothing could deter or swerve him.

At this point I should like to say a few words about his education and up-bringing. To begin with, he was fortunate to have as parents a father who had been the court sculptor to the King of Bulgaria and a mother who was a writer and intellectual who had fled Czarist Russia. Two liberal, creative and indulgent parents. It was his parents, infact, who brought the first piano to Israel. His schooling was of the best, in my opinion. Dancing, acting, music, athletic games took precedence over history, grammar and the sciences. He emerged from school a well coordinated individual, at peace with himself and the world (he had close friends among the Arabs and spoke Arabic after a fashion). He was an excellent soccer player as well as tennis player and between times learned to play the violin. What a difference, such a bringing up, from that of *our* children! In his teens he was reading the world's classics—Dostoievsky, André Gide, Thomas Mann, Anatole France and such like. *All in Hebrew*. To his home came people like Einstein and Elazar ben Jehuda, who made Hebrew a living language, the father of Zionism; the painters Marc Chagall, Diego Rivera, and so on. He never became a chauvinist, though he loved his country and was at home in it. Of course, it was at this wonderful school where he learned to draw and to paint. Today his work may be seen everywhere.

Somewhere along the line he lived and worked in Paris. Which made the tie between us even stronger. In addition to French he spoke German, Russian and Polish, to say nothing of English and Hebrew. (But no Yiddish!) In many, many ways, Lilik was thoroughly unlike a Jew or even an Israeli. He was truly a citizen of the world, at ease wherever he found himself.

When I first met him he was living in Berkeley. As my wife Eve's parents also lived in Berkeley I would visit him there

142

occasionally, especially during the production of *Into the Night Life*. But a couple of years later he moved to Big Sur with his wife Louise who was the sister of Eve, who was to become my fourth wife. Thus we became brothers-in-law as well as good friends. In Big Sur Lilik was to become my helpmate. For, in addition to his cultural and creative education, Lilik was also a fixer. If you had an odd job to do you could call on Lilik. He was always available, always willing, and often had original ideas as to how this or that should be done. I can never get over all the positive qualities and attributes he had. He was really a self-sufficient man. His only difficulties were with the British government officials. (Israel had not yet become a nation at this time.) This situation only sharpened his wits. He never allowed the situation to get him down. At the worst he muttered a few choice cuss words in Hebrew and Arabic. Arabic, as I understand it, is rich in foul language. (Listening to him talk to his mother over the phone I got to know one Hebrew word—*Ima* for mother.) It sounded good to me, better than mother. His relations with his mother were good, cheerful, wholesome, though in my humble opinion she was a bit of a trial. If Lilik were aware of her failings he never let on. During this period at Big Sur I had a number of Jewish friends. They all got to know each other but I can't say they fell in love with one another. Each one was unique and outstanding in his own way. I was a friend with all of them. Often, in fact, I was taken for a Jew. All my life, as I have remarked again and again, I seem to be surrounded by Jewish friends to whom I have always been greatly indebted. Only a Jewish physician, for example would say to a patient, a Goy like myself, that I need not pay him anything for his services *and* could he perhaps lend me a little cash? (No, I never met a gentile doctor who talked that way.)

It was while living in Big Sur, twenty-five or thirty years ago, that I first earned enough money to open a bank account. I mentioned Eve. After our marriage in Carmel we decided to spend a honeymoon in Europe. (I had not been back to France since 1939.) To our great surprise Lilik wrote us from Jerusalem and he and his wife would join us. All during the years prior to my success in America I had been corresponding with a Flemish poet named Pierre Lesdain. Now that I was in Paris I thought I would look him up. (We had never met.) Lilik wanted to join us, as I had told him a great deal about my friend Pierre Lesdain. But there was one big obstacle to be overcome first, namely, the fucking British government. Apparently Lilik had to have the consent of the British Consul in Paris. That was no easy matter. I don't know how many times Lilik visited this character in an effort to obtain the necessary permit. *Why* he could not go, *why* the Consul would not give him the go signal was an utter mystery. In desperation Lilik decided on one more visit. This time he took with him a portfolio of his work to show the bastard. Immediately the man saw Lilik's work his whole attitude changed. *So,* Lilik was an artist, and his parents received such wonderful guests as Einstein. "Marc Chagall was a frequent visitor," Lilik threw in casually.

"What!" exclaimed the Consul. "Did you say Marc Chagall?"

"Certainly." said Lilik. "He was a good friend of the family."

With this the Consul threw up his hands. "Why didn't you tell me this before?" he exclaimed.

"I never thought it had any importance," said Lilik.

"Marc Chagall happens to be my favorite painter," said the Consul. "Man, you could have had your visa weeks ago had you told me this. Here, let me arrange things for you ..."

And like that Lilik and his wife got permission to go to Brussels with us.

"So there was no real reason for him putting you off all this time," I exclaimed. "What a lousy hypocritical bastard! A typical Britisher. Didn't you feel like giving him a poke in the jaw?"

But no, Lilik was willing to forget the whole incident.

"I didn't tell you all," he suddenly resumed. "When I had the

144

papers in my pocket I told him I was going with Henry Miller and his wife. I thought he would throw a fit!

"'H.M.,' he mumbled. 'I never did care for his dirty books, but'—and he paused for a moment to reflect—'but I do think the bloke is a genius.'

"Then I took delight in telling him that you were not only a good friend but my brother-in-law.

"'Don't tell me H.M. married an Israeli girl?' he cried.

"'No, we married sisters—two Irish girls from—'

"He wouldn't hear another word. It was all too preposterous to him. He simply waved me away."

In Brussels the four of us put up at Pierre Lesdain's home. We wanted to go to a hotel but he wouldn't hear of it. He surrendered his bed to us and he and his wife slept on the floor, despite all our protests. Lesdain was one of those rare birds who, though poor as a church mouse, gave the impression of being well off. He insisted that we share all our meals with him and his wife. Happily both our wives were good cooks and aided Madame, his wife, in preparing the meals. We ate well, I must say, and the wines were excellent. The important thing, we soon found out, was garlic. At lunch and dinner we all joined in eating whole cloves of garlic. Lesdain insisted it was good for the health. The stench from our breath was fantastic. Add to this that Lilik had a habit of letting out a fusillade of musical farts, usually when enjoying a good meal. In fact he was capable of farting at will. He pretended to have taken lessons from the French vaudevillian who delighted his audiences with the variety of farts at his command. It included *musical* farts!

These times in Lesdain's kitchen were unforgettable. Needless to say we laughed abundantly all through our meals. For Lesdain it was a vacation, our staying with them. He did not go to work for ten days. It must have been a great relief, for his job was at the other end of Belgium. He had to leave the house at five a.m. and got back home about ten P.M. It was a job he hated

145

moreover. He wasn't obliged to work like a slave for he had a wealthy brother who was a minister in some branch of the government. But Pierre was too proud to accept his brother's help. He was a poet andhe preferred to live like a poet, that is to say, in poverty. At the same time he displayed no rancor, no bitterness; he was almost a saint.

Of course, his brother, Maurice, who was also a literary figure in Belgium, the owner and editor of a magazine of repute, insisted on showing the four of us something of his country. He had an expensive car with a chauffeur which enabled us to traverse most of Belgium in record time. Every noon and evening he selected a renowned restaurant. We ate like kings. The one town I shall never forget was Bruges. Walking along the banks of the canals I felt, as in Amsterdam, that it is only a town of such ancient beauty that a writer should create his work. While there I wrote a piece for a Flemish magazine. Flemish is a language I imagine I could learn easily. It seems close to low German. The street signs were easy to decipher, of course. I shall always remember him.

Among the little excursions or picnics we took with Lesdain and his wife was a visit to the monastery which was once inhabited by the Honorable Ruysbroeck. It was at one end of a wonderful forest of beech trees about two hours' walk from Lesdain's home on the outskirts of Brussels. Brussels itself seemed to me an utterly uninteresting town, a sister to Geneva, Switzerland.

In the famous cathedral of Ghent we saw the famous triptych of Van Eyck—"The Mystic Lamb." I was not only duly impressed, I was awe-struck.

The thing which was forever in my mind while in Belgium was that I was in the Lowlands, as it was once called. Also, although the official language was French, the people were Flemish and very proud of it.

Poor Lesdain! He was living in the wrong place. He should

have made his home in Bruges, a town never to be forgotten, and, as I said before, made just for poets. Even I might have written poetry had I lived there.

I believe we went directly from Brussels to London and thence to Wells to visit my old *copain* Alfred Perles.

Wells, as most everyone knows, has a cathedral whose façade is fascinating. Perhaps it would be more in order to call it surrealistic. Aside from that, I can't recall anything else of interest in Wells. Oh yes, the liquor store! Every time I accompanied Alf to purchase wine we were obsequiously greeted by the owner of the store, a typical Englishman who always called Alf *Mister* Perles and who was obviously impressed by the fact that *Mister* Perles was a writer who *had lived* in Paris many years. Watching the two exchange greetings I saw my old friend in a new light. He was no longer the clown, the rogue, the scoundrel, but an English citizen, a man of standing in the eyes of his townsfolk. Of course as soon as we got out of the wine shop we would burst into guffaws. "The old fart!" Fred would say. "They're all like him here, Joey."

Though there wasn't much to do in a place like Wells, we managed to eat and drink well and laugh our heads off. Lilik, who had never met Perles before, was taken by his wit and buffoonery. There was never a solemn moment.

Finally we returned to Paris, where soon after our arrival, Lilik decided that we must visit the painter Vlaminck. I was a bit surprised at first because I had the impression that Vlaminck's work had deteriorated since his days as a *Fauve*. However, like Lilik, I was curious to meet the *man*. By this time Vlaminck must have been well into his seventies. He was recovering from an illness. There he sat in an armchair a huge hulk of a man weighing over 225 pounds at least. He had always been a big man, even in his youth when he was a professional bike racer. Looking at his girth and his huge ass, I wondered how he ever managed to sit on a narrow Brooks saddle. I also wondered whether the weight of him didn't flatten those narrow racing tires. Huge as he was, he was nevertheless a sensitive, aesthetic creature. Before becoming a painter he had studied the violin and played in an orchestra.

In his rundown condition it is a wonder he received us at all. We found him most affable, most agreeable, and as he recovered his spirits a wonderful raconteur with a witty, biting tongue. He seemed willing to talk about most anything. Anything but Picasso, it seems. Picasso was his *bête noir*. As he put it in his raspy voice: "I have seen Picasso-negres, Picasso Cubism, Picasso this and Picasso that, but I have never seen a Picasso-Picasso!"

His home was now in Normandy where he owned a large farm and raised horses. He introduced us to his two daughters, very healthy, buxom teenagers who could put away a tumbler of pure alcohol without blinking an eye.

One of the painters of his time about whom he spoke most affectionately was Utrillo. Apparently they had been good comrades in the early days, as was Derain.

I could not help remarking the almost life-size statues of Negroes from Africa surrounding the fireplace. As is well known, Vlaminck was one of the first painters in France to collect these statues. I had seen some smaller ones at Zadkine's home but never any this size. It was most impressive and most fitting.

Vlaminck did most of the talking that afternoon. One had the feeling not of being in the presence of a human being, but of an epoch. My one regret was that I had never seen him ride a bike. During the days when I attended the six-day bicycle races in Madison Square Garden I had seen all types and all sizes but never anyone approaching the proportions of Vlaminck.

As we were driving away I said to Lilik: "Well, that's one man who never visited your home in Jerusalem."

"You're right," he replied, "but now that you mention the subject, let me tell you one man who did—I just thought of his name."

148

"Who was that?"

"Diego Rivera."

"That's strange," I said, "he was a frequent visitor at Anaïs Nin's home when they lived in the south of France."

We both felt like one does after having a very good meal. In fact, we felt stuffed. Later I read one or two of Vlaminck's books, for he was somewhat of a writer. There was a profundity in the books which did not appear in his talk. As a matter of fact, one might say he was a bit cattish in his talk. One incongruous feature of the man was his mouth. It was a tiny mouth, looking almost like a third eye stuck in that huge head. Perhaps of his illness his voice was not that of a man his size. To me it sounded thin and rather squeamish, but very effective when telling someone off or in mimicking, which he could do very well.

For several weeks we did nothing but visit art galleries and museums and excellent modest restaurants which we remembered from the old days. Then, with Fall approaching, we decided to make a trip to Spain. Neither of us had been there before.

We journeyed leisurely down to the south of France and at Montpellier we were taken by my friend Jacques Temple to meet the "great master of French literature," Joseph Delteil, who lived just outside the town of the famous *Tuilerie de Massane* with his American wife Caroline Dudley.

Perhaps I had met Delteil before, possibly through Lawrence Durrell. I definitely remember meeting him in Paris early in the 1930s when he was at the height of his surrealist fame. I remember distinctly the strange sort of baker's cap he was wearing when we met then. It reminded me of the character in that extraordinary Jewish play *The Dybbuk*. Needless to say Delteil and his wife treated us like royalty. We stayed several days in Montpellier going back and forth to La Tuilerie and sampling the excellent *vins d'ami* in his *cave*.

I suppose it was on one of those wine sampling occasions that we broached the subject of our proposed trip to Spain. Immediately we mentioned it, Joseph and Caroline asked if they could join us. (I believe Joseph had been there before, probably several times.) We set forth in two cars—Lilik and his wife in one and Eve and I with the Delteils in the other. Joseph was at the wheel. It wasn't long before he removed his jacket, keeping one hand on the wheel, and a little later his sweater under which he had several newspapers to protect him from the cold. I felt an immediate kinship with Joseph because I too am like a thermometer and barometer, susceptible to the slightest change of temperature or weather. Always turning the heat on and off.

Every now and then, as we drove through Le Roussillon, Joseph would get out of the car to ask directions. He knew the way perfectly but he wanted to exchange a few words in the *patois* of the region. He himself was born on the floor of a forest near the walled city of Carcassonne. I am sure he owes part of his mastery of the French language to the fact that he spoke Provinçal at an early age. Certainly I have never encountered a French writer with his verve, wit, acuity and invention.

We visited all the famous Moorish towns as we journeyed to that wonderful town of Cordoba and its mosque and, believe it or not, a Christian church inside the mosque—a veritable defamation. As with Amsterdam and Bruges, here once again I felt was a place for poets. And here again was the sound of water, water running through the gardens, water running through the rooms of houses to give coolth. Cordoba and Granada were the high spots for me. But there was also a town, Segovia, just outside of Madrid through which ran an ancient aqueduct. There we made the acquaintance of a coming bullfighter who was practicing the art of killing bulls on a bicycle. He said his parents were very poor and that if he became a bullfighter he could become rich quickly and take care of his aging parents. In America he would have tried to become a football or baseball player, in Mexico, a boxer.

The principal event of our trip was catching diarrhea. It began with Lilik, who was never too careful how or where he ate. And then it struck the rest of us one after the other. Some of the toilets in hotels and cafes are still engraved in my memory. People everywhere were warm and generous though usually quite poor. It was hard to believe that a bloody revolution had taken place two decades before. I should also mention the beautiful, immaculate hostelries, paradors, run by the government which were extremely modest in price. Also one famous hotel, the Washington Irving, in Granada, one of the best hotels I have been in anywhere in the world. Again immaculate, comfortable and not expensive.

The only reminder of the revolution were signs on the walls of cafés saying "no singing allowed." This was to prevent political slander.

It's hard to say enough about the Spanish people themselves. Though a poor country, they retain that air of ancient grandeur, hospitality, generosity and charm which makes them unforgettable.

There is one city I almost forgot to mention—Toledo, home of El Greco. Grim, proud, haughty, oozing Catholicism, it is almost fearful. Through it, like a black snake, runs the river Tagus. In the streets there are frequent religious processions, grim reminders of the Inquisition. Yet in this austere ambience is situated the charming abode of El Greco, adding a note of grace and lightness to the grim city.

It seems to me we often separate from one another. Thus one evening Eve and I came upon a small town or village near the sea where we saw on the beach a stone staircase leading nowhere. It was difficult to determine whether the staircase had once been attached to a building or whether it was a prank by some unknown Surrealist.

Somewhere before the border we left the Delteils. We had decided to leave Spain by way of Andora, the one principality I had yet to visit. I must confess it was not an ingratiating place, but we were well treated and the food was good. Our first stop in France was Foix where we had our first good French meal. Nearby was Montsegur where the last of the Cathares had been walled up. Out of respect for their memory I got out of the car, kneeled by the roadside and said a brief, silent prayer for their souls.

We were now headed for a town which was a railway junction. Here we were to separate, Lilik and his wife heading for Marseilles, where they would take a boat back to Israel, while Eve and I would return to Montpellier for a spell. We stood chatting there at the railway station for a long time. finally, I divided what money I had left with Lilik (not much) and he found that by dividing it a certain way it would reduce to the number three which to him meant good luck. And indeed he did have good luck. Shortly after his return, the Israelis got the British off their backs, and established an independent nation, and began to thrive. How many eminent individuals have gone to Israel, either for a vacation or to stay.

If I have not given much space to the Delteils it is because they went their own separate way most of the time. But the friendship formed with them on this trip has remained a solid one. Deteil has had luck, I might add. From being a renegade he has become perhaps the most notable French writer today. He continues nevertheless to cultivate his vineyard and to lead the simple life.

Vincent Birge

Vincent . . . good old Vincent. That's how I always think of him. Vincent never did anyone harm. That may not seem like a great virtue, expressed in negative fashion. Put positively, I would say he radiated goodness, generosity, sympathy, understanding.

To give an illustration of how he affected people let me tell how my mother reacted to him. She was on her dying bed when I happened to invite Vincent—or perhaps he had come of his own accord—to help in some way. Anyway, my mother is lying in bed. When Vincent entered the room and greeted her, she was as if electrified. She sat up in bed and nodding toward him she said, as if to herself, "If I had only had a son like that!"—and me standing right beside the bed, me the "renowned" author of dirty books, etc.

I met Vincent some years ago in Big Sur. I believe we had been in correspondence some time—he was then working for TWA and writing me from all over the world. And sending beautiful gifts too. Then, because they no longer needed radio operators, he lost his job. But soon he had another with a Texas oil company. Doing what, I never understood clearly.

From voyaging about the world Vincent had picked up French and Portuguese and seemed very proficient. I believe he also knew Italian. He seemed to have a gift for languages.

Finally he presented himself at Big Sur, loaded with gifts for me and the children.

It was easy to like a chap like Vincent. Though he had been raised in dire poverty, he managed to go through college in Waco, Texas.

His home life had been not too good. And it left its mark on Vincent. One of his characteristic virtues was his desire to be of help—this quality, I believe, stemmed from his life at home, the poverty and neglect. For example, he was sixteen or seventeen before he could afford shoes. His family were so poor they rented rooms from a Negro family. In other words, the poor whites were poorer than the poor blacks.

It was in Brazil, where he stayed for some time, that he picked up Portuguese. When, some years later, the two of us found ourselves in Portugal, I relied on him entirely. His French was also excellent as I discovered when we toured France together.

By this time we had known each other several years. When I had the chance to go abroad for a vacation I naturally chose Vincent as my secretary, chauffeur and handyman. He was like a miracle worker.

One of the reasons we became such good friends was because Vincent read good books and discussed them with me. (He himself never tried his hand at writing, but he always wrote interesting letters.) He read, moreover, in three languages. He also possessed an excellent memory.

I had been staying in Reinbek-bei-Hamburg for some time because I had fallen in love with one of Rowohlt's assistants, Renate Gerhardt. While there one day my old friend Emil White showed up and then Vincent. Emil was on his way to his hometown, Vienna. Some months previously Vincent and I had picked up the old Fiat which I had left with my good friend Albert

Maillet in Die, France. Vincent had driven it to Reinbek and was sort of waiting on my pleasure.

Meanwhile Renate and I had decided to join forces somewhere outside of Germany, preferably France. I then had enough money to purchase a house and perhaps a farm with it. I believe I have recounted this trip in detail elsewhere. (Vincent would remember, I don't; but Vincent is now in Louisiana and I don't have his address.) Anyway, the three of us took leave of Renate and her two youngsters, assuring her that we most certainly would find something in a few months. As it turned out, I must have been absent eight or nine months. When I returned to Reinbek without having accomplished my mission, I met a totally different Renate. She was glacial, uninterested in our odyssey, and obviously through with me forever.

Now that I look back on it all I can see that I was more fascinated by my travels than in finding a new home. We had gone through the best of Germany and Austria, then the south of France, the Roussillon in particular, part of Italy, the Ticino region of Switzerland and ended up eventually in Portugal. What I remember most vividly about this fantastic trip was Vincent's struggle with bugs—bedbugs, mosquitoes, flies, cockroaches, the whole gamut of insects. I recall vividly how, on finding a hotel for the night, Vincent would first pull back the covers of his bed to make sure there were no bedbugs. We usually slept in the same room and his bed would almost certainly have bugs whereas mine was free of them.

Once we were in a village in southern France, where Pablo Casals had lived. I had steered Vincent there hoping to meet Casals but he had already left for Puerto Rico. It was a beautiful, sleepy village and, for no reason at all, I suddenly suggested that we visit the church and say a prayer or two. We entered and had knelt down to say our prayers when suddenly Vincent started up and ran out of the church. I got to my feet quickly and went in search of him. Beside the church there was a public toilet. I went in and called his name. Suddenly I saw a naked arm above the toilet doors next to the opening. "Here I am!" he shouted. "I'm looking for those damned bugs. The church is infested with them." He had completely undressed and was thoroughly examining each piece of clothing.

About bugs . . . the worst places I remember were Vienna and Budapest. There were all kinds of bugs. In Athens the moment you turned on the light in the washroom and toilet the cockroaches came out of their lairs. And they were huge and made a disgusting crackle when you stepped on them.

I forgot that we also went through Spain—largely in the rain. From Lisbon to the French border it never stopped raining, which did not prevent poverty-stricken children from standing by the roadside with hands outstretched for coins, their faces drawn with hunger and sorrow.

Well, I lost a beloved but I had a marvelous romp through Europe. I took the plane back home from Hamburg. Where Vincent went from Reinbek I don't recall. The next thing I knew he married a French girl by whom he now has a daughter of six or seven years.

Twice he has tried farming. Once in Southern California and the second time in upper New York State. In California a scarcity of water made it very difficult to raise anything. When water was discovered a year or so later, it did not run through his property. Tough luck! But then Vincent had known nothing but tough luck. The loss of his TWA job was quite a blow. (He must have had a fairly good time of it in Brazil where he picked up his Portuguese.)

It was some years later that the oil company sent him and his wife and child to the island of Malta. Malta was not a very exciting place, judging from his letters. I spoke of his tough luck. In Malta he met with the worst luck to date. He was driving home one night with his wife and child when suddenly the car dropped into an unseen hole. His wife suffered the worst injuries. The child fortunately was unharmed. If anything had happened to that child it would have broken Vincent's heart. From the time she was born he idolized her. He always sends photos of her with his letters.

Anyway, on returning to America he settled in a small town in upstate New York. Again he tried a bit of farming. Vincent had what you call a green hand. He could make things grow in the desert. How well I remember his days in Southern California when, with a tiny cup of water in his hand, he would go from plant to plant. As a teenager he had to get up at three or four in the morning to catch the milk truck which took him to college. When he got to school he would finish his night's sleep on the lawn or on the steps of the college. Few Europeans realize what frightful poverty exists in this country, not only among the blacks and the Mexicans, but among the white trash as well.

There were some strange and some amusing incidents during our trip. For example, in Venice, the city of one's dreams. It was just as I had imagined it from all the photos and etchings of it I had seen during the course of my life. But oddly enough, I was not enthralled, not nearly so enthusiastic as upon entering Verona. In a day or so I fell into a terrible depression, a suicidal one, and apparently for no good reason. After a day or two I decided to write a rather famous astrologer in Hamburg whom Renate had introduced me to. Another few days passed, heavy as lead, and then suddenly at lunch while gazing at a big clock on the wall my mood disappeared as quickly as it had seized me and again for no apparent reason. That evening I sat down and wrote my astrologer friend in Hamburg. In a day or two came a letter from him saying that he knew the depression had disappeared, that he had *been praying for me!* I told Vincent, but he was unimpressed. It was some eight or nine years after leaving Renate in Reinbek that I received a letter from her telling me that the reason she had given me the cold shoulder was because our astrologer friend in Hamburg had advised her not to continue the relationship with me. That puzzled me greatly. Yet, upon sober reflection, I had to agree that he was right in thus counseling her. I had made a mess of four marriages already, with one more to come.

But to come back to Vincent and his skepticism—or should I say his common sense? Somewhere along the line I received an invitation to visit Georges Simenon. He was living in Switzerland in a rather beautiful old château. Emil White was still with us. I knew Simenon would not appreciate our barging in on him with two cronies whom he knew nothing about. So I asked Emil and Vincent to wait for me in Laussane. During my five or six days chez Simenon a friend of his told me of an astrologer in a village nearby who wanted very much to meet me.

I called Vincent to drive me there. The woman turned out to be another well-known astrologer named Mme. Jacqueline Langmann. We were only in her presence a few minutes when she asked if we would forgive her, that she would like to retire to her room and work on my horoscope. I naturally consented. In the few minutes we had been there she got from me all the data necessary to make a chart. I should add that from the moment we met we took to one another like old friends. She fairly sparkled as she spoke to me. Well, in about ten minutes she came out of her room beaming, with a pad of notes in her hand. She had unearthed enough about me to give me an astounding playback of my life. (I remember now one of the things she said which impressed me and that was I should never have married. Love affairs okay, but no marriage.) She read me like a book and, as a matter of fact, she later wrote a book (in French) about my life and chart. I was so impressed with all she told me that I urged Vincent to let her do his chart. But Vincent refused. He said it was all nonsense, adding that the planets she spoke of had long since ceased to be in the positions she took for granted. Fortunately, Madame Langmann did not waste much time refuting his arguments. Needless to say, since that day we have remained the very best of friends. About a year ago she visited me here in California in the company of mutual friends. Her book, unfortunately, has not yet been done in English. I say "unfortunately," for if it did exist in English, it would prevent many of my fans from asking the questions they do.

As I said before, we continued our supposed search for the right place into Portugal. By this time I realized that I was dreaming, that it would be next to impossible to make a menage with two American kids and two German ones and a German stepmother.

So I returned to Reinbek and seeing that it was over between Renate and myself, I returned to California alone, a sadder and somewhat wiser man. At least I trust so. Something in my make-up tells me I will never become worldly wise. I shall always be the innocent fool no matter what crimes I may commit.

Vincent and I are still the best of friends. He goes from one job to another, but always puts a good face on it. He is that rare thing in our society—an honest man, the man Diogenes was looking for. He is sage, broad-minded, but eschews anything that smacks of mysticism. He is a man for whom facts count, not theories, nor dreams, nor runaway ideas.

To my mind, though I hate to say this, it is just because he suppresses the dreamer in himself that life is so serious and his luck so poor. He is no man's fool, but it were better he were, in my humble opinion. One thing he definitely is, and it makes up for all his deficiencies—he is a true and loyal friend, a friend for life. And how much more important it is to be that than to be a successful this or that! God bless you, dear Vincent, you are the salt of the earth.

Emil White

You look into his eyes and you sense a profound, an inexplicable sadness. Yet he is a jokester of the first water and a raconteur who keeps you laughing and crying.

Which side of him is it that attracts women to him so easily? I have never decided this question, despite a long and intimate friendship. One can only shake his head and secretly envy him. For, even in remote Big Sur, his house is like a halfway station for transitory females, Orientals especially.

Of course he is an excellent cook, extremely considerate, always helpful, and truly compassionate. But these are not usually the qualities which draw women to men. Or, if they admire these qualities they do not lead them to the bed *tout de suite.* And Emil has this faculty (of quick work) *par excellence.* He has only to give a woman the eye and he knows instantly just how far he may go with her. Usually, it is all the way!

With Emil it is a curious melange of audacity and respect. You may arrive with your wife, your sweetheart or the woman you are hoping to lay. No matter. In the space of a few minutes Emil has taken her to one side or invited her to look at his petunias or whatever, and right under your very nose he is kissing and hugging her. Absolutely unabashed and seemingly behaving in

160

innocence. We got into the habit of referring to it as his "European way." This because in comparing the American and the European female Emil always implied that the American women asked to be raped rather than wooed. Or else she was a pushover. But in Vienna or Budapest, according to Emil, to lay a woman was as natural a procedure as moving from the dinner table to the salon. It went with good food and drink, *and* good conversation. In other words the sex had to be spiced, not served raw. But why Oriental women fell for such behavior was something of a mystery.

To be sure, for all his skill and technique Emil was also a born admirer of women. He knew what pleased them, he knew where to touch them, he could make them laugh or cry without great effort. In addition his house was always something of a museum, whether it was a shack or a nice little cottage such as he now inhabits. It gave him pleasure to show a guest around. There were his paintings, his books, his photos and always somewhere a bit of erotica. Naturally, while extolling the beauty or the wonder of an object he let his hand roam freely over the fair one's body. He was especially fond of teats *and* a cute ass. He could pat one's ass so lovingly that even if she were a duchess she could not be offended. This was all part of his "respectful," even worshipful attitude. Later he would move for the kill. Often, instead of an afternoon's visit, the gal would remain a week or a month—and return for more.

We, his friends and neighbors, had all observed his tactics time and time again. Sometimes, indeed, he would seem to show off. It was as if he said to you, "You think she's hard to make? Watch this!" and he would begin operating. His maneuvers were so effective and performed so casually and boldly that we began to believe that women in general liked nothing better than to be goosed in public. Of course not all women liked this treatment. I had a few women complain that he was callous, a male chauvinist pig, and so on.

But to do him credit, most all the women who knew him loved him. And this reminds me of my first meeting with Emil. I was in Chicago, visiting Ben Abramson at his Argus Book Shop. I had never heard of Emil White. As I'm walking along Michigan Boulevard a man suddenly darts across the street to greet me. It was the familiar "Aren't you Henry Miller?" which I've heard hundreds of times. But this time it was different. Emil knew me inside out, from reading my books. (To this day he has a better memory of what I have written than I myself. When I am unsure in which of my books to look for a certain passage I write to Emil and I always get the right answer.) The sequel to our chance meeting was an invitation to have lunch with him and a few of his friends at his flat. I accepted readily, having realized quickly that this was no ordinary fan, but more of a blood brother. And so I went. To my surprise there were several young attractive women already seated at the table. They were for me, as Emil put it. Very much as if he were offering me a bouquet of red and white roses. The meal, by the way, was delightful. It consisted of cold cuts of meat, caviar and a variety of smoked fish. A treat. I took it for granted that the girls were all bedmates of Emil's in addition to being Henry Miller fans. They were all at my disposal, according to Emil, a fact which I did not take advantage of immediately. I forgot to explain that at Ben Abramson's shop I had met another ardent fan and collector of my work. He had insisted that I come and stay at his home while in Chicago. It was an invitation I could scarcely resist, being broke as usual. This individual was a University of Michigan graduate, extremely well read, married and obviously well off. He had a penchant for dirty books, dirty photos and pornographic films. He kept these possessions in a safe hidden behind a rolling door. Every night after dinner he would get out his treasures and display them to me. I very soon grew tired of looking at the dirty photos, but not the films. Night after night, he, his wife and I sat in the living room, with a drink in hand and watched still another film. After which his wife would tuck me in bed.

But to come back to Emil's harem. One of his girl friends ho had not attended the lunch, heard of my presence in Chicago and invited me to her flat of an afternoon. She made no bones about the fact that she wanted to be laid. Having read the *Tropics* I suspect she thought I would make a good instructor. She was a strange gal, a virgin at thirty-two, and extremely passionate. Passionate *and* hygienic. If I toyed with her cunt she had a box of Kleenex handy so that I could wipe my fingers. I told her I preferred not to wipe my fingers, that I enjoyed inhaling the perfume of her cunt. For some reason this shocked her. I mentioned that she was extremely hygienic. Naturally she had to douche first; then she brought a basin of warm water and washed my prick, not realizing of course that this was the usual procedure in brothels. In addition to these attributes she was athletic—almost a contortionist. She must have read up on Tantric Yoga and all the fantastic positions employed by members of the cult. For a virgin of thirty-two I must say she was a real adept. I almost broke my back trying to please her. When we had finished—get this!—she knelt at my feet and kissed my feet, then my balls and prick, and finally my belly button, all the while gurgling profuse thanks for breaking her in.

It was probably a year after my meeting with Emil in Chicago that I landed in Big Sur. I was now living on Partington Ridge in a cabin lent me by the then mayor of Carmel. I was alone, a city lad who had never held an axe or a saw in his hand before. Somehow Emil, who was in Alaska working at some lucrative job, heard that I was in Big Sur and wrote me that he would love to join me. He offered to be my cook, dishwasher, secretary and bodyguard all in one *and* for free. I agreed and in a week he arrived, bringing gifts as usual. One of the packages contained some special delicacy from Alaska which I served to my cats, being all out of cat food. (Cats were very important on the Ridge as it was infested with rats, field mice, gophers, rattlesnakes and other pests, not least of which was poison oak.) When I told Emil what I had done he was not only shocked but deeply hurt, for which I could scarcely blame him. However, he soon forgave me and, true to his word, began helping me in every possible way.

During the lonely evenings I would often get out my water-color set and begin painting. Emil used to watch me work very attentively. After a time he got the notion that he too could paint, if he tried. He began by cooperating with me on a joint endeavor. If I made a tree, for example, he would embellish it with more bark and more leaves and branches, somewhat like Douanier Rousseau. Sometimes he would add a figure, a nude. The result was usually a monstrosity, but it gave Emil courage together with a little conceit. In a very short while he had developed a style purely his own, something bordering on neo-primitivism. People liked his work: he sold his paintings at good prices. A little later he tried to buy back some of his work. Somehow he has acquired strong doubts that he will ever paint again. Had he continued, I believe he would be famous and in demand today.

During his stay with me on Partington Ridge in that little cabin I had no car. Neither did he. One day he fixed me a sort of go-cart, such as kids make for themselves in the ghetto, and with this I was able to haul up the two-mile hill the laundry, the groceries, the kerosene, etc., which the mailman delivered to the mailbox on the road. I did this clad in nothing but a jock strap and a fedora hat.

Emil was never at a loss for words. In addition to being a good storyteller he loved to discuss politics—*world* politics.

Myself, I found politics boring. I knew next to nothing about it, but would sometimes attempt to cross swords with him, always to my utter defeat. The curious thing about this kind, gentle soul was that he was hypercritical, authoritarian and stubborn as a mule. If I wrote him a letter he would inevitably reply by pointing out what I had omitted, what I said incorrectly and so on. He was scrupulous to a fault, exacting as a schoolmaster.

If one took a glance at his desk one would think him completely disorganized. Papers, documents, letters were piled in heaps, even on the floor and bed. But, like Blaise Cendrars, he knew exactly where everything was and could find it in a jiffy. (Cendrars once showed me a little room in his hotel which was strewn with books. They lay *pêle mêle* in a huge heap. In that disorderly pile he always stashed away a wad of paper money which he could lay his hands on at a moment's notice. This money was a safeguard against penury. Every time he made a long trip he took this precaution.)

Another thing, regarding work—Emil did everything single-handed. He had no use for a secretary. He also had a great memory and therefore needed no file cases. In short he was "the compleat Angler." He was also handy with his hands, could repair anything. The two shacks he occupied after we left the cabin on Partington Ridge were largely his own handiwork. Attached to a shack he had on the highway near Anderson Creek was a sort of open shed which served as his art gallery. It's a wonder no one ever stole any of his paintings because I don't believe he took them into the house overnight.

As I hinted before, Emil had a flair for what might be called neo-primitivism. His mania for detail and exactitude which I alluded to earlier displayed itself in his art. He could do streets and houses like an architect—a dreamy architect, to be sure. His color was good, despite the fact that he was color-blind. (It's amazing, when one stops to think of it, how little color-blindness matters in painting. Didn't Picasso used to say—"When I run out of red I use blue?") In some of his work—I think of one called "The Tiger" particularly—he evoked memories of Rousseau. Though Emil knew Rousseau's work I doubt that he was influenced by him. Like Rousseau, he tried to paint things as they are.

We all see the world through different eyes and Emil's eyes were very definitely his own. In some paintings he was a poet, albeit rather a Dadaist. (See the one called "I am a Stranger here Myself." It's in a class by itself and very Emil Whitish. Or if not Emil Whitish then Kurt Schwitterish.) Why, after a few years, he stopped painting I don't know. As best I understood it, he had a perpetual fear that he could never do another like the ones before. He even bought up some of his own work. (Like a hen afraid of losing her brood.) But then some very great painters have done the same, though for different reasons.

I mentioned his obsession about *Welt Politik*. I must add in all fairness that it was not all talk with Emil. He was born in a hamlet in the Carpathians, but was raised in Vienna. During an aborted revolution he journeyed to Budapest to aid the revolutionaries. He was only fifteen or sixteen years old. To make it short, he was caught and sentenced to be shot. Lined up against the wall, he was prepared to die. Suddenly, the guard caught sight of some Austrian currency in Emil's shirt pocket and let Emil give him the slip. Two years later he managed to get to New York where he found a relative who aided him for a while. I wish I could remember the story about the relative. It is one of his comi-tragic ones, right out of Emil's book of "Droll Stories." A companion tale to "My Life as an Echo."

It was a cruel blow which Fate dealt him twice. As one might gather from the foregoing, Emil was not the marrying type. In his horoscope there can be no doubt that as far as marriage goes he was accursed. The first wife was one of the most ravishingly beautiful women that ever passed through Big Sur. She was Hungarian by birth and had a bit of paprika in her temperament. But that wasn't the root of their trouble. It was something much worse and more difficult to cope with. It was partially the fact that she had two children from a former marriage and one of them was gaga in a peculiarly annoying way. In addition to the two children, she brought along a piano which was most welcome. She had a beautiful voice and played quite well. But that one son! He was just too much for Emil. In a few weeks they had separated.

With all the women who threw themselves at him it is a wonder he wasn't married ten or twenty times. A few years after his divorce he married his second wife. Whatever induced him to marry her is beyond me. To my mind she was rather a moody, lazy creature. I said she was not gifted. She bore Emil two sons, but was no mother. Emil became the mother. Emil loved children and particularly his own. It was depressing to visit him now. All the sparkle had left his twinkling eyes. He and she rarely spoke to one another. They were deliberately giving each other the silent treatment. If you stayed for lunch or dinner it was Emil who fixed the meal. If the children needed attention it was Emil who had to look after them. He was inordinately attached to them. They grew to be bright obedient boys and Emil was very proud of them. Then one day his wife up and announces that she is going off with another, younger man to live in Australia. And she is taking the boys with her. For Emil this news was tantamount to the earth opening up beneath his feet. He was heartbroken over the prospect of losing his children and did his best to retain them but to no avail.

After a few years he decided to take a trip around the world and stop off in Australia to see his children who had now become teenagers. One may wonder how Emil, who knew how to live on ten dollars a week when I first knew him, could pick up and become a globetrotter. (The answer to this will appear shortly.) Anyway, when he arrives at their home in Australia there is not even a bed for him in the house. He is obliged to sleep in a shed on a rude iron cot amidst a welter of junk. The children remembered him, but are not as jubilant as he expected them to be. In short it was a sad, disappointing reunion. However, from Australia, Emil decided to visit Japan. This constituted a lucky break. Japan, or the Japanese, was Emil's meat. Here he met with nothing but courtesy, kindness and beauty. He fell in love with the country in no time. (I always wondered why he ever returned to America. I certainly wouldn't have.) Naturally he fell head over heels in love with the Japanese girls. One in particular he wanted to bring back to America, but her parents wouldn't let her go. I remember the lengthy correspondence he carried on with her upon his return to the States. Now and then he would show me one of her letters. Despite the halting English her letters were full of charm and tenderness. There were also, of course, quaint turns in the English—not *Japlish*, but thoughts thoroughly Japanese. One which I liked very much and transcribed on the wall of my studio was: "Thank you for always calling me darling." Certainly there is nothing wrong with the English in this sentence. But whoever heard of an American girl being grateful for being called darling? I believe he went to Japan a second time in order to convince her to marry him and return with him to Big Sur. Of course he was unsuccessful. Japan is hardly the land of romance. If anything, it is the land of love-and-suicide.

Fortunately, as I said at the beginning of this chapter, Japan came to Emil. One seemed to recommend him to another. It is almost impossible to visit him without finding a Japanese girl also visiting him, either for an afternoon or evening or for a week or a month.

In the early days of my stay in Big Sur I had many female visitors, all fans. Once I happened to remark to Emil that there were too many coming, that they interfered with my work. His ready response was: "Send them on down to my place!" Which I did to the satisfaction of all concerned. Indeed some of the more romantic fans would write me, after a sojourn at Anderson Creek, thanking me for introducing them to such a charming host as Emil White.

But I have forgotten to explain Emil's rise from rags to riches. As far back as I can remember Emil made a living selling books through the mail. The remuneration was certainly not magnificent. He earned about ten dollars a week on which he managed to live quite decently. Of course he had no vices; he never drank to excess, he smoked only three or four cigarettes a day, he needed no radio or T.V. His only vice was women, but they cost him nothing. Usually they brought him practical gifts. I think his rent never came to more than seven or eight dollars a month. He lived fairly near the Hot Springs which were then free. Here he not only enjoyed a hot bath and a sun bath but he did his laundering there too. In other words, strange as it may seem today, in 1975 Emil was living the life of Reilly. Better—he was living like a pasha.

As I said before, Emil was indeed well read. During his Chicago days he had been a frequent visitor of the Dill Pickle Club, made famous by such writers as Ben Hecht, Maxwell Bodenheim, Theodore Dreiser, Sherwood Anderson, William Faulkner and other celebrities.

I mention the Dill Pickle Club because Emil always had to do with writers. He was not only a great reader, but a perceptive one with a very retentive memory. I never saw him reading a trashy book, which is more than I can say for most of my intellectual friends. In addition, he was a confirmed letter writer. Sometimes, it seemed to me, he was in touch with the whole world. In the bottom of his heart I believe Emil considered himself a writer—much more so than a painter. Perhaps his long association with writers had something to do with this. At the same time, Emil was what is called a very practical man. Not only was he a do-it-yourself man, but he had ideas of all sorts floating in his skull. How it came about I no longer remember, but one day the idea hit him to get out a magazine about Big Sur. He not only put the magazine together but he wrote articles for it himself. More, he even delivered copies of the magazine up and down the coast which was no mean job. And if people wrote in asking about the magazine he answered them himself. In this day and age what he undertook was little short of miraculous. The question remained—had he done the community a service or a disservice, for soon after the appearance of his publications tourists began pouring into the almost unknown Big Sur. I suspect that I started this business myself, all unwittingly to be sure. My letters were traveling all over the globe. Besides the fans who made my life difficult there were the occasional freaks who sometimes created untold mischief. Anyway, Emil capitalized on the fame and beauty of this Paradise and began reaping a small fortune. After a time he brought out two more "Guides," one on Carmel and vicinity, and the other on the Hearst Castle. The one on the Hearst Castle sold over 300,000 copies. It was on these earnings that he was able to take a trip around the world when he felt like it. Let me quickly add that wealth did not spoil him. He remained the same modest, frugal Emil who ate the same sort of meals every day. Perhaps the one luxury he permitted himself was to buy a good station wagon which he needed to deliver his "Guides" up and down the coast from San Francisco to San Luis Obispo.

Just a very few years back he seemed to be in a bad way. He wrote me once that he had the palsy, which everyone construed as meaning Parkinson's disease. Emil accepted the situation stoically. In no way did he change his mode of life. Happily in a year or so he regained his health and now, whatever his real age, looks fit as a fiddle. His Japanese girl friends have not deserted him, nor the others either, for that matter. The one thing which remains for him to do is to write the story of his life, but I doubt he will ever do it. If it weren't for his failing sight his friend Henry Miller would do it for him. Or perhaps some feminist like Kate Millet will do it for Women's Lib!

If I were to write his epitaph it would go something like this: Here was a man who genuinely loved women despite their faults and frailties, or maybe *because* of their very shortcomings.

Ephraim Doner

Encore un juif! (Another Jew!) But this one from the Diaspora not the ghetto. A Chassidic Jew, b'Jesus, for which there is no counterpart in Jewry. One has to look for his equal among the Persians or Arabs—the mantic sects, what! I have never met the likes of him before. He is absolutely unique, undiluted, integral. One would like to write about him in Polish or Old French. English is too dull, too flat, too weak, to render his nature, his soul. For, of all the friends and acquaintances I have had, he is the only one with a predominant soul.

Chassidic as he is, he is always whirling about you, snapping his fingers and muttering prayers. He makes one dizzy immediately. Dizzy, thirsty and talkative. For he is an electrifier! He makes the heart and soul dilate. He turns everything topsy-turvy. Jew that he is, he is nevertheless more of anything and everything else than a Jew. Which is to say he is 101 percent Jewish. He is a Jew twenty-four hours a day—even when working on a canvas. For, no matter how seriously he takes his work (as painter), in his heart is is always *singing*—from the Bible. The Bible and *Don Quixote* are his two favorite books. The latter he reads every year—in Spanish. He could also read it in French,

171

Polish, and Yiddish, if these translations were available. Though he knows five languages thoroughly, he gives the impression of knowing ten or twenty. He always knows more than one is supposed to know about everything.

I know almost nothing about his early life. I am not even certain if Poland was his birth place. It could just as well have been Minsk or Pinsk. I suspect his father, or else his grandfather, was a rabbi. No, I don't suspect . . . I am certain of it. How else could he have come by his exalted condition?

It was in Big Sur that I first became acquainted with his phenomenal being. He lived in Carmel Highlands and each week we passed within a few yards of his home on our way to Monterey to shop for the week. On the way back we would usually stop off at his home and have dinner with him, his wife Rosa and sometimes his young daughter. The latter was often a bit of a trial. Brought up by two extremely liberal parents, she seemed to take delight in expressing her rebellion. Rebellion against what? I used to ask myself. Her most daring utterances were old hat to both her parents. However, Tasha, as she was called, never could get her father's or mother's goat. Their indulgence used to amaze me. They seemed capable of understanding anything and everything.

The meals *chez* Doner were always festive ones. Excellent cooks, both he and his wife. Excellent wines, cognac, whatever. But best of all, were the conversations, in which *mon cher* Ephraim usually took the lead. He was like a man out of the early Middle Ages. He could discourse on most anything. But his favorite subject (presumably) was the Old Testament, the ancient prophets, the miracles, the very language, whether in Hebrew, Yiddish or English. What a treat to listen to him dwell on one of his favorite chapters—"The Book of Job" was definitely one. He made the Bible come alive, especially for a goy like myself. The figures he chose to expatiate on were all grand, whether male or female. He spoke of them as if he had a real

172

acquaintance with them. (How different, his rhapsodies, from the dull aired sermons I had to listen to in my Presbyterian Church, as a boy!) One would not know they were the same characters that were being extolled.

The very preparation of the meal was a treat to behold. For Rosa usually assisted him, one taking care of the meat, fowl or fish, and the other the vegetables and sauces. Between times one of them would go out to the garden to gather some herbs. Parsley was the key word. Never a meal without parsley or watercress. And *garlic*, to be sure. It made no never mind if before the meal the two of them had been arguing or disputing. Come time for dinner and they automatically fell into step. During the preparations for the meal Ephraim would usually give a little discourse on the "heavenly" virtues of parsley or garlic or whatever. All of which helped to whet one's appetite. At table, which always opened with a rapid prayer (in Hebrew) Ephraim would soon begin reminiscing about some books he had just read or was in the process of reading. This led to a vivacious discussion about authors past and present—Cervantes, Hamsun, Proust, Joyce, O'Casey, and, not least of all, Isaac Bashevis Singer, whom we both adored. Doner read in three of four languages, which made his observations all the more acute. He never tired of praising Yiddish as a written language. He used to make me feel ashamed of myself for neglecting to study Yiddish, or at least read translations in English. (From all I could gather, Yiddish was preferable to Hebrew, as a written language.)

The talk did not center around literature exclusively. We touched on many subjects, including astrology.

After the meat course we always had a divine dessert coupled with Cognac, Armangac or Kirschwasser. The drink would set Ephraim's tongue wagging again—this time perhaps about the splendors of French wines and liqueurs. Whatever he chose to dwell on he spoke like a connoisseur. Sometimes I suspected him of inventing things but I never caught him in *flagrante delicto*, so to speak. The same with ping pong, our favorite pastime. I cannot say that I ever saw anyone, amateur or professional, beat him. Not that he was such a skillful player, but rather that he was indefatigable, a veritable bull. (I'm sure he was a Taurean, by the way.) A completely different side of him came to the fore when it came time to tackle the canvas. He went through a certain ritual before attacking. Here is where he displayed his holiness. First came the donning of the blue apron—with a short prayer; then the mixing of his paints. I feel certain that before he touched brush to canvas he made another prayer to his Jehovah— and that was, to be permitted to do something extra good that day. Whatever he undertook it was with heart and soul.

I have only seen him once or twice since leaving Big Sur ten or twelve years ago. At that time, though highly esteemed by a few of us, he was relatively unknown in the art world. Not that that mattered greatly to him. He had been poor all his life; he took it as part of an artist's life. As a matter of fact we were both poor at the time I speak of. But Ephraim was the more resourceful of the two. On the day my wife and I sent to town Ephraim would be standing at a gas station near his home, waiting for us to pass by. "How are you fixed today?" he would ask. "If you need any dough, just say the word, I can always borrow from the gas station attendant." Many is the time he slipped a ten dollar bill in my hand. I doubt that he himself had a penny in the bank. But, if he needed anything, there was always a way to get it. He literally "trusted the Lord." And he was always protected. Whether it was through divine mercy or utter faith in life, it's difficult to say.

I used the word phenomenal in referring to him earlier. His ebullience, his vivacity, his never failing enthusiasm endeared him to everyone. His energy was boundless. He was a giver. If you saw something in his home you liked veryuch, he would say, "Take it home with you. It's yours." In this way he was never poor as others sometimes are. For the more he gave the more he

174

received. And he could accept just as easily as he gave. Poverty to him was a sign of holiness. Though he could argue a point till Doomsday he was truly liberal-minded. He could understand the beauty and logic of other religions. In his practice of Judaism he was universal. As I said earlier, he was really a man of the Middle Ages, learned, rounded, jubilant, forever worshiping his Lord and Master. I have listened to much talk about holiness, but it was *chez* Ephraim Doner where I saw it actualized. His little house was a refuge for those in need, who thirsted after knowledge and truth.

He didn't live long in this Carmel abode before visitors began to stream through his place. They came from all over the world and were royally received. He was literally inexhaustible. He gave himself up to his guests entirely. He never said, "I'm sorry, I'm too busy to see you today" or "I'm sorry, we don't have enough food for an extra plate." He knew how to make a little do. (The loaves and fishes, the water that turned into wine . . .)

One day a real miracle took place. His wife Rosa had been deaf for years. Then, quite by accident, she discovered a physician who promised to restore her hearing. And he did. I shall never forget her account of how it affected her to hear the birds singing again. Being quite deaf myself, I know what a heavenly feeling it is to hear birds chirping in the trees.

As I said before, theirs was a holy place. And they were protected as holy ones usually are. In accordance with Jewish tradition they never attempted to make converts. Like St. Francis of Assisi, they treated the atheist and the Catholic as they would their own. Theirs was a true liberalism, not an intellectual one.

I remember going through a marriage ceremony with Eve, my fourth wife, in the patio of their home. It was a civil ceremony, as neither Eve nor I espoused any particular religion. But it was also a religious ceremony because it was arranged by the Doners. In any case, it was a joyous, festive occasion, celebrated with excellent food and wines.

Though, as I said before, I have only seen Ephraim once or twice since leaving Big Sur the impression he left on me never fades. From him I learned more about the art of living than from anyone else. I suppose a Jew would refer to him as "a good Jew," but to me he was so much more. To me he was a good China-man, a good Gentile (not a Christian)—in short, a good human being. And that is saying a lot these days. Nor do I need to give my blessing. He was blessed long ago. His very presence is a blessing never to be forgotten. There was another strong reason for my attraction to Doner. He too had lived and worked in Europe. In fact, he was born there. But at some fairly early age, he had come to Paris. He knew the city, intimately. He had starved there. It's true there were other friends of mine who had lived in Paris for awhile, but they had not been inoculated, so to speak. Some who hadn't been there knew about the life from books they had read. But with Ephraim it was like doing a waltz together. One name, whether of an author, a painter, a street, a church, would suggest another. With no one else in Big Sur could I talk ecstatically about men like de Nerval, Marcel Duchamp, Vlaminck, Matisse, Utrillo, Francis Carco, Man Ray, George Grosz, Duhamel (the Salavin series) Reverdy, Roger Vitrac, Zadkine, or the works of André Gide, Anatole France, André Breton (his Nadja) and others. We intoxicated one another with our recollections. Even street names could set us on fire. The rue Mouffetard and the Place Contrescarpe, for example. Or the rue de Seine and the rue Mazarin. Or the Grands Boulevards! The Portes, the Place Violet, for example. Each of us had his store of anecdotes to tell and they fell on appreciative ears. Just to mention the name André Breton was enough to cause us to explode for an hour or so. Because around Breton there had clustered a whole group of Surrealists and former Dadaists. Who in American had ever heard of Jacques Vaché, who was to have such an influence upon Breton's life? Who ever spoke of Max Jacob and his early days with Picasso?

176

Who had read that most engaging book *La Nostalgie de Paris*, by Francis Carco? Who ever mentioned Blaise Cendrars or Jean Giono? With all these writers and painters there were associated the names of streets dear to our memory, streets we had walked on empty bellies, streets (and hotels) where famous artists had lived and died. What a difference between being a temporary resident of Paris and working there as an artist! All those little restaurants where one ate cheaply—how we adored them! How wonderful to know some kind Frenchman from whom one could borrow a few francs when in dire need! How inviting the park benches when one was footsore and defeated, ready to give up the game! Yes, over those dinners *chez* Doner we relived our blessed poverty-stricken days in Paris. (Who has not starved in Paris doesn't know Paris.) Though neither of us attended church, even the churches bore gracious memories. And last, but not least, were the *clochards* and prostitutes. Sometimes the dregs of society carried themselves like royalty. Some of the prostitutes in Montmarte were like cornerstones, unforgettable in carriage and demeanor. To the great credit of the French people those exiles of society were permitted to walk the streets, to enjoy of restaurants and cafes when they could. They were a very important ingredient of Parisian life.

In a sense the attitude of the Parisian was to be surprised at nothing. It was out of such a sense no doubt that one day Mary Reynolds, then mistress of Marcel Duchamp, made me a gift of my own *Tropic of Cancer* bound in human skin. (I can't recall what happened to this book. Did someone steal it from me or did I make someone a gift of it? I would give anything to know into whose hands it has fallen.)

Speaking of Duchamp, whom I have referred to as the most civilized man I ever met, I am reminded of an encounter with him I shall never forget. As everyone knows, early in his career he had abandoned painting and taken up chess. One day on visiting him at his home he asked if I knew how to play chess. I told him I did, but that I was a poor player. He wanted someone to play with badly that day, for the next thing I heard him say was—"I'll give you my Queen, a rook and a bishop, and if that is not enough, I'll throw in a few pawns."

Hearing these words I was already defeated. We began playing and in a few moves I was checkmated. Since I had arrived in Paris in 1930 I was in time to imbibe some of the surrealist spirit. André Breton was still alive and by now regarded as the "Pope" of the movement. I had read a few of his books and was intrigued. To tell the truth, I was more impressed by Celine than by Breton. At any rate, what I am trying to say is that it was a period full of highly interesting individuals, whether sane or insane. I knew a few of these artists, such as Max Ernst, Kokoschka, Man Ray, Duchamp. Breton himself I met just once at some crazy party. A fight had broken out. I happened to spy Breton at the fireplace with his head resting on his hand, watching the fracas detachedly. He looked exactly as everyone pictured him—a lion (or a defrocked priest). Something propelled me to go up to him and introduce myself. He was warm and friendly and not at all diffident, as I had expected him to be.

I mention these incidents because our conversations were full of them.

I notice that I have given little space to Doner's paintings. As I said earlier, his approach to his work was a holy one. There was beauty and sincerity in everything he touched. Now and then he sold a painting. The fact that he sold his work at long intervals did not deter him from working. He went to his studio religiously everyday—like a priest to the mass. He looked upon everything, no matter how commonplace, reverently. Whether he did a still life or a portrait or a landscape was all one to him. He admired, nay *loved* his own work. And rightly so. They all contained some part of him—heart, liver, kidneys, no matter what. And all were imbued with soul. Without soul a painting like an individual, was to him dead. When I think back on these days, I

178

realize that he was one of the very few American artists who understood the blessings of poverty. Though he was one hundred percent Jewish he understood and admired a great spirit such as St. Francis of Assisi. I think he preferred him to Jesus, *as I do myself.* At the same time there was in my friend Doner a touch of Don Quixote. Whatever he did had a Quixotic touch. He made even the prophets seem Quixotic—and weren't they?

In conclusion I must add that I have never known anyone beside him who could argue strenuously for hours without getting angry. He knew always how to give the soft answer that turneth away wrath. Always, at the finish of a dispute, he was on his feet, whirling and snapping his fingers whilst reciting or chanting a prayer.

I have not dwelt on his faults. They were insignificant compared to his virtues. *Pax Vobiscum, cher ami!*

Jack Garfein

He lived his early years in a German concentration camp. Even there he was like a darling of the gods. It was there also that he learned the art of discrimination.

What amazed me about him on our first meeting was the range of his knowledge and his mastery of English, a foreign language to him. When we meet the sparks fly. He is not only most affable, charming, exciting, but a great raconteur who holds you spell-bound.

His career as a director began quite early, in New York City, with O'Casey's first play, *The Shadow of a Gunman.* The school which he later established has turned out a number of excellent actors.

One is not long in his presence before one realizes that, next to the theatre his passion is women. He loves them as a gardener loves flowers. He makes no bones about it, he is a sensualist. And as such, he is like a famous violinist.

Like Napoleon, he believes that the best defense is the attack. He attacks everything with the same gusto. He is endowed with an enormous appetite for life. He *devours* things, human beings as well.

Talking to him, one feels he had an extraordinary education. He gives the impression of knowing any and everything—and thoroughly! He probably has prejudices, as do we all, but he does not reveal them. He seems more like a "master" from the Middle Ages than a contemporary individual.

When he talks he sets everything in motion. He says things which stun, startle and confuse you momentarily.

One of his characteristics is that he seems always to be beaming, always infatuated with whatever he is doing.

Strindberg is one of his favorite playwrights. He is particularly fond of *Miss Julie, The Stranger,* and *Creditors.* He knows his characters inside out. Just to mention Strindberg or Dostoievsky is to set him talking for hours. Of his students he expects the utmost. He himself always gives his utmost. Besides, he is never through explaining. No matter how well you may think you know a book, a scene, a character, Jack can explain what you failed to see or understand. He is as ruthless with his pupils as with himself. He can talk as interestingly about the Talmud or the Old Testament as about modern or ancient drama.

He is tenacious as a bulldog, a perfectionist—no letting go until a thing has been mastered He is also possessed of great tenderness as well as reverence. In a man whose tastes are so varied and whose intellect is so keen this tenderness of his is or is not a great surprise. One thing he is *not* and that is an intellectual snob. He is so many things, always involved, always searching for answers, usually for the truth of a situation, that he has become the "compleat" human being. He is like an organ from which one can wring the finest, noblest music.

He lives on a grand scale, whether he can afford it or not. His heart is abundant and the range of his interests is simply staggering.

If I have not seen him for a few weeks he will in that time have read all the great Russian authors, for example. Or the Scandinavian playwrights. Or perhaps he will have done some research on the Gnostics. I am always surprised to learn what he has just been up to. He is, to put it simply, a cosmological man. His world is the cosmos.

His female pupils are always falling in love with him and he with them. "All for Love" is his motto.

As a conversationalist he is one of the most stimulating men I have ever known. He is always full of surprises, sometimes erotic ones, other times erudite ones.

He is deeply religious without belonging to church or synagogue. He would have made an excellent rabbi, for example, particularly because of the way he can split hairs.

Being a perfectionist he is somewhat hard on his pupils. He has the endurance of a giant and the knowledge of an encyclopedist.

I mentioned his reading. He is a voracious reader with a retentive memory. When he reads a book he knows it by heart. He retains a memory of books read which is nothing less than phenomenal. And such a diversity of reading matter! Myself, though I am no longer a great reader, I can seldom relate the story or plot of the book I have just read. But I can talk about the book—endlessly, it seems.

Jack has two wonderful children in their late teens. The product of a stormy marriage, they show no neurotic strain. Half the year they live with their mother, the actress Carol Baker, and half the year with Jack. Living with the mother they have seen something of the world. They speak several languages fluently. They are a remarkable tribute to both parents. Jack's life with Carol Baker reminds me somewhat of my life with one of my wives. Stormy, tumultuous, fascinating.

As I said before, he is deeply religious without going to synagogue. I repeat this bit about his religiousness because at first blush he gives the impression of being nonreligious. A great Jewish writer said somewhere—"the man who constantly talks about God is an ungodly man." Precisely. It's when Jack is talking

182

about some simple thing that one feels his godliness. To me he is similar to Krishnamurti, who is against masters and gurus and all so-called holy people. Was it Ramakrishna who once told his disciples not to follow in his footsteps, confessing that his love for God was a vice?

I hope I have made my point clear. To put it more simply still I would say that Jack is in love with life. But he includes *all* life. There is no "holier than thou" in his make-up. All is holy, and out of evil often springs good. *Voilà* a man after my own heart.

I mentioned earlier that Jack gives the impression of being a well educated individual. Oddly enough it began in the concentration camp. One of the guards took a liking to him and made it his business to teach him what he may have learned at school. A strange business, this tenderness among the killer Nazis, but a true paradox. On Christmas day, for example, he was treated to a piece of cake and a glass of wine by his jailers. Apparently even monsters have a heart. As a result of these occurrences Jack has a most forgiving and understanding heart. I believe it was he who once quoted a line out of Eckerman's *Conversations with Goethe*. Said Goethe one day: "I doubt that there is a crime, however heinous, that I have not felt capable of myself." This from "the first European."

Jack has a mind like a razor's edge and a heart to match. A rare combination. If he had followed his head he might have become a celebrated rabbi; if he had followed his heart alone he could have become a saint, a *Jewish* saint, *bien entendu!* But he is, as I mentioned earlier, the whole man, the rounded man, the man of a bygone epoch. Today we turn out great scholars, great pundits, great scientists, even great musicians, but no great men of heart. We turn out men of learning who can also be monsters, masters (in a religious sense) who turn out to be fakers. Everything we touch in this world of today has something phony about it. It's the age of plastics, nothing being what it seems to be.

And now I feel like saying something that may shock some of

my readers. I think that Jack Garfein's experience as a boy in a Nazi concentration camp demonstrates that sometimes out of evil springs good. Certainly I know no other way to explain his benevolence, his sense of humanity, his understanding and compassion.

After all, is it so very strange what I have just written? Do not the Christians owe their god Jesus to the treachery of his disciple Judas?

Only the other day, from the lips of a physician who had served in the war, was I informed of the fact, according to him, that over half the guards in the concentration camps were volunteers from other countries than Germany.

But enough of this . . . one may begin to think I am making a plea on behalf of the Nazis, than which nothing could be further from the truth.

What I am stressing, I must repeat, is that good and evil are mixed in the human being. We have not yet seen the perfect man, though we have had some noble examples of a human being. Suffice to say, they were not all saints. We also know that there were so-called saints who were nearer to being monsters.

To change the subject abruptly . . . To see Jack Garfein put his arms around a woman and kissing her is a very special treat. If it was lust which inspired his behavior then lust has to be regarded as one of the virtues.

This is only a feeble example of why I said before that Jack is a holy man. Perhaps a holy man who, out of the greatness of his heart, permits himself to sin on occasion. (And not go through the farce of repenting afterwards.) No, his behavior reminds one more of that of a Zen master whose religion is no religion. No repentance, no guilt, no shame! How refreshing!

Joe Gray

This was supposed to be Chapter the Last.
But I won't risk putting it off any longer since my hold on life
may break any time now. And I wouldn't want the "Book of
Friends" to be minus Joe Gray who meant so much to me. *Meant*
did I say? I mean *means*, for in my memory he is still alive and
kicking, still as vivid as ever.

Joe was loved by men, women, children and animals—or else
detested. Born and raised on the East Side, Manhattan, he had all
the characteristics of this breed from which so many celebrities
sprang. Only Joe was not what you would call a celebrity. To be
honest, and this is one of his qualities which endeared him to me,
Joe had no ambition. He was quite content to be a stunt man, a
stand-in, a bit actor which hehad become after a brief career in
the ring. In fact, he would have enjoyed doing nothing at all,
getting along on a small pension. That is, so long as he could go
to the beach every day, read his favorite authors and have three
or four good-looking women on the string. Oh yes, and his dog
Byron, from whom he was inseparable.

Though his career as a pug was brief it nevertheless marked
him. It had altered his physiognomy—for the better! Born with a

real Jewish nose, he had had it smashed during one of his early bouts. He didn't remain long as a fighter because very early in his career he was knocked out. That seemed to bring him to his senses. He quickly realized that he would never be a Benny Leonard, who was then his idol.

His older brother, Mack Gray (Killer Mack, he was nicknamed) was living in Hollywood and had a cushy job managing one of the very popular stars. Mack urged his brother to join him, promising to find him work in the movies. Before joining his brother in Hollywood Joe had a new nose built for him by a plastic surgeon. From a tough mug he became a handsome guy whom women looked upon favorably. And so Joe took the train and came to sunny California, which was just to his liking.

But he did not come before having one or two heart-breaking experiences with the opposite sex. *Unrequited love.* How often we discussed this subject at the dinner table. Joe apparently was one of those who never get over a woman's betrayal. It made him bitter toward women in general, unforgiving, hard as nails. Nevertheless, he was never without a woman on his hands, usually several at a time. He maintained that he never fell in love with them; he simply could not resist the flesh. He no longer thought of them as persons, but as possessors of big boobs, marvelous thighs, big asses and so on. He always took them apart immediately. I used to drive about with him sometimes of a weekend. He wanted to show me how easy it was to pick up a cunt—*any* cunt. And to observe his tactics it was indeed easy, but also rather embarrassing. What he liked best, he used to say, were maids, maids from South America, who worked for slave wages in rich Jewish families in Beverly Hills. They were "always grateful" for a good lay and a meal. He didn't put any stock in the actresses who were sitting around waiting their turn, however beautiful, even ravishing they might be. They were too proud, in his opinion. However, he often brought these glamour girls to my home—*"for you"*—he would whisper on the side. I must say I

186

never saw such a bevy of beautiful women in my life. But, as he was quick to point out, there was always something missing in them. His contempt for actors and actresses was undying. "All they know how to do," he would say, "is to read the lines." As a generality, this was of course quite true. Most of these folk *are* empty-headed, when you get to know them. I don't think I need to indicate those who were the exception to the rule, or vice versa.

Perhaps it was his rough masculinity, perhaps it was the cute nose the plastic surgeon had given him, but there was something about Joe which made him extremely attractive to most every woman. I was often surprised by the kind of women he would bring to meet me. I should have said earlier that shortly after I arrived in L.A. I ran into Joe at the home of a mutual friend. We became friends immediately. In a way, it was something of hero worship on Joe's part. He had only just begun to read me when we met. Prior to this he was not much of a reader, though strangely enough, his favorites were Byron, Shelley and Keats. Byron he could recite by the yard. He even named his dog Byron.

I mention all this only to explain that when Joe did bring a woman to the house it was to give her the privilege of meeting "the great Henry Miller, Henry Miller the genius," etc., etc. It was as if he were bringing me fresh flowers.

The women, usually gullible, were ready to see whatever Joe indicated. What often annoyed him, though he wouldn't show it till after the gal had left, was the free and easy way I accepted her presence, the way I put my arms around her and kissed her, for example. Tough and rough as he was, Joe was not used to such behavior. Or, to put it another way, he probably felt the girl should have shown a little more resistance. At bottom it was a hang-over from the Puritan days, a quality which lurks in every American male. Presumably, my years in Paris had rubbed off some of this nonsense. In another sense I was far more naïve, far more innocent than Joe. He called me a romantic, not without scorn.

It would infuriate him if I said that I didn't mind being hurt by a woman, if I loved her. If I loved, I would say, I love body and soul. This made me a masochist in his eyes. Or a blind fool, or a dozen other things. None of which, however, prevented him from coming to me for advice. For, despite the fact that he was supposedly through with women, he couldn't help but get caught now and then. Of course he never took my advice. No siree, not Joe Gray. It would end up by him giving *me* unasked for advice. What Joe liked more than giving advice to a friend was to badger and bully him. To me his antics were amusing. I would encourage him to lay it on thicker. For example, some time after I met Joe I fell in love with Hoki Tokuda, whom I later married. Now Joe took a violent dislike to Hoki almost from the very first. Unlike me, he did not see the unusual qualities in the Japanese woman. In fact, he suspected them all of being blood suckers. She was out to get something, that was his idea. I knew of course that there was a strong element of jealousy in Joe's behavior. This Hoki was going to rob him of his best friend. She was a menace. And so on. What he could not understand was that I got a kick out of his ranting. I would incite him to continue, to say his worst. This bothered him. My passivity, or endorsement, seemed to him like a betrayal of my love for Hoki.

Finally the day came, when over dinner for three, Joe urged me to marry her. "She'll make you a good wife." he said, a remark unthinkable a week previous.

We damn near took Joe along on our honeymoon, because Joe had never been to Paris and wanted very much to see how artists behaved there. (Probably influenced by *Tropic of Cancer*.)

From the day of the marriage, he watched Hoki like a hawk. Every other day he'd ask, "How's it going?" "Is she living up to expectations?" And so on. He was relentless. Any little fault he discovered became a dramatic incident.

Soon he was telling me that he had always warned me she was no good. It was a veritable merry-go-round. Since I never said anything one way or another he assumed (and rightly) that it was a fiasco.

However, playing ping pong wiped out a lot of the bitterness. We used to play, Joe and I, occasionally joined by two or three friends, almost every day and for several hours at a time. Joe played best to the music of Scriabin's Fifth Piano Sonata or Ravel's *Gaspard de la Nuit*. He was as violent in his likes and dislikes for composers as he was for authors. As for the authors he disliked I usually shared his opinion. But for composers, no! Joe was best in his appreciation, or lack of it, for authors. For a man who had had no great education it was amazing how keen his judgement of authors was. For a man who could so easily ingratiate himself with women, it was amazing to observe the affection he bestowed on his dog. Byron came first in everything. Of course this lavish affection for a dog came about through some heart-breaking setbacks with women. He had been betrayed three or four times, with the result that he was absolutely adamant as regards showing any further affection toward the other sex. All his attention now centered on Byron and me. He couldn't avoid fucking the women occasionally, but he could never fall in love again. He was absolutely unforgiving. Having been betrayed two or three times he was absolutely relentless in his aversion toward the other sex. Which did not prevent women from throwing themselves at him. To mollify them he would give them a lay and then forget them. Yet he could not resist flirting with them, leading them on, but he never said "I love you!" The word love had dropped from his vocabulary. What he frequently did was to bring his women to me and offer them to me, like a nice bit of juicy fruit. Fortunately, his women weren't always satisfied to take the substitute he offered.

It wasn't only women Joe brought to the house, but gifts of all

189

sorts. Books especially, followed by health food products, wearing apparel (often the cast-off suit of some movie star) and usually recordings of Scriabin, Ravel, Debussy, *et alia*. Or a new set of ping pong balls, for we wore them out fast. In addition to bringing gifts for me he also brought gifts for my children, Tony and Val.

If he stayed for dinner, which he frequently did, he would get a little high on wine and whiskey—or sometimes Armagnac, if I happened to have any on hand. If I warned him to take it easy driving home he would tell me not to worry, if he got too drunk Byron his dog would see him home safely.

One night, after imbibing rather heavily, he drove home so cautiously that he aroused the suspicions of the police. Just as he pulled up to his front door out came the cops and took him to the brig. He begged them not to do any harm to Byron, offered to pay for his board and keep, and so they set Byron free.

That was a night Joe never forgot. Tough bimbo that he was, he was not used to associating with the dregs he met in his cell. He emerged from the experience a thoroughly crushed individual. Had he been a devout Catholic or even an orthodox Jew he would certainly have done penance for a month or so. It didn't stop his drinking, it only moderated it.

There was a serious side to Joe, the eternal student, you might say. Books enthralled him, probably because he had neglected them for so long. Nothing daunted him in his reading ventures. As he explained to me one day, when he began reading my books, he paid attention to the books and authors I mentioned in passing. And so, like that, he found himself reading Blaise Cendrars, Jean Giono, Ferdinand Celine, Richard Jefferies, many authors indeed whom he had never heard of a few months before. What's more, he would discuss their work with me or anyone who happened to come along. Often, on returning a book he had borrowed, he would slap the book down and exclaim: "That's one hell of a good book, do you know that?" To which I would reply, "Yes, Joe, that's why I told you to read it." Whereupon he would say, "Where do you dig up all these books?"

A book like *Song of the World* by Giono or one of Isaac Singer's books would put him in a trance for a week.

To be honest, I never found Joe guilty of reading a trashy book. He despised people who did read such books. On the set at the studios he always had two or three books with him. He carried them to lend if he found a good listener, or, as he would put it, someone who wanted to be healed. For Joe regarded good literature as therapy. Though Jewish he went to Temple only on Yom Kippur—out of respect, he said. Otherwise he had no use for sermons whether delivered by a Jew or a Christian minister. They were full of shit, according to him. Joe never wasted time talking politics or religion. Nor did he waste much time talking about films. He felt sorry for the deluded gals who poured into Hollywood every day, hoping to become a star one day.

However, his sympathy for them did not prevent him from taking advantage of them. If he took a fancy to a tyro he would play his cards like any Hollywood bum. He would promise her the earth, let alone a good part, in order to get his end in. You might say he gave her a sympathetic fuck. If he met her six months later sitting on the bench he would say, "What's the matter with you, didn't I tell you who to pay attention to? You're wasting your time, you're fucking the wrong guys. Here you don't fuck for pleasure, but to climb a little higher up the ladder. They're all bums, I told you that months ago. Not a decent one in the lot. See that guy standing over there (pointing to a well-known male star), he'd fuck your grandmother if he thought it would help him. Watch out for the wolves!"

Funny, Joe could play the seducer and the protector at the same time. And they all loved him for it. He wasn't a bum like the others. He really had a heart—and a conscience of sorts.

Playing ping pong to the tune of Scriabin's Fifth Piano

Sonata—we had at least six or seven different virtuosi recording this piece—Joe would spice his talk with his latest favorite author, the cunt he picked up the day before—her teats, her ass, her thighs—together with tidbits about famous prize fighters and the values of certain health foods which he ate religiously every day.

He got me so riled about his fucking health foods that one day I composed a list of my favorite dishes and tacked it on the closet door of the kitchen. They were all dishes inclined to increase cholesterol—juicy, fatty, tasty bits. At the bottom I wrote in big letters "NO HEALTH FOODS PLEASE!"

In addition to books Joe loved my watercolors. He was always begging me to give him one as a bribe for this guy or the next in the casting department. For himself he was content to take only my failures—he finally plastered the walls of his joint with these. As with literature, so with painting. Joe soon caught on to the good ones. Modigliani was his favorite, followed by Bonnard, George Grosz, Renoir and Matisse. Picasso he considered a fraud. And nobody could ever convince Joe that he was wrong in his predilections.

About everyone and everything Joe had very definite opinions. If, on meeting someone for the first time, he took a dislike to the person he made no bones about telling him so. It didn't matter if it were a man *or* a woman. With a woman he might soften his speech somewhat, but never his attitude. With a man it was a positive treat to hear him carry on. Such abuse as he handed out—only an ex-pug could get away with it. But Joe didn't behave this way because he knew he could beat the shit out of the other guy. He just couldn't keep from speaking his mind. It made no difference to him either that the person might be a friend of mine. After the individual had left he would say to me, "And he calls himself a friend of yours! How can you tolerate such shits? They're all just ass-lickers." It made no difference if the person in question happened to be a man of some prominence—a doctor, an artist, an analyst, For analysts Joe had only a supreme contempt. Instead of shrinks Joe offered people good books. He had a whole string of such therapeutic works to recommend, ranging from Herman Hesse to Jean Giono. There were certain titles of mine, for example, which he always had on hand, and would read aloud from on occasion.

He also kept a wonderful notebook filled with quotations from his favorite passages from all the books he had read. I tried to induce several publishers to take it, but they couldn't see as I did. To me this notebook was in itself the key or the door to the best in literature. When Joe liked a book he never stopped talking about it. He recommended it to all and sundry regardless of education or culture. "Read!" he would say, "It will do you good."

Though he had begun life as a boxer, boxing held no great interest for him. "They're all fakers," he would say. "All bums." As for wrestling, it was absolutely beyond his comprehension that a person like myself could watch it on TV week after week. I would tell him it didn't matter to me if they were all phonies, I liked it. I got more of a kick watching these fakers than listening to an intellectual lecture or watching a TV performance.

It was rare indeed that Joe recommended a movie. Sometimes he would recommend a not-so-good one because one of his buddies was in it. Joe was good friends with a number of well-known movie actors. George Raft, for instance, was one of his great favorites. He only had praise for him, no matter what the gossips said. It was surprising indeed the sort of friends Joe had—they were from all walks of life, including the best and the worst, a point in his favor, I thought. And with them all he spoke the same language. As a stand-in or stunt man for certain well-known actors he acquired an excellent wardrobe of their cast-offs. Now and then one of those $350 cast-offs fit me perfectly. "Take it," Joe would say, "it's yours."

Like that, he never had to buy clothes, nor I either. (For most of my life I have worn other people's clothes. Now in my old age I was beginning to look like a dude.)

In the early days of our acquaintance Joe liked to invite me to rather good restaurants. Often, I discovered, he had chosen the place not for the food but because of a certain waitress he had taken a shine to. For a few years we went frequently to Stefanino's on Sunset Blvd. He liked the bar and the women he could pick up there. He also had a great admiration for the woman who ran the wardrobe. She was what Joe called "a real woman," a rare compliment from his lips. She was an Italian actress who had come to Hollywood, thinking to hit the jack-pot, but go nowhere. I too admired her. I thought of her as a "lady, a lady of parts."

Most everyday Joe could be found at the beach, foot of Chautaugua Boulevard. He needed the sun, he would say. Actually what he went there for was *Cunt*. How often he would point out a woman of forty or so and say to me, "Jesus, Henry, you should have seen her twenty years ago when I first knew her! What an ass, what teats! One of the best lays I ever had. Look at her now. An old bag already."

At the beach he was always surrounded by a coterie of friends, of both sexes. They were drawn to Joe like flies to fly paper. To most of them he addressed cutting remarks, like, "Why don't you do something about that belly of yours?" Or, to a woman, "Aren't you getting a bit sloppy? Look at your teats—they're like two heads of cabbage!"

All of which his cronies took in good part. Now and then he would be hit up to pay for an abortion or a divorce. It didn't bother Joe. He took everything in its stride. "It's life," he would say, and begin to talk about Gauguin or Van Gogh. "Look what they took!" he would say.

Most young, striving artists he had no respect for. They weren't "serious," in Joe's opinion. All the artists he admired were dead.

194

He was usually in good humor. If he felt bad he wouldn't show up. Needless to say, he was always in good shape, even if he did booze it up a little too much.

With all the failed watercolors I supplied him with his walls were soon filled. Now and then he would try to wheedle a *good* watercolor out of me. Anything he wanted badly he usually succeeded in getting. And so, over the years, he managed to obtain a few of my very best paintings. To tell the truth, even the failures didn't look so bad.

When he received a visit from some broad he had been chasing he always made her examine my watercolors first. Then, little by little, he would work out his usual strategy—a glass of cheap wine, a cracked Debussy recording, a nice rug by the glowing fireplace, and before you knew it, he was undressing her. Everything with Joe was a matter of technique. If you knew what cards to play you had her without trouble. If you didn't you were a loser. And Joe had no use for losers.

Every now and then he had to leave the country, as a stand-in for Dean Martin or some other star. Joe enjoyed these trips abroad. Like any other tourist he would head for the show places—in Italy the burial grounds of Shelley and Keats, in Switzerland, the castle on Lake Geneva which inspired Byron's *Prisoner of Chillon,* in Germany the lake (Starnberg) where the mad Ludwig of Bavaria was drowned. Naturally his job had taken him to many famous places. In Switzerland for example, he tried in vain to visit one of Herman Hesse's residences—the one in the Ticino on a mountaintop. Joe was crazy about Hesse's *Siddhartha*—to him, and to me too, I must confess, it was like a New Testament. We could talk about it for hours.

To hear Joe talk about his favorite authors in his own jibe language was something. In this lingo he could discourse for hours on such authors as Proust, Elie Faure, Thomas Mann, even James Joyce, though he confessed that Joyce was over his head.

In passing through his bedroom to go to the toilet I always stopped a few minutes in the bedroom to look at two objects: one was a pair of boxing gloves given him by his idol Benny Leonard; the other was a small framed photo of his mother. This photo intrigued me very much. The first time I asked Joe who it was he said, "My mother. A wonderful woman. I loved her very much. She was very good to me." Almost every time I passed her image I asked him more about his mother. His replies always made me envious. If only I had had a mother such as Joe described, I might well be a different man today. Perhaps not as famous, but a *better man*. Not to have a mother you love and believe in is a serious handicap. I have often noticed that some of the toughest bimbos had the greatest reverence for their mothers. A famous French writer whose work I adore says somewhere in his books that a man who does not love his mother is a monster. And I hated my mother all my life! One may ask how could a man have such respect for his mother and treat women so bad? (Well, think of Napoleon.) Actually, Joe loved women though he could never forgive their betrayal. And it had happened not once, but two or three times. I have never got over the loss of my first love. I never will, no doubt. I am fortunate that I don't take it out on other women, though I realize that is exactly what some of my female readers think I do.

No, Joe was drawn to women very naturally. He accepted them as you would flowers or exotic birds. But he wouldn't trust them. *Never.*

What crazy conversations I have listened in on when trying to take a nap at his joint. Suddenly I would be awakened by Joe's cussing and swearing at the top of his lungs. I would open ;my eyes and find him at the telephone with a grin from ear to ear. Meanwhile he is bawling out the young woman on the other end of the line.

"You bitch! Didn't I tell you never to phone me again! What's the trouble this time? Another abortion—or what? I can't help you out any more. I wouldn't if I could. It's no good. You'll never learn. You're a stupid bitch if ever there was one. All your brains are in your cunt and by the way, don't come knocking at my door at two or three in the morning. Lay off the booze! Keep your legs crossed! If you have to, why not masturbate once in a while. It won't hurt you. Listen, I suppose you're a Catholic, aren't you? I feel sorry for you. All that shit and still you're shit out of luck. . . ."

The girl is trying to get in a few words. Joe is saying—"I don't want to hear any more about that cocksucker. Fuck him! He's no good for you. He's an ass-hole. Why don't you find yourself a regular guy, *like me*, for instance? But don't bother me. I ain't got no time for sick cunts like you."

The girl is trying to tell him something. I suspect that she wants him to know she loves him, just him.

"I've heard that crap before," says Joe. "You don't fool me. You can't really love anybody. Got that? So long now, I'm busy." And he hangs up.

Joe never came to see me, and he came frequently, without bringing a gift of some sort. He never came in a depressed or downcast mood. He was always boisterous, jovial, full of stories. Real life stories. He had just picked up an unusual broad—what legs! What teats! And so on. Or he had picked up a writer, sometimes an actor down and out. Or something would remind him of so-and-so, a guy whom everyone in Hollywood knew, according to Joe. Anyway, this guy was known for having an enormous prick—a horse cock. The joke of it was that sometimes he would be walking with a guy, chatting away, and suddenly he would take out his huge hunk of meat and place it in his friend's hand. Joe was full of pranks too. If he detested a guy, what he called "a creep," he would take pleasure in calling him on the phone at four in the morning and say, "Hey, what's the matter with you? It's half past eight already. I thought you were going to meet me at seven." And with that he'd hang up. Naturally the guy wouldn't be able to go back to sleep.

He made it a point to have brunch every Sunday at a famous delicatessen in Hollywood where actors usually met. Joe knew them all. And despised most of them. At these gatherings there usually came a well-known film actress who was fond of dogs. "She loves her dogs more than men," Joe would say. And then he would add in a whisper, "I know she wants me to fuck her, but I'm not interested. I talk dogs to her."

When it comes to loving dogs no one could love a dog more than Joe loved his Byron. He took Byron with him everywhere. Now and then he would recite a few lines of Byron's poetry to him. This animal was quite unique, as everyone admitted. He wasn't a dog—he was partly human. He hung on Joe's every word as if it were the Scripture. When he looked at Joe it was such tenderness, such adoration, that it was almost beyond love. If anyone didn't happen to care for dogs Joe had no use for him.

If, on the other hand, Joe liked someone, he couldn't do enough for him. Speaking of the gifts he used to bring me, often it was food. Though he was not an enormous eater, Joe had a great respect for food. It hurt him to see the way I wasted food. Yet I had starved more than Joe by far, which did not prevent me from throwing good food into the garbage can when I had had my share. (I had always hated my mother's command to finish what was on my plate. Sometimes I would get up the courage to tell her that I was not a garbage can. But with stupid, conventional Germans, such behavior was like committing a sin. And Jews often felt the same way, I noticed.) It also hurt Joe that I did not relish the health foods he brought and which I never touched.

Though he was Jewish, I noticed that he didn't have much traffic with Jews. And the learned ones bored him to tears. Often he would interrupt a conversation (say about psychoanalysis) and say, "C'mon, let's have a little ping pong." For that he could have got a good crack in the jaw from a goy, but Jewish intellectuals never made much use of their fists.

Joe was full of surprises too. Like one day he comes in raving about Montaigne, the famous French writer. (His notebook was full of quotes from Montaigne.) Now Montaigne, though highly regarded, isn't usually the subject of table talk. Yet Joe could go on for hours about him.

One day he asked me for a piece of crayon, got out a chair, and wrote on my studio wall this: "A man who marries his mistress is like a man who shits in his hat before putting in on his head." Joe signed it—Montaigne.

Joe wrote a number of things on my studio wall. One was from Celine and went like this: "I piss on it all from a considerable height." Joe adored Celine, as we all did. One day I surprised him by telling him that the French considered Celine an anti-Semite. "What if he didn't like Jews," said Joe. "He was a great writer. Give me Celine any day to some of those Jewish punks who are handing us a lot of shit."

That was Joe—always direct, never pulling his punches.

I liked Joe because he had no ambition and also because he was a self-educated man. I'll never forget the day he discovered Zen. He had a book under his arm and a wide grin on his face. Proffering me the book, he said, "Henry, this is it. This makes sense. It cuts clear across this Jewish-Christian nonsense. It opens your eyes, makes you laugh, and lets you let out a good loud fart. Why didn't I hear about this sooner? It would have saved me lots of agony." On and on he went, happy as a lark. Then one evening, when we were watching TV, he heard Alan Watts for the first time. The look he gave me was one of utter amazement. "Why haven't they got guys like this in the synagogue?" he asked. "Jesus, Henry, I hever heard a man make so much sense as he did. And you say you knew him once? I envy you. Here I am hanging around with all these half-assed actors, these crack-pots and shit heels." And once again he went off into a spiel about what nobodies actors are, how all they know what to do is to read the lines, not a thought in their heads, and so on.

Nobody could forget Joe Gray once they met him. He was like a shock of electricity. In the beginning of our friendship he used to haul me with him to Hollywood parties. What dull affairs! But Joe would always say, "Wait a minute, there'll be some hot-looking dames come in before the night's over." Funny thing was, he could go up and talk to anyone, man or woman, as if he were an important guest. If he took a fancy to a broad he would promise her a job, anything she wanted. He always had printed cards in his wallet, with his name and address. As the night wore on he was handing out his cards like laundry tickets. It was amazing to me how many girls kept his card and telephoned him a day or two later. By that time Joe had, of course, forgotten their names.

"Wanda?" he would repeat, "Oh yes, you're the blonde girl, aren't you?"

"No," she might say, "I'm the short fat girl with dark hair."

"Then fuck you!" he would reply and hang up.

Of course, wherever he took me Joe would embarrass me by saying "This is my friend, Henry Miller, *the writer*. You know—*Tropic of Cancer, The World of Sex*...."

The person he was addressing often did not know the names Henry Miller, *Tropic of Cancer* and whatever, but would pretend with great gusto that they did. Some would even remind me that they had met me in Paris, London, Berlin or some out-of-the-way place in South America, all places which they themselves had never been to.

The question I was always asking at these parties was, "When do we eat?" Or, "Are we going to eat?" Joe would rustle up some food for me, one way or another. "You're always asking about food," he would say. "Listen, I brought you here to see the dames. Look at that one over there with the big teats! Do you want me to introduce you to her?"

200

"Do you know her?"

"Of course not. That doesn't make any difference here. Besides, you're a famous writer. They'll only be too happy to meet *you*. They'll piss in their pants. I *know* these bitches!"

What interested me in Joe Gray, more than all the cunts he brought to see me, was the joy and the appreciation he showed for the books he liked. Over his fireplace were lined up some of the most bewitching titles anyone might desire. When Joe read a book he devoured it hook, line and sinker, as we say. It stayed with him for days, weeks, months. Not only did he make notes and copy passages from his favorite works, but he read the books which the author may have mentioned in passing. (I know no better way to detect what books are worth reading.) Incidentally, let it be said in his favor there was only one other person I knew who collected and read wonderful books and that was John Cowper Powys. When I visited him in Wales my eye fell on the range of books beside me. I could read the titles clearly. They were all classics—Homer, Virgil, Dante, Villon, Rabelais, Dostoievsky, Shakespeare, Marlowe, Webster, the Greek dramatists, Ovid, Lucretius, Longinus, etc. I was rather surprised, I remember, and asked him (rather audaciously) if he ever looked at them now and then. To my amazement he replied: "Why Henry, I read them all once a year." And he read them all in their own language! Of course Powys was an exceptional individual. Reading and rereading the classics did not dry him up. On the contrary— they increased his lust for life.

What endeared me to Joe the reader was the reverent way he referred to certain writers. I shall never forget how he took to Richard Jefferies, author of *The Story of My Heart*. He carried that book with him wherever he went and was continually lending it to people, whether they wanted it or not.

I also remember his reaction on first reading Dostoievsky. "How come nobody ever told me about this guy before!" he exclaimed. "He's not a writer, he's a magician, a giant."

But the strangest thing was to see him working on a broad with one of his favorite authors. For, as the reader must have surmised already, in Joe's eyes most cunts were "dumb cunts." To observe him making it with one of the latter say with a Dostoievsky in his mitt, was like watching the artful Dodger. If one of these cunts truly liked the book Joe had shoved on her he was ready to kiss her ass. It just wasn't in the cards for "dumb cunts" to appreciate the likes of Dostoievsky or Herman Hesse, another favorite of his.

In the way he took to authors and painters, so he took to women. It was incredible to hear him extol the virtues of some slob he had become fond of. "You don't know her," he would begin. "She may be a slob but you can *trust her.*"

"How do you mean, Joe, trust her?"

"I mean if you're short and need help, go to her. She'll help any damn fool out—because she doesn't know any better. I've seen her shell out a hudnred bucks to some worthless bastard who didn't deserve to wipe her ass."

"Sure, what if she *is* a hooker, she's a friend in need. She'll even give you a free fuck if she likes you."

Another one he might like because she was a health food addict like himself. And another because she loved dogs. "Between you and me," he would say, "I think she lets them fuck her. Byron is always sniffing her, if you ever noticed. Yeah, she sure loves dogs, but she hates cats and birds, can you beat it?"

Living in that crazy world called Hollywood he came to know lots of freaks, I mean real freaks who belonged in the side show. There was a female midget he took quite a fancy to. She interested him profoundly, largely, I believe, because she was a great reader.

The people he didn't like, and they were often Jews, strange to say, even his dog Byron didn't like either. As I said earlier, Byron was partly human. He picked up things which even Joe's dumb broads never got wise to. He was a horny beast too. Always

202

humping something—a leg, a piece of furniture, a palm tree or whatever. Yet Byron never had a good fuck in his life. Strange, considering his lord and master was such an expert about cunt. The trouble was, as I gradually discovered, Joe didn't think the bitches available were good enough for Byron. Many of Joe's friends were on the look-out for the right bitch for Byron, but none ever came up with the right one. Byron was worth his weight in gold, as Joe would say.

When Joe took a job out of town he wanted to leave the receiver off the hook so he could talk to Byron at odd hours. Thus, if he heard Byron bark at the sound of his voice Joe could carry on a one-sided conversation which even a dog fancier would find incredible. Often Joe lacked the price of a good meal, but not for Byron. Byron ate only the best, the most expensive food. And that made Joe happy.

One day I happened to meet Joe coming out of his pad. He's all smiles, I notice.

"What happened, Joe," I say, "what makes you so happy?"

"Come along with me," he says. "I'm just walking up the street in hopes of running into a dame who lives on this block. I've been flirting with her . . ."

When I heard the word "flirting" I couldn't believe my ears.

"Yeah," he continues, "I think she's the romantic type. Good looker, dresses well, polite and all that."

"Tell me more," I said, wondering if this was going to be one of his infatuations.

"I can't tell you much," says Joe, "because I think it's finished already. I'm not her type."

He goes on to tell me how he happened to notice that she came home exactly the same time every evening. He would be walking his dog and thus run into her, as she lived only a few doors away.

One evening, instead of saying "Hi" and passing on, he stops and says "Hello beautiful, aren't you a little early this evening?"

She answered coldly, "Is it any of your business? Why do I see you outside my door every evening?"

"Because," says Joe, "I have a yen for you."

"Oh yeah," says she, "well stick it up your ass."

Somewhat surprised by this sort of language coming from her, Joe says, "Is that a nice way to talk to a gentleman?"

"Whoever told you you were a gentleman?" she retorts.

"Come now, *lady*," says Joe, "be human, I'm a neighbor of yours, don't you know that?"

"No I don't," she snaps. "Go and get lost."

At this moment Byron rushes up from somewhere and begins to paw Joe. Somehow Byron appeals to the girl. She softens a bit.

"Beautiful dog," she says. "Where did you get him?"

Here Joe makes up a long story just to keep her from running out on him.

The girl leans over to pat Byron. As she does so Joe pats her on the rump. The girl pretends not to notice. Joe quickly follows with a "Why don't you come to my place for a few minutes. I'll fix you a cup of tea or whatever."

To his surprise she falls in step with him and before you know it she's in his pad examining my watercolors on the wall.

"Are you a painter?" she asks.

"No," says Joe, "I'm in the films. I'm a stunt-man. Sometimes I stand in for Dean Martin."

That's all he needed to say. From then on the conversation quickly switched to more interesting things. Apparently, like all the rest, no sooner did she hear "films" than she melted. Joe didn't have to make her any tea—she gulped down a few bourbons straight, flung her arms around him and groped for his prick.

"It was like falling off a log," says Joe.

"What happened then—did you give her a quick lay?"

"No," he replied, "I decided to make her beg for it. I told her to come back tomorrow. You'll see, tomorrow she'll be ringing my

204

doorbell, I know these cunts. She doesn't want me, she wants a job in the movies. When she heard 'Dean Martin' I could see the change come over her. Maybe she thinks he'll give her a quck lay and make a star of her. What shit! They never learn."

"Where are we going, Joe?"

"Nowhere. I just wanted to give Byron a run."

In trying to give a full portrait of my friend I am afraid I have magnified his faults and foibles.

Joe was one of the three best friends I ever had in America. There was nothing he would not do for me if I needed his aid. He was usually cheerful, if a bit feisty also. He liked and disliked intensely. There was no in-between for him.

There were many people who referred to him as their friend, but Joe was the sort who acknowledged only two or three friends—the others were simply acquaintances, bar flies, and so on.

If he disagreed with your opinion, he disagreed violently. He was intense in everything. Above all, he hated hypocrites, people who said one thing and meant another.

He did not hate women, he merely distrusted them. As for the women themselves, they were attracted to him as if to some magnet. Joe attributed a lot of this to the nose the plastic surgeon had given him. But I am sure everything would have been just the same had he never lost his old schnozzle. For Joe emanated warmth, enthusiasm, confidence. He never let anybody down. If he thought of himself as somewhat of a healer there was truth in the assumption. Everyone he came in contact with felt somethng unusual in Joe's vibrations. Even the men he worked for in the film studios acknowledged this gift.

He laughed easily and heartily. He never appeared if in a bad mood, nor did he have many bad moods.

I used to tell him he was a natural born healer, that he should have been a rabbi instead of a stunt man. Joe's method of healing was somewhat unusual:he healed through books. He kept a huge notebook of quotations from the books he read and when the opportunity presented itself he would read a few passages to the poor devil who was suffering. If one had told him that that was the method employed by Christian Scientists he would have scoffed.

All in all he was an original. No one ever forgot Joe Gray once they had a taste of him. Joe and his dog Byron. People would ask after Byron as if he were a human being. And Joe treated Byron like a human being.

It's been my good fortune always to have two or three good friends I could count on in time of need. To be blessed with just *one* good friend is usually sufficient. Friends more than made up (for me) the absence of money. And when I say friends I mean ordinary individuals, not exceptional ones. But they were exceptional in their ability to give, to serve, to be at one's beck and call. Nearly always these friends possessed a good sense of humor. They were never preachers or advisers. In fact there was always something a bit dotty or eccentric about them. One might say clownlike, I suppose. Above all, they were always unselfish. In Joe Gray's case he was unselfish where women were concerned. That was not because he despised them but rather because he looked upon them as gifts from above. He may have treated them outwardly like dogs, but anyone who knew him knew differently. It wasn't cunt that put Joe at their mercy but the fact that he saw their angelic side. He was always trying to preserve them from some threat of harm or humiliation. In his own peculiar way he was a Knight of the Round Table. He was one *in disguise.* As for the friends Joe made, they were all *close* friends. He couldn't tolerate anything lukewarm. Because he had once been a professional boxer he sometimes took insults that were unbelievable. At the height of an altercation at a bar, for example, he would often grab me by the arm and say "Let's get out of here!" Outside I would say "What's the matter, Joe, why didn't you give him a poke in the jaw?" and Joe would always reply, "Because I'm not allowed to. Besides, he was too much of a punk for me to bother with. He had a big mouth, that's all."

Later, when I saw the film *A Bad Day at Black Rock*, in which Spencer Tracy plays a one-armed man versed in jiu jitsu, I appreciated Joe's words. I also took another look at myself, I who usually relied on his ability to *talk* his way out of a bad situation.

One of the unusually bright days with Joe was spent in Big Sur. Bob Snyder was then making the documentary film of my life and all we needed was a glimpse of Big Sur. We brought with us Michiyo Watanabe, who had been living in my home in Pacific Palisades. I had not been back to Big Sur for ten years or more. It looked more attractive than ever, the little house on Partington Ridge. Of course my companions fell in love with the place. Who wouldn't? It was the nearest thing to Greece imaginable. We spend the night there and on the way home fell to singing old songs, like "Meet Me Tonight in Dreamland," "You Great Big Beautiful Doll," "Roses in Picardy," and such like. Even Michiyo, who had been born and raised in Japan, caught the spirit. It was a wonderful way to finish off an exciting trip. It also made Big Sur seem more precious than ever. (It was probably my very last trip there. My days of travel are over, along with my days of travail.)

As I have said before, Joe was not only a stunt man but a stand-in for Dean Martin. In photos they bore a remarkable resemblance to one another. Joe enjoyed working for Dean. On several occasions Joe had traveled abroad with him as well as to Mexico. Now Dean was getting ready to make a film in Mexico. It was a rough region but Joe liked the Mexicans and, besides, he was short of cash. So, in spite of his premonitions, he accompanied Dean to Mexico. In a few days, to my great surprise, he was back in L.A. To my even greater surprise he complained of not feeling right—was going to see a doctor. I say "surprise" because Joe was not only a health specimen but a health food addict, a believer in Dr. Bieler and absorbed as much sun and oxygen as he could.

Well, I believe that Dean urged him to see his own doctor—or perhaps it was Elizabeth Taylor's. I saw him the day after he entered the hospital—in the evening. He seemed (to me) fit as a fiddle. When I inquired what he was suffering from he couldn't tell me exactly—probably the poor Mexican diet, he thought.

Anyway, the next day he was dead. He was in his late forties, a remarkable specimen of good health and *joie de vivre*. I never did learn what the doctors thought killed him.

His last words, it seemed, were about his dog Byron. I found out later that one of Dean Martin's daughters adopted Byron. Bless her! To this day people ask me, "What ever became of Byron?"

My Best Friend

Believe it or not, it was my bike. This one I had bought at Madison Square Garden, at the end of a six-day race. It had been made in Chemnitz, Bohemia and the six-day rider who owned it was a German, I believe. What distinguished it from other racing bikes was that the upper bar slanted down towards the handle bars.

I had two other bikes of American manufacture. These I would lend my friends when in need. But the one from the Garden no one but myself rode. It was like a pet. And why not? Did it not see me through all my times of trouble and despair?

Yes, I was in the throes of love, my first love, than which nothing is more disastrous, as a rule. My friends had become disgusted with me; they were deserting me, or vice versa, one by one. I was desolate and alone. Whether my parents knew of my sad plight I don't recall, but I am sure they knew that *something* was bothering me. That "something" was a beautiful young woman named Cora Seward, whom I had met during my high school days.

As I have told elsewhere, we were such naive creatures that perhaps we kissed two or three times—at a party, for example,

209

never elsewhere. Though we both had telephones, we never telephoned one another. Why! I ask myself. (Because it would have been too bold perhaps.) We did write each other, but our letters were far apart. I remember how each day when I came home I turned first to the mantel piece, where letters were kept, and it was almost always a blank absence that greeted me.

It was a period when I spent most of my days job-hunting (presumably). Actually, I went to a movie or the burlesk, (if I could afford it). Suddenly I stopped doing this, *and* did nothing. Nothing but ride the bike. Often I was in the saddle, so to speak, from morning till evening. I rode everywhere and usually at a good clip. Some days, I encountered some of the six-day riders at the fountain in Prospect Park. They would permit me to set the pace for them along the smooth path that led from the Park to Coney Island.

I would visit old haunts, such as Bensonhurst, Ulmer Park, Sheepshead Bay and Coney Island. And always, no matter how diverse the scenery, I am thinking of *her*. Why doesn't she write me? When will the next party be? Etc., etc. I never had obscene thoughts about her, never dreamt of fucking her some day or even feeling her twat. No, she was like the princess in the fairy tale—untouchable even in dream.

Nor did it ever occur to me to ride to Greenspoint, where she lived, and ride up and down her street in the hope of catching a glance of her. Instead I rode to the faraway places, scenes associated with my childhood—and happy days.

I thought of those idyllic days ruefully, with a heavy heart. Where were they now, these dear pals of my early youth? Were they going through the same anguish as I—or were some of them married already perhaps?

Sometimes, after having finished a good book, I would think of nothing but the characters in that book. The characters I speculated about most were usually out of Dostoievsky's novels, particularly *The Idiot, The Brothers Karamazov* and *The Possessed.*

Indeed they were no longer characters from a book, but living creatures, people who haunted my reveries and dream life. Thus, thinking of some absurd individuals like Smerdyakov I would suddenly burst out laughing, only to quickly check myself and veer my thoughts toward her. It was impossible to rid my mind of her. I was obsessed, fascinated, bereaved. If by some great chance I may have run into her I would doubtless have been tongue-tied.

Oh yes, once in a blue moon I would receive a letter from her, usually from some summer resort where she was spending her vacation. It would always be a short letter, couched in conversational language—and, to my mind, completely devoid of feeling. And my reply would pretty much match her letter despite the fact that my heart was breaking.

Heart break! There was a subject I gave myself to totally. Did other people my age suffer the same pangs? Was first love always as painful, awkward and barrèn as this? Was I perhaps a special case, a "romantic" of the first water? The answers to these self-addressed queries were generally written in my friend's faces. The moment I mentioned her name a look of total uninterest would emanate from them. "Still thinking about her?" "Haven't you had enough already?" And so on. Implicit in their reactions was—how stupid can a guy become? And over a girl, no less.

As we spun along (me and my double) I went over these fundamental facts backwards and forwards. It was like studying a theorem in algebra. And never once did I run into a compassionate soul! I became so desolate that I took to calling my bike my friend. I carried on silent conversations with it. And of course I paid it the best attention. Which meant that everytime I returned home I stood the bike upside down, searched for a clean rag and polished the hubs and the spokes. Then I cleaned the chain and, greased it afresh. That operation left ugly stains on the stone in the walkway. My Mother would complain, beg me to put a newspaper under my wheel before starting to clean it. Sometimes she would get so incensed that she would say to me, in full sarcasm, "I'm surprised you don't take that thing to bed with you!" And I would retort—"I would if I had a decent room and a big enough bed."

That was another grievance I had to put up with—no room of my own. I slept in a narrow hall bedroom, decorated only by a shade to keep out the early morning light. If I read a book it was at the dining room table. I never used the parlor except to listen to phonograph records. It was when listening to some of my favorite records (in the gloomy parlor) that I would go through the greatest anguish about her. Each record I put on the machine only deepened my sorrow. The individual who moved me the most—from ectasy to absolute despair—was the Jewish Cantor Sirota. Next to him came Amato, the baritone at the Metropolitan Opera. And after these came Caruso and John McCormack, the beloved Irish tenor.

I took care of my wheel as one would look after a Rolls Royce. If it needed repairs I always brought it to the same shop on Myrtle Avenue run by a Negro named Ed Perry. He handled the bike with kid gloves, you might say. He would always see to it that neither front nor back wheel wobbled. Often he would do a job for me without pay, because, as he put it, he never saw a man so in love with his bike as I was.

There were streets I avoided and streets I favored. In some streets the setting or the architecture actually gave me a lift. There were sedate streets and run-down ones, streets full of charm and others horrendously dull. (Didn't Whitman say somewhere, "Architecture is what you do to it when you look at it"?) As a dromomaniac I was able to carry on an elaborate interior dialogue and at the same time be aware of the stage setting through which I was moving. Riding the bike was a little different; I had to watch my p's and q's or take a bad spill.

About this time the champion sprinter was Frank Kramer,

whom of course I idolized. Once I managed to stay right behind him during one of his practice spins from Prospect Park to Coney Island. I remember him slapping me on the back when I caught up with him and, as he slapped my back, said, "Good work, young feller—keep it up!" That day was a red letter day in my life. For once I forgot about Cora Seward and gave myself up to dreams of riding in Madison Square Garden some day, along with Walter Rutt, Eddie Root, Oscar Egg and the other celebrities of the track.

After a time, habituated to spending so many hours a day on my bike, I became less and less interested in my friends. My wheel had now become my one and only friend. I could rely on it, which is more than I could say about my buddies. It's too bad no one ever photographed me with my "friend." I would give anything now to know what we looked like.

Years later in Paris, I got myself another bike, but this one was an everyday sort, with brakes. To slow up demanded an effort on the part of one's legs. I could have had hand brakes put on my handle bars but that would have made me feel like a sissy. It was dangerous and thrilling to race through the city streets at top speed. Fortunately the automobile was not then much in evidence. What one really had to watch out for were youngsters playing in the middle of the street.

Mothers would warn their children to be careful, to keep their eyes open for that crazy young man who loves to speedthrough the streets. In other words I soon becaue a terror in the neighborhood.

I was both a terror and a delight. The kids were all begging their parents to get them a bike like mine.

How long can the heart ache without bursting? I have no idea. I only know that I put in a grueling period courting a girl *in absentia*. Even on my twenty-first birthday—a great event in my life—I sat some distance apart from her, too timid to open my mouth and tell her of my love. The last time I saw her was

213

shortly after, when I plucked up the courage to ring her doorbell and tell her I was leaving for Juneau, Alaska, to become a placer miner.

It was almost harder to separate from my wheel from Chemnitz, Bohemia. I must have given it to one of my cronies, but to whom, I no longer remember.

It should be borne in mind that, although my heart was breaking, I could still enjoy a good laugh. When I had the dough, I would often take in a vaudeville show at the Palace or spend the afternoon at the Houston Street burlesk or some other burlesk house. The comedians from these shows were later to become figures in radio and television. In other words, I could literally laugh on the wrong side of my face. It was this ability to laugh in spite of everything that saved me. I had already known that famous line from Rabelais—"For all your ills I give you laughter." I can say from personal experience that it is a piece of the highest wisdom. There is so precious little of it today—it's no wonder the drug pushers and the psychoanalysts are in the saddle.

BOOK THREE

Joey

*A loving portrait of Alfred
Perlès together with some
bizarre episodes relating to
the other sex.*

Joey

PART I

Sometimes I called him Alf, sometimes

Fred, and sometimes Joey. He usually called me Joey, seldom
Henry. We met in 1928, I believe, on my first visit to Europe. I
met him through my then wife June who had been to Paris the
year before with her beloved friend Jean Kronski. Jean and Fred
had met and Fred had fallen in love with her—"madly," as he
always professed to do. As for my wife June he later told me he
didn't think very much of her; she was to him a typical "Central
European type," whatever that means.

As I came to know him better, during our years together in
the Villa Seurat, I realized that he knew and was adored by quite
a few unusual females. Oftimes he would stay at their hotel for
a spell or they at his, which was usually a crummy hotel of which
Paris boasts aplenty now and then.

The interesting thing about his relations with women is that
they all *loved* him and adored him. He never married or even
entertained the idea of marriage. He would talk as if he were

215

passionately in love with each creature, but the way in which he declared his passion usually betrayed him.

It must be recognized at the outset that Fred or Alf or Joey was a bit of a rogue, perhaps even a scoundrel, *but* a lovable one. (I never met man or woman who hated him.)

He was born, so he always said, in Vienna, and indeed he seemed to retain a great affection for his native city. Oddly enough, my wife and I had visited Vienna the same year we met him in Paris. By this time (1927) Vienna had a woebegone look, the look of a city which had been through a great war. It was falling apart at the seams. My wife's uncle, who had been a colonel in the Hungarian Hussars, was now distributing reels of films by bicycle for a movie house, a job for which he received a mere pittance.

I have spoken elsewhere of the vermin of Vienna. Never in my life have I seen so many bedbugs climbing up and down the wall as in this famous city. And nowhere else in the world have I met with such wretched, abominable poverty. Some twenty or thirty years later I returned to Vienna with a Viennese friend from Big Sur. This time it looked somewhat better, but not much. It reminded me strongly of the Brooklyn neighborhoods I grew up in.

Between visits I had spent some time in Germany. There I learned that the Viennese (and the Austrians in general) were not held in very high esteem by the Germans. They were always referred to as "treacherous."

I make this detour about Vienna to throw a little light on Joey's character, his origins, etc. From all he told me he came of a high class bourgeois family. He had received a good education and when the dread First World War broke out, he found himself a lieutenant in the army. Fortunately for him it was at this early stage of his career that a very important incident took place. I believe his company was defending a certain position from the enemy. The order had been given not to fire until one could see the whites of the enemies' eyes. Fred was in command at the time. As the enemy came nearer and nearer Fred lost the courage to give the order to fire. A top sergeant, realizing what was happening, assumed command and thus saved the regiment from utter annihilation. Fred of course was court-martialed and promptly condemned to be shot. But his parents had influence with the higher ups and instead of being sent to meet a firing squad Fred was remanded to an insane asylum. He spent the war years as a lunatic. And then, upon the declaration of peace, the gates were opened and all the inmates rushed to freedom. It was then that Fred worked his way to Paris. He had had a French governess at home and consequently knew enough French to get by. (He also knew some English.)

From then on until I returned to Paris in 1930 to stay a few years, Fred led the usual precarious existence of anyone who possessed an artistic soul. It was also during these rather somber days that he made the acquaintance of the various women who later dropped in on him from all parts of the world.

But, the time spent in the crazy house must, I am sure, have had its effect upon Joey's subsequent career. Though he never became a loony, he was definitely eccentric. *And lovable.* Always, no matter what his faults or defects, one had to add—*but lovable.* Was it at the bughouse that he read all the good books he later talked about? Certainly, by the time I caught up with him, he possessed a wonderful acquaintance with literature—German, French, and English. Of all the authors he admired or revered, Goethe took first place. He could quote him by the yard. Most of the celebrated French authors he also knew intimately. Both prose writers and poets. He began with Villon, then the nineteenth century "decadents" and symbolist poets—Villiers de L'Isle Adam, Mallarmé, Baudelaire, Rimbaud, all the famous novelists and essayists. Samuel Putnam, who was something of a scholar and translator, always referred to Perles as a scholar of the first water. Among German poets he was at home with

Schiller, Heine, Holderlin, etc. Naturally, if one knew Joey, he made light of all this learning, or on occasion would even deny it to be true. As Joey, he was the clown, the "always merry and bright" companion who kept us all in stitches. He might be on the verge of tears, quoting a verse of Holderlin's and the next moment guffawing like a jackass.

His countenance was almost always radiant, always with a grin or a benevolent smile. (Recently he sent me a photo of himself—same exuberant expression; not a day older in looks.) Only once did I see him angry. That was at Clichy where we shared a small apartment for a time. He was shaving and I, while watching him, was twitting him about his faults—mere pecadillos. Then I must have begun teasing him in earnest and I saw his face darken. Evidently I was laying it on too thick for suddenly he dropped his razor in the sink and swung at me. It was a good crack in the jaw I received and with it I tumbled into the (empty) bathtub giving myself a good crack in the skull. I immediately scrambled out of the tub and apologized to him. He then apologized to me—and soon everything was "merry and bright." Nor was there ever a recurrence of this sort.

Yes, when I look back on these marvelous years together I see his face ever wreathed in a smile. One might call it a "Viennese" smile, as one often refers to a Japanese smile. As I mentioned earlier, Joey was a bit of a rogue, sometimes a downright scoundrel, or as we would say in America, a real son-of-a-bitch. (But, once again, a lovable one.) Elsewhere I have recounted (or did he?) how we robbed our friend Michael Fraenkel of petty sums. It was always a collaborative event. While I engaged Fraenkel in hearty discussion of this or that Joey would remove the wallet from the inside pocket of Fraenkel's coat. He always hung it over a chair when overheated. To top it all, we would then take him to dinner—to his amazement—as he knew we were always broke.

When I became acquainted with Anaïs Nin, Joey naturally fell

218

madly in love with her. He wrote her beautiful letters, disguising his passion: they were artful and highly literary, which was his forte. At first she inclined to look upon him favorably, never taking him seriously. But as time passed Fred became more and more infatuated. Despite all the women he had known, none compared with Anaïs. She was someone from another world, an ethereal world. He resolved to write a book about her—I believe it was in French. (He only began writing in English after going to England to live.) Unfortunately for Joey, Anaïs did not take kindly to the script he showed her. The reason? He had been too frank; he had mentioned names and circumstances which offended her sense of propriety. Or so she put it. Actually, what I believe disturbed her was his "truthfulness." Anaïs, as everyone must know who has read her *Diaries*, was a very adept, adroit prevaricator. To use a more kindly word, she was a "fabulist," or "fabulator." I believe she was possibly more honest with me than with any other of her friends or acquaintances. But, well as I knew her, I cannot help but remark that she probably told me, too, some tall stories.

At any rate, Fred was now in disfavor. I use this peculiar expression because with Anaïs one was either in her favor or not. She was like a *duchesse* dispensing her favors or withholding them at will. Often one fell out of her favor over a trifle. To regain her good graces was like climbing Mt. Fuji.

Fred, who had put his heart into writing about her, was not to be daunted. He hit on the novel ideal of, à la Solomon, dividing her into two different characters—one a dancer, the other a writer. He went to great trouble to accomplish this piece of literary surgery and once again brought the manuscript for Anaïs's approval. This time she was not only indignant but furious. Poor Fred was banished from court—irrevocably. (He never regained her friendship, I should add.)It was more a reflection on her than on him. I might add that later on Lawrence Durrell also fell out of favor, but he was either more artful or more persistent than Fred, for he won his way back to her favor not only once but several times.

What I think made Anaïs so hard on Fred was that she did not appreciate the clown in him. Unlike Wallace Fowlie, she did not make the association between clowns and angels.

Though at first blush Anaïs was always taken as angelic, I must say she was far from it. She was a very ambivalent creature, to put it mildly.

This time Fred was thoroughly crushed. He made no attempt to regain her favor. He simply abdicated. I think it was along about this time that a fan of mine, a Swede, used to come to visit, always unannounced. He was probably the most frightful bore I ever met in my life. And, to make it worse, I didn't know how to get rid of him. He would stay on and on until we had drained the last drop from the last bottle.

If he happened to barge in on me while Joey was there, the latter would promptly get off his ass, reach for his beret and say, "See you tomorrow, Joey!" This happened a number of times before my Swedish friend caught on. Then one evening, after Fred had left hurriedly, he turned to me and said in all innocence,

"Meelah, why does he always leave when I arrive? Does he dislike me?"

"Dislike you," I repeated, "he despises you. He can't stand the sight of you."

"Why is that, Meelah? I have never spoken to him."

"Because, if I must tell you myself, you are a horrible *emmerdeur.*" (French for bore.)

"And do you feel the same about me?"

I answered promptly—"I most certainly do? You are the worst bore I have ever known."

You would think that after this rejoinder he would either have socked me in the jaw or got up and left without another word. But no, instead he remained another half-hour trying to get me to explain to him *why* he was such an *emmerdeur.*

220

I have only known three or four Swedish men in my whole life—and they were all terrible, frightful bores. One of them was a renowned poet who translated some of the famous French symbolist poets into Swedish. We had exchanged a few letters and then one day he wrote he was coming to see me—where could we meet. I named a café on the corner of the Boulevard St. Michel and the street that leads to the Pantheon. It was four or five in the afternoon. I had looked forward to the meeting, knowing of his literary reputation. However, in less than ten minutes I had had a bellyful of him. All I could think of was what excuse to make and be able to duck. Finally I simply said that it just occurred to me that I had made a previous engagement for the same day, same hour. And with that I got up, shook hands and said good-bye. I remember turning the corner and walking towards the Pantheon, but soon turning down a side street for fear he might follow me. And that's that for the Swedes. . . .

Finally one day after I had been in Paris almost a year I got an attack of homesickness. I wanted to send a cablegram to my parents in Brooklyn asking for boat fare home. But I didn't have a cent to my name. I remember sitting on the *terrasse* of le Dôme and scratching a note to Fred which I put in his mailbox. It was asking him if he knew anyone who could lend me the money to get back home.

In a surprisingly short time he appeared at the café, sat down beside me and said, "Joey, you're not going home. I won't let you. Have another drink. Try a Pernod this time. It will pass. I've experienced this feeling many times, But you've got to stick it out."

Like that we sat, had a few drinks and soon were talking about other things, possibly about his beloved Goethe, his *Dichtung und Wahrheit*. Toward the end, he had a happy idea—he would get me a job on the American newspaper in Paris, *le Chicago Tribune*, as a proofreader like himself.

"Will I get paid?" I promptly asked, recalling my recent experience as an English teacher in the Lycée Dijon.

221

"Of course you will, Joey," he replied. "It won't be much but it will keep you alive." And on that we parted for the morrow.

It must have been shortly after this episode that I managed to rent a typewriter and began writing *Tropic of Cancer*.

From here on my whole lifestyle changed. I began to see the whole French world with new eyes. Bad as things were they were never as bad as in America. For one thing, I began reading French in my spare time. I don't know how I ever managed, considering that my spoken French was literally atrocious.

Anyway, I had the good fortune to stumble on Blaise Cendrar's *Moravagine*. I remember vividly reading a bit of it each afternoon at the Café de la Liberté, near the Cimetière Montparnasse. To my surprise, Fred, who was acquainted with Cendrar's work, was not particularly enamored of him. Neither was Anaïs. To me he was a giant among contemporary French writers. I would ask every Frenchman I met if he knew Cendrar's work. As time went on I read virtually everything he had ever written. Often I felt I would go mad, reading one of his never-ending passages with the vocabulary of the editor of a lexicon. That was part of the charm of Cendrars—he borrowed from all professions, all trades.

But let us leave Cendrars for the moment. I will speak of him a little later, after I had finished writing *Tropic of Cancer*. Let me return now to another bore, this one an American from Topeka, Kansas. He was considered an expert in the advertising world, at least in America. He was pompous, vainglorious, a braggadocio and God knows what else. I had met him just once, briefly, at some reception. In the interim I had become acquainted with his wife who was a fascinating woman, a writer no less. She had already produced several books, one of them a biography of my favorite American writer, Sherwood Anderson. We got along famously each time we met. Then one day I asked her if she would not like to have dinner *chez nous*—I said I was a fair cook. She was delighted, then immediately added—"May I bring my husband along? I think you met him once or twice," and she repeated his name. I did indeed remember him and when I informed Fred of the dinner date I added "Let's show him a good time."

From the moment Fred laid eyes on him he disliked him, couldn't stand him. Though he was an American, our guest, he had the appearance of Eric von Stroheim. He was arrogant, rude, and knew everything better than his fellow man.

I excused myself to watch over the *gigot de'agneau* I was preparing for our dinner. Fred soon joined me. Suddenly he whispered, holding up a bottle—"This is all the cognac we have." With that both of us had the same idea—to piss in the decanter and serve it to this bastard as an apéritif. We knew that he was a lush and suspected he wouldn't know the difference. Of course, we were discreet—we didn't piss too much into the remaining cognac.

Well, we sat down to dinner and before tasting a bite I poured some cognac in our guest's glass and just a drop in the other glasses. We also had some delicious vintage wine to go with the food.

We watched his face as he emptied his glass—he just threw it down the hatch. He made a slight *moue* but made no remark about the foul taste. Soon we were all talking at once and devouring the *gigot*. His wife had begun to talk about André Breton, the pope of the surrealist movement. Suddenly her husband turned to me and asked very bluntly—"What is this surrealist movement I hear so much about? What *is* a surrealist, can you tell me?"

Blandly and innocently I answered with a smile: "A surrealist is a guy who pisses in your drink before he serves you."

With that his face dropped. He had got the drift of my reply instantaneously. (Besides, Fred was grinning like a Cheshire cat.) Without betraying his feelings he asked for his cane and his fedora, rose stiffly, à la von Stroheim, and bade us all good-night. Well, that was one bore I had really taken the measure of. The joke was that his wife was not insulted; in fact, she seemed rather amused as if it served him right.

This little joke—a *bad* joke—was probably a hangover from my early days in Paris. Though the Second World War was impending and sensed by most everyone, still there was time to play. Indeed, it was just because of the disaster which lay ahead that people, particularly the artists, could launch all manner of crazy movements. Dadaism had flourished for a decade or more before Fred and I endeavored to start a movement which we labelled "The New Instinctivism." It was largely a movement *agin* everything. I think I mentioned elsewhere how Joey had endeavored to put over his (or our) crazy ideas in Samuel Putnam's serious literary review, *The New Review*. This was the kind of bad joke typical of the times.

It was probably my third year in Paris. Almost from the start I had begun writing the *Tropic of Cancer*. At last it was finished. But before thinking about a publisher, I knew it had to be edited, trimmed down especially. I looked about me in vain for editorial guidance. Anaïs Nin was out of the question. It was not her type of book. One day, perhaps at Fred's own suggestion, I asked him if he would help me. He immediately agreed. We were still proof-readers for the Paris edition of the *Chicago Tribune*, which meant we worked from 8:00 or 9:00 P.M. till 2:00 or 3:00 A.M. And then an hour's swift walk home. During the "break," around midnight, all of us except the printers used to repair for a drink to a café called Les Trois Cadets on the rue Lafayette.

I don't recall anymore for what reason, but we decided that we would edit the *Cancer* book in the afternoons at this same café. It was a lucky choice for after a few sessions we noticed that we were very attentively watched by a dwarf who frequented the café everyday at the same time. One day we broke into conversation with him. We soon learned he was bilingual and not only that but a bit gaga to boot. Just made to order for us. Especially the rapport between him and Fred. (Now we had two Joeys.) If our little friend was a trifle gaga he was also something of a scholar. He knew all about the surrealist writers and painters and even professed to know André Breton himself. Fred and I were naturally more attuned to the Dadaists than the surrealists. Talking to one another about my script at the café we resembled a trio of comedians working out a new script. We seemed to do nothing but laugh and joke—*and* drink. Nevertheless the day arrived when we actually finished the job. We had mixed feelings—one of joy about finishing the work and one of sorrow that the three of us had to part. The dwarf took it best of all. He said we would probably all meet one evening at the *Cirque Medrano* where he was going to put on an act with some monkeys from the jungles of Brazil.

Three or four years after the publication of *Cancer* Fred had two of his books published in French. One was *Sentiments Limitrophes* and the other *Le Quatuor en Ré Majeur*. With neither of these was I able to lend him a helping hand. Poor though my French was I read these two books and appreciated them thoroughly. He said he had written before (in German) but I believe with these two books he broke the ice. Of course they did not become best sellers but he did receive excellent reviews from the French critics and personal tributes from some of France's top writers.

Somewhere in between these two events I wrote a pamphlet intended to help him out of his economic misery; it was entitled *What Are You Going to Do About Alf?* We sent leaflets and letters about his *plaquette* to a number of prominent French and British authors. The idea was to raise contributions so that Alf might go live in Ibiza or some other sunny and more hospitable clime. To our amazement we received contributions from André Gide and Aldous Huxley, among others. Here I must confess playing a dirty trick upon my beloved *compain*. As the return mail was addressed care of Henry Miller it was I who opened the mail. Being rather hard up myself, I took the liberty of filching the contributions at times, vowing that I would make up for them

225

when I got on my feet. (Which I never did all the time I lived in France. I remember distinctly arriving in N.Y. from Greece, with my steamer trunk as security and not a cent in any pockets. Indeed, the first thing I did on entering my hotel room was to call one of my old friends and ask for a quick loan of a few bucks.)

I must say Fred took my pilfering in good spirit. He probably would have done the same had the situation been reversed. He was also very grateful for the meals and drinks we shared when I at last became established at the Villa Seurat.

Somewhere about this time, or was it after the publication of *Cancer,* which took a year or two, Lawrence Durrell wrote me from Greece. He was enamored of the *Tropic of Cancer* and threatened to visit me soon.

And he did. Fred was there when he arrived and the three of us hit it off immediately. Though in his later writings Durrell became a hermetic writer, in character and behavior at *this* point in his career, he was a jolly, lusty Dada-surrealist son-of-a-bitch like Joey and myself. To go with him to the cinéma was bound to be a treat. For, when Durrell started laughing the whole theatre broke into a laugh. Once or twice we were requested to leave the movie. (How strangely similar was the deliberate surrealist act of going to the cinema and suddenly opening a basket noisily to produce some sandwiches and uncork a bottle of *vin rouge* and begin to talk loudly.) At this sort of shenanigans Joey was made to order. For example, if the three of us went for a walk and happened to be in the vicinity of a *commissariat* or police station, Joey would suddenly dart ahead of us, mount the steps leading to the station (the door of which was usually wide open) and shout at the top of his lungs: *"Je vous emmerde tous! Salauds! Imbéciles!"* Then he would quickly run down the steps beckoning us to follow, which we would do leisurely, only to find him standing at the corner quietly smoking his *Gaulois Bleu.* At that period, and I assume for many many years, the French police were hated and

226

despised by the ordinary citizens, especially the youth. They were recruited largely from the mountainous Auvergne region and were naturally of peasant stock within sensitive hides. To do what Joey did was therefore tantamount to running the gauntlet. He would do these things to show off, to prove to us that though he was not a *costaud* he was fearless just the same. Also because he despised the Paris police. In addition to being a clown, a buffoon, a wit and a *bon compain*, there is no doubt that Joey was also a zany. During the period that Durrell and his wife stayed in Paris—a year or two—most every night was a gala night. Oddly, or perhaps not so oddly, Anaïs never participated in any of these riotous *soirées*. For one thing, she was not a drinker. (She could more easily have been tempted to try opium.) Also, as I may have hinted before, she loathed vulgarity and boisterousness. And these gala evenings of ours were anything but refined. Incidentally, it was noticeable that Durrell's wife was never present either. If she had, I am afraid it may have been disastrous. They had hot tempers and were not above using their fists on one another.

There was one evening in particular which I shall never forget. I believe there were just the three of us. I had made the dinner and the others had furnished the wines and cognac. (On these occasions we drank only the best wines.) It was the period when Hitler was causing a commotion everywhere. Sometimes Joey and I ventured out to hear him in some public place—over the radio, to be sure. We listened for enjoyment, I must confess, because of his atrocious German. Going home Joey would imitate his speech—he could do it marvelously.

And so, on this particular evening at the Villa Seurat, Durrell egged Joey on, plying him with liquor and laughing his head off at every fool remark Joey made. Suddenly he knocked a bottle over, broke a few glasses (in his hilarity) and with this became even more grotesque than ever. For some reason he was in bare feet. When the accident occurred he was a first unaware that the floor was covered with broken glass. He only noticed it when he observed the blood streaming from the cuts in his feet. This seemed to make him more elated, more gaga. Now he began singing in German as he continued to prance about the table. Each time around he had another good sip of wine, cognac or whatever. Now he imitated Hitler frenziedly to our great amusement. (By the way, civilized creatures that we were, no one thought to stop the bleeding or beg him to stop his crazy antics. Durrell and I were by this time hysterical with laughter. We never dreamed of begging him to look after his cuts and bruises.) "More, more!" we kept shouting. And more we got! Now he began reciting German poetry, good and bad. We all joined in singing *"Die Lorelei"* and other well-known German songs.

Finally Joey collapsed on the couch, his feet looking as if he had been crucified. Durrell left to return to his lair and I went to bed in the next room. The place looked frightful, what with the uneaten food, the broken glass, the bottles on the floor, and the blood stains just everywhere.

I awoke about six in the morning on hearing Joey pass through my bedroom to go to the bathroom. He acted as if he could not understand what had happened.

He muttered to himself, something about vomiting and falling off the couch into his own vomit. Next morning when the *femme de ménage* came to clean up, she was thoroughly horrified. She told me she had always taken me to be a gentleman *but*—such a pig sty, no, she had never seen anything like it in her life. I assuaged her feelings by giving her a good tip and she quieted down. (With the French, no matter what station in life, a few francs always work wonders.)

Today, after the frightful carnage of the Second World War it seems impossible that that monster Hitler could have unknowingly provided us with such a glorious evening. It's hard to believe that once upon a time he was just a nasty joke. But such is life, alas.

PART II

It was about the time that his *Sentiments Limitrophes* was published and reviewed in the literary chronicles that he received a wonderful letter from Roger Martin du Gard, a writer whom he revered. It was the sort of recognition he longed for and deserved and it put him in a state of ecstasy.

He was no longer living in the Hôtel Central but was now a house guest at the apartment of a mutual friend named Eugene Delacourt. Eugene was a poet of sorts who expressed great admiration for both my work and Fred's. He was a good fellow in every respect except for one little fault—he had no sense of humor. At best I have seen a flickering smile hover about his lips. But he was warm-hearted, sympathetic and extremely generous.

In addition to these virtues he had a raven-haired mistress, Ariadne, who was something of a sculptress. The four of us often ate dinner in some modest restaurant and from there to the cinéma or to a familiar café. Eugene incidentally picked up the tab—for everything.

One evening he announces in his usual grave manner that his grandfather had just died and that he would be leaving in the morning to attend the funeral ceremonies. He was going to the

Isle d'Oleron in the south of France and might not be back for three or four days.

Hearing this somber news Fred promptly said he would come stay with me until Eugene returned.

"Why would you do that?" queried Eugene.

"To avoid complications," Fred replied.

"Nonsense!" exclaimed Eugene. "I want you to remain and look after Ariadne."

"Are you sure you can trust me?" says Fred.

"What are you talking about—of course I can trust you. *Nous sommes des amies, quoi.*"

Nothing more was said. The next morning early Eugene left for the south. By noon Fred was already in bed with the dark-haired ward. On the third day, in the evening, Fred comes to my place in the Villa Seurat with his charge, Ariadne. The two of them were all smiles—and why not since they had been fucking their heads off ever since Eugene left for the country.

We chatted for a while and then Ariadne seated herself on the couch in my studio, with her back to the wall. We were drinking a cool white wine and getting very *amoureux,* the three of us. Suddenly I leaned over her and planted a few warm kisses on her lips. She responded avidly and slipped her tongue into my mouth. Fred had lowered the lights—we were virtually in the dark. After a few minutes I decided to try the other hole. As I reached for the spot I felt something hard and hairy. A weak voice, mirthful too, called out "It's me, Joey." The three of us burst out laughing and disengaged.

Turning the lights up a bit we spontaneously decided that we would go at it in a natural, more comfortable way. My bedroom was next to the studio. We would have her one at a time. Ariadne smiled agreeably. The question was—who was to tackle her first?

Joey thought I should, since they were my guests. I saw no sense in standing on punctilio and so off Ariadne and I went to my double bed. As she didn't have much on it took no time to strip. She was beautifully built, a delight to all the senses. We hugged and kissed and caressed, did all manner of fool things, but for the life of me I could not get an erection. (Perhaps because it was all too *facile*.) Finally I gave up trying and called to Joey in the studio. He came in on the double trot. I confessed that I was impotent and told him it was time to try his luck. He jumped into the bed immediately and was all over her.

However, in about ten minutes, I heard him calling for me. I went into the bedroom to find him lying dejectedly beside his Ariadne. He too had found himself impotent.

Instead of taking it tragically we all got dressed and went to the *Coupole* for drinks and a light snack. Ariadne took it like a brick. She said it was one of those things—it even happened to women sometimes. "By the way," she added, "Eugene will be back tomorrow. I had a letter from him today."

Two days later Fred appears at my place about eight in the morning—early for him. "Can I use your bathroom?" he said. "Of course," I replied, whereupon he loped off to the bathroom. He was hardly gone when there came a harsh knock at the door. I opened and who do I see before me but Eugene. I started to say *"Bon jour!"* but he cut me short with—*"Où est'il?"* (Where is he?) I shrugged my shoulders, not realizing at first whom he was referring to. He pushed me roughly aside, walked through my bedroom and opened the bathroom door. There was Joey waiting for him and trembling no doubt. The first word out of Eugene's mouth was "Salaud" followed by what sounded like a slap in the puss. More epithets flowed from Eugene's lips, always followed by slaps or blows. Now I heard Eugene berate him for not defending himself. "Coward!" he yelled and then more bang bang. It sounded bad. I didn't dare go to Fred's rescue as I was due for some of that punishment myself—or had Ariadne only told on Fred and not me?

Anyway in a few minutes Eugene appeared, brushed by me

without saying a word and disappeared. A few moments later Joey made his appearance, looking rather battered and bruised but with a grin on his face.

The first thing I said to him was—"How could you take a beating like that and not defend yourself?" He grinned some more, sheepishly this time, and replied: "I didn't try because I deserved what I got."

"You mean you kept your hands at your sides and let him make a punching bag of you?"

"Exactly," he said. "I was guilty. It was a lousy thing to do to a friend. I deserved every bit of it. I even feel good about it. Sort of soothes my conscience."

With that we dropped the matter. I even forgot to ask him where he was going to sleep hereafter. (I couldn't offer to put him up in my place because it would risk displeasing Anaïs.)

The more I mulled the matter over—I mean his refusal to defend himself—the more I had to admire him. We have all taken beatings at one time or another but rarely voluntarily. He was dead right too about the punishment soothing his conscience. There was one puzzling factor which was never resolved. Why had Ariadne told on Fred and not on me? Was it because the whole truth would have been too much for Eugene to take? Or was she endeavoring to preserve the friendship which Eugene and I had shared for years? One never really knows what motivates a woman's behavior. To men they always seem to have an affinity with cats. In a word they are "treacherous." Men are too, of course. But women seem to be born that way. Men only acquire it with growing experience of life. In a way there was also something feline about Joey himself. Women adored him, loved him, helped him, but usually sensed that at bottom he was not to be trusted. He amused them, flattered the pants off them and used them—and, for some inexplicable reason they did not mind too much. His continuous air of cajolery seemed to have a mollifying effect on them. Besides, it's no great secret that women are easy prey for rogues, liars, scoundrels. They may refuse to give themselves to the good and earnest man who reveres them, and allow themselves to be seduced by the first Romeo who comes along. Not only that, but at bottom their behavior is often far more shocking than that of men. A woman, for example, who passes for the incarnation of virtue may be discovered eventually to be a lascivious bitch—worse, an unacknowledged whore. She may have a vicious streak, demanding to be fucked only in certain ways, certain positions, all this, mind you, while playing the role of good wife and devoted mother. And sometimes, by Jesus, she really can be both things at once.

Of course there are plenty of men given to the same deceit and treachery, but usually they are not as artful as women. They betray themselves more readily. They are more insouciant.

Why is is that the man who has been made *"cocu"* (cuckold) always appears ridiculous to our eyes? Raimu, the famous French actor, played this role in its dual aspect marvelously. He was at once naïve and ridiculous and then tragic in the real Shakespearean sense.

I don't think Fred ever suffered from a broken heart. Oh, perhaps yes, when he was still a youth, but not after he had matured. The trouble with him was that he was very silent, very reticent about his youth. It was almost as if he had never known such a period. He probably went from the university to the army and thence to the bughouse. It was here at the that I imagine him to have done his greatest reading. Trust the Germanic instinct for learning to have provided even their insane asylums with good reading matter. I feel almost positive it was there he got to know his Goethe—*Conversations with Eckermann, Dichtung und Wahrheit, The Italian Journey;* perhaps *Faust* too and *Wilhelm Meister.* When tipsy and acting the buffoon the line which often came to his lips was: *"Das ewige Weibliche zieht uns immer hinein."* He would mouth this famous phrase with the same mock solemnity that a Jesus freak might quote the Golden Rule.

He could also recite in this manner with one hand up his girl's dress, tickling her clitoris. Or he could recite it sitting on the toilet. There was something delicious about his pranks, his roguery. One hears of men who would betray their own mother if they badly needed a meal or a pair of new socks. What's more, the likes of them often are not at all detestable—on the contrary. That is why I return again and again to the congruity of the cat and the rogue. What to me is so despicable in the cat is the way it curries favor by rubbing itself against your leg, or purring so gently and softly—like wheedling a blind man out of a bit of cash.

With all his feline qualities I want to emphasize once again that whatever lousy thing Joey might do he remained a lovable guy, *a friend*. He could rob you barefacedly and with the other hand give you a caress. Perhaps there is a bit of truth in the Germans' reference to Austrians, especially Viennese, that they are "treacherous." One hears the same about the Italians, how they smile at you as they put a stiletto in your back. But they too, the Italians, are a lovable sort and are always forgiven their faults. Tourists (women especially) are fond of telling how awful the Italian men are, that they will pinch a woman's ass even if she is walking with her own husband. But once again one must bear in mind that women secretly enjoy being pinched in the ass, and especially in that sly way the Italians do it.

After *Tropic of Cancer* had been out a month or two there appeared a review of the book by none other than my favorite writer Blaise Cendrars. It came out in a little review called *Orbes,* run by one of Cendrar's most devout admirers. One day shortly after this happening Cendrars and his friend came unexpectedly to visit me at the Villa Seurat. To their dismay they saw posted on my door a printed, or rather handwritten, sign reading—"Do not disturb! Genius at work." Cendrars took it good-naturedly and refused to disturb me but his friend to whom Cendrars was a god was highly incensed. He wanted to break the door down.

A week or two later Cendrars came alone. This time I responded quickly. Fred was in my place at the time. Again we were short on drinks and broke to boot. But no thought of any funny business. I explained the situation to Cendrars frankly, knowing he would understand. In any case we rationed the little that was left of the cognac and husbanded our tiny portions as best we could during a two or three hour session with Cendrars.

What a marvelous afternoon we spent together, talking of everything under the sun but mostly of his adventures in various parts of the world.

I recall now two things he mentioned which surprised me. One was his dislike of Marcel Proust's work and the other was his fascination with Remy de Gourmont—both the man and his writing. He told of one strange incident that sticks in my crop. I believe he had just informed us that de Gourmont was a leper and went out only at night. One evening as Cendrars was about to cross one of the famous Paris bridges he thought he recognized a figure bent over the parapet, gazing idly at his own image in the water below. He looked again and was certain now that it was one of two men he most admired at the time—the other being Gérard de Nerval. Yes, he was sure it was Remy de Gourmont—he had seen enough photos of him to be certain.

Not wishing to obtrude upon his idol, Cendrars nonchalantly advanced a few steps until he was almost touching de Gourmont and then he too leaned over the parapet gazing into the Seine. He wanted badly to talk to de Gourmont but was too shy to introduce himself. So he began talking to his own image in the water, but about things which he knew would interest his idol and let him know he was talking about him. I believe he began by talking of some of the authors de Gourmont wrote about in his less well-known work about Latin authors. I don't remember whether de Gourmont responded in any way but at least he didn't move away. It was a characteristic gesture on the part of

Cendrars. Rough adventurer that he was, he was also one of the gentlest, most sensitive men I ever met.

The afternoon wore on most agreeably, with Cendrars doing most of the talking whilst Fred and I listened open-mouthed and dumbstruck. Finally Cendrars announced that he was getting hungry, wouldn't we like to have dinner with him; he knew, he said, a wonderful modest restaurant in Montmartre near where Picasso and Max Jacob once had a studio. It was on the rue de l'Abbesse, if I am not mistaken.

To make it easier for us to accept his invitation he lied about having just that morning unexpectedly received a check from one of his publishers.

In the street around the corner from us was a cab rack. (Rue de la Tombe-Issoire.) The restaurant was indeed a cozy little joint with a bar which was already occupied from one end to another by a group of whores. Cendrars was well-known to the proprietor and to the girls also, it appeared. The first thing he did on taking our seats was to order *un coup de champagne pour les jeunes filles en fleurs* (mocking Proust) adding aloud, glass in hand, that these were France's true ambassadors. This immediately created a genial atmosphere.

When it came time to eat, Fred and I offered to cut his steak for him. He politely refused, saying the waiter was used to doing it for him. A few moments later he was to get up and stand in the show window to show us all how he could touch any part of his body with his sole left hand. (But not cut his own steak.) On the other hand it is well-known that he drove a Bugatti not only through the heavy traffic of Paris but up the Amazon. It was there among the headhunters that he learned the trick of showing how he could reach any part of his body with just the left hand. He told us it had saved his life, as the natives (headhunters) found this exploit highly amusing.

It was interesting to note how his familiarity with the whores at the bar did not alter his gentleness. This man, who had lost his good right arm as a *Legionnaire* was the same man who in answer to a questionnaire—"What quality in women do you admire most?" wrote "Innocence."

Well, we had an excellent meal, probably cooked especially for him and his friends, washed down with his favorite wines. It was a royal feast and we, Fred and I, were slightly tipsy.

When Cendrars suggested that we now go bar-hopping (along the *grands boulevards de Montmartre*), Fred made some excuse and took leave of us. (He did this out of delicacy, not wishing to impose further on Cendrar's hospitality.) I *had* to go along with Cendrars because he considered me a genuine pal. Often during our conversations he would remark about the parallelism of our lives just before the First World War. He liked to remind me that he too had been a bum and a beggar in New York, that he hated work, that his one passion was reading, etc., etc.

So we began stopping off—a bar here, a bar there. Everywhere immediately recognized by the proprietor, bartenders and *clientèle*. Tough *hombre* that he was, I noticed he stuck to his white wine (usually *un Meursault*) rather than Pernods and cognacs.

At one bar where there was a cluster of whores at the counter he opened the blouse of the girl standing next to him, pulled out her planturous teat and turning to me said: *"Regarde-moi ça! C'est beau, n'est-ce pas?"* What he wanted me to observe closely were her lovely *"nichons"* (nipples) which were the color of grapes. All this in good fun, not with vulgar ostentation. The girls seemed to know him and respected him as a famous writer, though I doubt any had read him.

Towardfour in the morning I managed to break away, saying (the truth!) that I had to go to the Central Post Office to deposit some mail which would just catch one of the fast ocean liners going to New York.

A memorable, an unforgettable evening. Never repeated, alas!

Well, back to *mon copain*, Alf, Joey, Fred... *Les Degourds du Onzieme*, by Courteline. A book I often wanted to talk to Fred

238

about but never did. There were certain authors both French and English, I never heard him mention. And yet he was extremely well-read. Which reminds me that there are two characters I have neglected to mention thus far—Hans Reichel, the painter, and Betty Ryan, the girl downstairs. It was one Christmas morning that both Reichel and Fred happened to visit me about the same time—early morning. Though none of us gave a damn about Xmas, nevertheless we felt the occasion warranted some modest sort of celebration. As so often happened there were just the dregs of a bottle of white wine available. All the empty bottles of the nights before were lined up like sentinels beside my desk. Nothing daunted, Reichel suggested we pour the remains of the wine bottle into three tiny glasses— like thimbles really. This we did, then toasted one another and, as we began to converse, did our best only to take the barest sip from our tiny glasses.

Somehow this procedure reminded Reichel of his days in a French concentration camp during the First World War. (He had had to flee Germany at a moment's notice because he was guilty of harboring the Communist playwright Ernst Toller.) Anyway, in the concentration camp, when the rations were scarce or nil, he would don an apron and pretend to be a waiter, going to each prisoner in turn and asking what he would like to eat. (He would first rattle off an imaginary menu which would make everyone's mouth water.) He repeated some of the antics he employed. Like Fred, he too was a good clown. We enjoyed his imitation immensely. From this he went on to talk of his friendship with Paul Klee, whose painting he was often accused of imitating. Anyone who knew both men's work intimately could never make this assertion. However, it now gave him pleasure to tell us in his inimitable way (using French, English and German) how very much alike the two of them were in many ways. In fact, as he put it, they were like brothers. As I recall it now, many years later, Reichel informed us that not only did they think and paint in similar fashion, but they both played the violin, and fell in love with two sisters, among other things. "How could we help but paint alike?" he added. "We were like twins."

Now it happened that just below me on the ground floor was a young lady, also a painter, who was an ardent admirer of Reichel's work. And Reichel, for his part, was an ardent admirer of the young woman. In fact, he was conducting a secret love affair with her. The young woman was not only highly sensitive and angelic but somewhat eccentric. She preferred the company of men to women.

One day she invited about fifteen or twenty of her men friends to a banquet downstairs in her quarters. In addition to a choice selection of wines she also offered us cognac, chartreuse and other cordials. The dinner was going along fabulously until Reichel took one drink too many, whereupon he changed as usual into a demonic, quarrelsome individual. Now Reichel had always suspected me of having designs on the young lady—and in truth he was not far off the mark. And so, in very blunt Germanic fashion he began talking sheer nonsense. Pointing to one of his treasured watercolors on the wall he said it meant nothing to him, that he could destroy it as easily as he had created it. For some crazy reason I was in a somewhat diabolical mood myself. And so I began to twit him. Finally, rising from my seat, I went to the painting in question, put my hand on it, and dared him to destroy it in front of us all. I really believed he was capable of doing this, but to my great surprise, he refused, and grabbing his full glass of wine smashed it against another wall. With this our hostess became positively alarmed. Reichel, seemingly humiliated, called for stronger drinks and began to curse and swear in German.

With this, several of the guests (Frenchmen) took their leave. And in a little while, one by one, they all bade their hostess goodnight and left. I was left alone with her. I saw that she was quite drunk and I wanted no part in what might follow. So in a

240

moment I too said goodnight and started upstairs to my studio. The young lady was now not only indignant over the failure of her party but outraged. She picked up several half empty glasses as I started up the stairs and flung them at me. I kept mounting the steps, never turning a head to look back at her. That positively enraged her. More glasses were hurled and smashed to smithereens against the stone steps.

For almost an hour all was quiet. I had gone to bed to take a nap. Suddenly I heard the young woman calling my name. I opened the door and there she was at the bottom of the stairs, making ready to come up.

"But the glass!" I shouted.

"I don't give a damn," came the reply.

And so, over the broken glass she came up the stairs with bare and bloody feet.

Our course I washed her feet and did my best to staunch the flow of blood.

She was still in a somber mood. "What ever got into you?" I asked.

"You!" she replied. "*You* egged Reichel on. You knew he was in love with me. You did it deliberately."

I could not deny the truth of this. All I could do was to bandage her feet and invite her to get in bed with me.

Will the reader kindly regard the foregoing about the broken glass as an interlude to the Christmas passacaglia which I am about to continue....

We left Reichel, Fred and myself slowly draining the thimblesful of cognac which Reichel had doled out in three equal portions.

During the conversation which took place all that morning—or rather "the reminiscences"—it occurred to me, as it had on previous occasions in which the past was celebrated that Fred never seemed to have had a youth or else had completely forgotten it—or it was simply lost in the night of history.

Whereas myself, not only on this occasion but often in my life I could recollect (and delighted to do so) many, many things out of my days from five to ten years of age in "the old neighborhood."

Back to that Christmas Day in 1930 something or other. The morning visitation—then a sleepy afternoon with Fred popping in again around four in the afternoon to see if by some miracle I had rustled up some food. "Sorry, Joey, but no luck. We'll just have to pull our belts tighter." But then in about an hour the miracle occurred. About 5:00 P.M. there was a rap at the door. I go to open it and there stands a charming couple—young man and woman of indeterminate age—just over from England. Hoping to spend part of Christmas Day with Henry Miller whose books they have devoured. I had barely introduced my pal Joey when it occurred to me to tell them the truth about our situation—that we were broke and not a morsel nor a drop of liquor in the larder.

"Have you any money on you?" I asked bluntly.

Of course they had. They would be only too happy to go look for some food for us all.

What a godsend! We blessed them and told them where to look for the food.

When they returned about half an hour later, they were laden with good things—a roast chicken, vegetables, fruit, wines, liqueurs, cigarettes. They had thought of everything. The woman, whom I will call Pat, went to work immediately to prepare the dinner. The young man, who was an unknown writer, helped set the table, talking books all the while. I soon discovered that he was familiar with my own favorites—Cendrars, Max Jacob, et al, and the French painters, Braque, Matisse, Bonnard, et al.

Fred meanwhile was helping Pat prepare the food. They were having an animated conversation, it seemed. Later he told me that she had confided to him that she was a poet, "a little mad," and had only recently been released from the insane asylum. And British to boot!

We sat down to table in a little while and tackled the *hors d'oeuvres*, which they had remembered to bring, including *celeri remoulade* (sic). At table we gradually learned who the young woman with the white hair was. She was a poetess, not known in every household in England but well-known in the halls of poesy and lunacy. At table the rapport between her and Fred (they sat opposite one another) was striking. I hardly ever had seen Fred in such a joyous and serene mood. He recited from French and German poets. She in turn quoted from her own work, which was excellent and extremely modern. Not crazy either. Rather a mixture of coolth and passion, restraint and abandon, immanence and permanence, nightly emissions, *asamara, fragile jonquils.* The wines they had bought were superb—château vintages no less. And with the dessert came the Armagnac, the chartreuse, etc. A royal feast, if ever I had one!

In the midst of it Pat suddenly gets up, goes around to Fred, and embraces him. A long, warm embrace. They were both reeling beside the table. Suddenly, without a word, Fred takes her by the arm, and leads her to my bedroom. There, as I later learned, he gave her a quick fuck—but, as he put it—a *good* one. In a few minutes they came out, looking perfectly nonchalant, and resumed their places at the table.

From here on until they left it was poetry and song. What I could not help but notice was the remarkable affinity between the two. Could it have been that her recent release from the asylum reminded Fred of his own four years in the nut house, as a casualty of the war? Though there was probably no connection between the two events, it was a fact that not long after their meeting, Fred went to England to live, became a British citizen, and when the war began, enlisted in the British Pioneer Corps, as I believe it was called.

It was some half hour or so after they had gone, and we two

243

were still sitting at the table. From where Fred sat he could see the window up above my balcony. It was a small window but large enough for any sized moon to shine through. Suddenly he glanced up at the window and let out a shriek. A three-quarter moon (on the wane) was mirrored in the little window. It was a cheesy looking moon, as if chunks had been bitten out of it.

Fred immediately jumped to his feet and moved to the other side of the room. He repeated what he had told me several times before—that the sight of the moon always unnerved him. He was very much like a woman in a tantrum. I offered him some more Armagnac but he decided he had had enough, grabbed his beret and left.

I was left with the garbage and dirty dishes. The place was a mess. In my excitement I completely forgot that the *femme de mènage* was due next morning and so, as I hustled about, cleaning up the mess, I began humming to myself and recalling scenes out of my early childhood, then scenes at the piano in my sweetheart's home, playing her favorite melodies. In retrospect I had risen from the piano stool, embraced her warmly, then run my hand up her dress and felt her warm, throbbing cunt. That was as far as I permitted myself to go. Suddenly at this point I thought of my old friends and acquaintances in the old neighborhood. "Merry Christmas! Mrs. Reynolds!" I shouted. "Merry Xmas Mr. Ramsay, you old goat! Merry Xmas Mr. Pirossa, may your bananas slowly ripen! Fuck Jesus! Fuck the Virgin Mary! Fuck Gautama the Buddha! Peace on Earth with neutron and hydrogen bombs! Vive the clap! Vive Syphilis the brother of Satan! When you are in love you must destroy right and left! Long live the street cleaners. Long live Insanity! A new day is dawning, an even worse one. Run for your life! Take cover! Fuck your sister, your mother, your aunt, your cousin! Not a crumb of the past will be left. Not a morsel, not even a speck. A clean sweep. Pure, beautiful annihilation."

"Roses, roses, roses bring memories of you dear...."

"Fuck you all! The earth rejects you. Satan rejects you. The cherubim reject you. You are disappearing into nothingness and leaving not a shred of memory behind. You are not even so much horse shit! Ta Ta!"

During the war Fred and I corresponded. I learned that he intended to write a book about me, about our friendship. He intimated that he would like to visit me in Big Sur for a few months, if I could put him up conveniently. I was then married to Eve McClure. The children were down south staying with their mother and her new husband. They weren't too happy about the new arrangement. Tony, my son, took it especially hard. I used to telephone him once a week. I noticed that he answered in monosyllables—yes, no, maybe, etc. That made me feel wretched.

However, vacation time was soon due and then they were free to stay with Eve and me a few months.

Fred had already arrived and taken to the life immediately. I'll never forget the look of wonder and pleasure on his face when we took him to Monterey to shop. As usual we stopped for lunch at a lunch counter which served hamburgers. I don't think Fred had ever seen a hamburger before, much less eaten one. He wore that expression of glee which one sees on the faces of kids on TV when attempting to down a monstrous sandwich.

Eve, my wife, found Fred to be a darling. We had a Mexican, or rather Panamanian friend (female) who also took a great liking to Fred and offered him sexual satisfaction if he got hard up. Then there were the hot springs where we usually went once a week.

All in all, everything was just ducky.

Finally it came time to pick up my kids for their vacation. We were to meet at a bus station in Santa Maria, if I am not mistaken. I had an old beaten up jeep, which looked rather like a museum piece. Fred wanted to go with me. He had heard a lot about the children not only from Eve and myself but from the neighbors also. Everyone described them as "darling." Fred seemed surprised that I could drive as well as I did. (I was always the most unhandy bugger imaginable.) But I learned to do many things living in the country which I never thought possible in New York or Paris.

Well, we arrived at the bus station and there, sitting placidly on a bench were my two kids with their mother and stepfather. One could see at a glance that they had been scrubbed clean as a whistle, been arrayed in their best clothes and told to sit quietly until we arrived.

The moment I appeared they jumped from their seat and shouted and climbed all over me. "Daddy, daddy!" they yelled. They acted as if they had just been released fromprison. I could see that Fred, who had never had anything to do with children, was already somewhat apprehensive.

Well, we quickly piled into the jeep, the kids occupying the rear seat, and started homeward. The moment I put my foot on the gas pedal and veered toward home pandemonium set in. They flung a hundred questions at me at once.

I glanced now and then in Fred's direction and thought I detected a look of growing terror in his face. Certainly the kids behaved as if uncontrollable—a pair of wild animals. (But *lovable* ones!) I of course was thrilled at this unexpected reception. I realized, without their saying a word, what a disciplined life they had been leading at their mother's house. And so I allowed them to carry on in their own sweet way. They sang, they yelled, they asked a thousand questions about their old (young) friends and so on. Sheer insanity. After driving a bit I noticed that it was getting dark and that we would have to stay at a motel and continue on in the morning.

I believe I chose Andersen's, a well-known hotel and restaurant. We took one large room with three beds. First we had hamburgers and tea or coke. This revived their spirits and so, when we entered our room they went absolutely berserk. Fred gave me a look as if to say—"Can't you calm them down just a little bit?" But I was so happy to see them in this joyous, if crazy mood, that I made no attempt to put the brakes on them. I didn't care if they ripped the place apart.

Naturally, there had to be a debate as to who would sleep with whom. I suggested that Tony and Val sleep together and Fred and I separately in our own beds. I think it was Tony who wanted to sleep with Fred or me. Not getting his way he began a pillow fight. Soon all four of us were throwing pillows at one another. I thought because of the pandemonium that the manager might order us to leave, but fortunately he let us be.

It must have taken a couple hours before they were ready to sleep. I could see that Fred was already worn out. Our gambits in the Villa Seurat days were nothing compared to these shenanigans.

Well, next day we arrived home and received a warm greeting from Eve. She immediately set about preparing a beautiful lunch for us all.

Tony meanwhile had found some of his old toys and a big top hat (for the opera) which he donned and began his antics in the garden. It was curious to watch my son, a Virgo like Fred (born the same day of the month) act the clown which was Fred's forte. They definitely had something in common, though I don't think Fred was quite aware of it as yet. He regarded the "two monsters" as if they were freaks from the circus. He always kept a little distance between himself and them, much as Moricand had tried (unsuccessfully) to do with Val.

What a misfortune not to have children of one's own. Certainly they can create trouble but whatever the pain or discomfort it is worth having them. I only wish I had been able to produce a round dozen.

Well, Fred stayed on two, three or four months, and finished his book, *Mon Ami Henry Miller,* there in Big Sur. And what a beautiful, loving book it is! Written from the heart, if ever a book was thus written. No bullshit, no academic appraisals—just the simple, plain, natural truth.

I wind up this chapter about him with tears in my eyes. He was a friend indeed, an unforgettable one.

I wrote was instead of is. He is still alive and still living in England, only now he is living in Dorset (Thomas Hardy's country). My son, Tony, who has always had a secret admiration for Fred, intends to visit him sometime this year. This time Fred will not meet with a wild Indian but a handsome, intelligent young man who is a chip off the old block. May the two Virgos have a rollicking time of it.

EPILOGUE

Dear Joey,

As you probably know, Anaïs died a year or so ago. Before dying she left instructions for two of her very dear friends to republish the *Diaries* exactly as she wrote them, to translate into English the early childhood diaries, and to write a biography which would tell the whole truth about her life. All these things are now being done.

You may also know that an erotic book she had withheld until her death has been selling like wildfire. It's called *The Delta of Venus*.

One other little, but touching item. Before her death she wrote a letter to Hugo, her first husband, asking him to forgive her for all her "capers," her lies, the tricks she played behind his back; in short, for all her misdeeds as a wife, which, needless to say, were legion. To her delight and *soulagement* he told her that he had always loved her, that he was aware of her "shenanigans" (my word, not his) and that there was nothing to forgive. All this made me recall how she treated *you*, how unforgiving she was. And you were only trying to let her and everyone know how much you loved her.

With her death she left behind a host of admirers and idolaters, mostly young women. How they will react when they learn the truth I cannot at this moment conceive. (In my own case, when I learned the truth about Kunt Hamsun's behavior during the Second World War, it made no difference whatever in my feelings toward him. He still remains a hero to me.)

We (you, I, Durrell) knew about Anaïs's lying and deceit long, long ago. I mentioned earlier in this narrative about "falling out of her favor." You were not the only one to be dismissed, as it were. There were others. But what always stuck in my crop, Joey, was the utter unfairness of her behavior with you. And what, after all, was your crime? That you told the truth about her and her relationships. But you did it innocently, without malice. *That* she simply refused to see, unfortunately.

Anyway, before very long, the whole world will be made aware of her inveterate lying, her chicanery, her duplicity, and so on. I myself, who was perhaps her best friend, have referred to her as a monstrous liar or prevaricator or fabulator, however one feels like expressing it. I have discussed this aspect of her being with her most loyal, devoted female friends. We are all that this inability to tell the truth was based on her inability to accept reality. She had to alter reality to suit her own view of the world. You may remember her abhorrence of vulgarity, that it was worse than sin to her. (I have mentioned in this narrative that she was not ever present during our "orgies," so to speak.) And it was this compulsion of hers which drove her to write her *Diary*. In it one is tempted to say—everything was upside down.

And now I come to the point of this long detour, which is—why not get out your original manuscript about her and seek a publisher for it. After all, it is not a piece of gossip but an adoring tribute to her. Yes, Joey, a "loving portrait," far better than what I have done for you.

Now is the time. Her *Delta of Venus* was on the best seller list for a number of weeks. How ironical that she who detested "vulgarity" should win posthumous fame by a highly erotic work!

Unfortunately, I only remember the flavor of that book you devoted to the super-terrestrial aspect of her being. In those days I used to say to myself (mockingly), "Joey is good at that sort of thing." You were indeed far closer to understanding her very special nature than I who was her intimate friend. Many times, as I look back on those years, I can see again the expression on your face which told me what a brash, insensitive American I was. Often this would happen when I would question you about some famous old German writer whose name I happened to run across. You would simply say "He's not for *you*, Joey," and that was all. But you cannot realize how crushing those simple rejoinders were. It told me not only that I was Brooklyn born, without a real education, and that, like most Americans, I know little or nothing about Europe, but that, try as I may, I would never have the insight, the sensitivity that most Europeans are blessed with. How right you were! Arriving in Paris a whole new world confronted me—language, literature, culture, social behavior, eating habits, just about everything. And Anaïs, though born in France, never really understood or appreciated her native land as did you, a foreigner like myself. It was not with Anaïs but with *you* (and with Larry too) I held lengthy discussions about French authors, French habits, French streets and so on. Anaïs, who was quite a reader, always seemed to skim the surface.

In a profound sense she lacked a religious instinct. Having renounced Catholicism she closed the door on all mysteries. Yet, in spite of her faults and shortcomings she remained in our eyes a creature not of this world, nor of the heavenly world, but someone floating felicitously between Heaven and Earth. She was forever ethereal, forever guileless, forever innocent. And withal a helper, a sort of Mother Earth. She could no more shut her eyes to distress than she could to vulgarity. If she sinned,

251

and God only knows how she did, it was as a child, a child who had not yet opened her eyes on the world.

And Joey, my dear, my abiding friend, *you* knew all this better than anyone. In my crass American way I used to think of your writing then (particularly about Anaïs) as so much "embroidery." "He's good at that sort of thing." When, however, you came to write *Sentiments Limitrophes* and *Le Quatuor en Ré Majeur*, I began to realize whom I was living with, what a truly wonderful view of life you possessed. I would give anything to be able to reread those books now.

Although throughout this book I may seem to have dwelt more on your "scabrous" behavior, your perpetual clowning and deviltry, I am sure you know that, just as Anaïs floated between Heaven and Earth, so you always hovered between the clown and the angel. Perhaps "idiot" would be better suited to express what I tried to convey. Of course, I mean "Idiot" in the Dostoievskian sense and not as our born idiots take the word to mean. The older I grow the more meaningful and beloved that word has come to be for me. So, Joey, as one idiot to another, farewell for the time being. May you continue to live your happy-go-lucky life right to the end. You have brought laughter and tears to us all. Bless you,

—Henry

POSTSCRIPT

One other little item remains to be touched upon. Strangely enough, you and Anaïs had this whatever you may call it in common. I mean a seeming lack of childhood. An absence of childhood friends. Try as I may, I cannot recall either of you dwelling on early friendships. Whereas in my own case, the years from five to ten seem now more than ever to have been the most important, the most wonderful years of my life.

252

Furthermore, it is hard for me to imagine a childhood without friends. Even a doll or a wooden horse is something to remember in later years, something endearing.

But no, with both of you there existed this vacuum. I am not going to try to analyze this lack or gap—this is for the psychologist to do, if he can. There is only one little trait you both shared which I will dare to mention—a need for secrecy. Often I felt that neither of you had anything to hide or to be ashamed of, but that you simply did not wish to share *everything* with even the best of friends.

I am probably all wrong, but I thought I ought to give voice to my suspicions. It doesn't alter my feelings about you; it simply makes you more "mysterious," closer to the angel than to the clown. *You* were the one who believed in miracles, remember? I can still hear you saying to me—"Don't worry, Joey, something will turn up." And, by crickey, something usually did. I used to attribute this gift of yours to some sort of spiritual legerdemain which you carried with you from infancy, from a world I knew nothing about. Which reminds me now how farcical must have seemed my attitude of perpetually baring my soul. Do you remember the little story I once told you about going to a woman, a Jewish woman, who was a psychic individual? I had hardly crossed her threshold when she exclaimed "My good man, what have you done with your soul?" I instinctively felt in the neighborhood of my heart, where we imagine as children, the soul is located, and thought to myself—"She's so right, I must have lost my soul a long time ago." But enough of this. I feel now we shall meet again in the next world whenever and wherever.

épreuve d'artiste — Good News — Henry Miller 1973

Other Women in My Life

A few days ago I had a birthday—my eighty-sixth. I had thought that I would do very little further writing, if any at all.

But two disparate occurrences in the last few days threaten to alter this decision, at least for one more book. The first factor was the absence of a fairly large sheet of watercolor paper which had been resting on the piano. It had been there for a couple of weeks and suddenly it was gone. On it, scribbled in helter-skelter fashion, were the names of almost all the women who had played some part in my life. I recall telling my son Tony, who had accidentally discovered this sheet, to take good care of it. Not that I then thought of writing about all these creatures.

The second factor was a remark by Simenon in his book *When I Was Old*. He stated that he was not a writer (regrettably) but a novelist and that being a novelist produced pain rather than ecstasy. This remark stuck in my crop. I asked myself how I would categorize myself. And immediately concluded that I was definitely not a novelist. Good or bad, from the very beginning of my literary career I thought of myself as a writer, a very important writer to be. I had no use for fiction, though many of my readers regard my work as being largely fictive. I myself am at a loss to give it a name.

But to come back to the women whose Christian names I used to cover a sheet of Arches watercolor paper. For some reason unknown to me I now have the urge to write about them. I may not use their right names, nor do I promise to be totally truthful or accurate in what I shall say about them. Rather I prefer to think of them as Proust so aptly entitled his one volume—*Les Jeunes Filles en Fleur*. Scott Moncrieff, Proust's translator, named the volume *Within a Budding Grove*, which was nothing less than a stroke of genius.

My main motive in writing about these women is to evoke the aura of the times in which they lived. I will not pretend to give their life story, but only the essence and the fragrance of them as I sensed these at the time. Also, I shall not pretend that I slept with them all. On this score Simenon would seem to have broken all records. Much as I have dwelt on the sexual aspect of my relations with women in my previous work I must nevertheless now state that there were many others aspects in all the women I have known than what I chose to write about. Woman, as a subject, is endless. Like everything else, the skeptic may say. But in my humble opinion there is even more to her than the infinitude of sex would indicate.

Pauline

Pauline was my first mistress. I met her
while giving piano lessons. It was at the home of a friend of hers
whose daughter was taking lessons from me—at thirty-five
cents an hour. I was still madly in love with my first love Cora
Seward. I was teaching the piano in order to supplement my
meager salary working as a clerk for the Atlas Portland Cement
Co. On my way home after giving a lesson I would stop off at an
ice cream parlor near my home and eat two banana splits. They
cost me thirty cents. The nickel that was left over I often threw
in the gutter out of sheer disgust. I preferred to dig into my
mother's purse for carfare next morning. One can see what little
sense of reality I had.

But to come back to Pauline. She was usually seated in a chair
some distance from the piano. Always neatly groomed, as if
ready to go to the theatre or a concert. Hair always beautifully
arranged and a pleasant smile on her face. Her friend, the
mother of the girl I was teaching, was on the other hand something of a slut, careless about her apparel or her make-up. What
the two women had in common was hard for me to tell.

To begin with, Pauline was from a small town in Virginia. She had a most pleasing Southern accent. Louise, her friend, could have been from anywhere or nowhere. Louise had a boarder, a black man, whose mistress she soon became. I knew him as the man who ran the bicycle shop where I took my bike to be repaired. But I was not aware immediately of the relationship between the two. That I discovered later from Pauline.

Pauline had taken to calling me Harry. She thought Henry too nondescript. We didn't fall into each other's arms immediately, I must confess. In fact, it *seemed* as if I was likely to fall for her friend first. Louise was a lascivious bitch who could hardly wait for the lesson to be finished before throwing herself at me.

(Both women were in their thirties—I was eighteen.) Another fact I discovered later about Louise was that she had syphilis. That helped to resist her advances.

Usually, when the lesson was over, I escorted Pauline to her flat. She was poor as a churchmouse but kept a neat, cozy flat for which she paid a reduced rent in return for acting as janitress. She had a son by a divorced husband who had been a musician in the army. (She always referred to him as "Shooter"— his last name, which was spelled "Chouteau.") Her son George was just a year younger than I and worked as a shoe salesman. He had a light tenor voice, very agreeable. He and his mother often sang softly together—under their breath, so to speak. Alone, especially doing her housework, Pauline usually hummed to herself, something I found enchanting. (I've only known one woman since who sang and hummed.)

From the foregoing it's obvious that I was now living with Pauline. (And still madly in love with my first love.) I was supposed to have gone to Cornell University but at the last minute my father decided he could not afford to send me to Cornell, even though I had been granted a scholarship in German. I had elected instead to take a job—at $30 a month. Naturally, these nightly walks past my true love's home were seriously curtailed.

Once during this period I ran into her by accident one evening at Coney Island. A most embarrassing moment, as Pauline was hanging on my arm. On another occasion, after moving to another flat, I discovered through a friend that my Cora Seward lived now in the house facing ours—and was married. I said nothing to Pauline about this, but now and then she would catch me looking through the window facing her yard with a dreamy expression on my face.

During this whole crazy adolescence I kept myself in good shape physically. I smoked a cigarette or two when I went to a party and drank wine when I went to an Italian restaurant, which was rather rare. No hard liquor. Lots of physical exercise. As I have explained elsewhere, for a good long time I virtually lived on my bike. In addition, I would run three, four, or five miles before breakfast. Before I took to living with Pauline I used to pass her flat every morning on my way back from Coney Island. She would be on the stoop waiting to see me pass. All we did was wave to one another. But that evening, after dinner, I was sure to be at her place, raring to get my end. Though she was old enough to be my mother—she had given birth to her son at the age of fourteen or fifteen—what a difference there was between the two women! Pauline was delicate, petite, beautifully proportioned, always of a cheerful nature. Uneducated but not stupid. In fact, her lack of schooling rendered her even more charming to me. She had taste, discretion, and a sound understanding of life. As I said before, she had not fallen for me at first blush. I believe she sensed what she was letting herself in for. She must have known from the beginning that it would end tragically for her. I, on the other hand, acted as if I were blind, deaf and dumb. I questioned nothing. I never looked ahead a millimeter. Of course it was my initiation into the world of sex. And it was a most beautiful one. As for Pauline, I am certain she had been deprived of a sex life for a number of years. She had never remarried and, so far as I knew, had had no lovers. We were both hungry for it. We fucked our heads off.

There was a strange interlude during which she met with an unexpected rival. It was the piano. I had given up teaching the piano and decided to become more proficient at it myself. I rented a piano—it cost almost nothing then—and took to practicing at her place. She would lie abed waiting for me to quit. She was pregnant at the time, I remember, and probably needed much more attention than I gave her. Gone were the winter evenings when we sat by the kitchen stove, she in my lap, and fucked and fucked. We would take to bed and sleep before midnight. George, her son, was due home around midnight. We could always hear his footsteps as he mounted the stairs. When we did I would slide further down in the bed so that George would not notice me when he bent over his mother to kiss her goodnight. Actually he must have surmised that I was in there with her, but he never let on.

In the Cement Company, where I was still working, I had an idol named Ray Wetzler. He lived at the N.Y. Athletic Club and was something of an athlete. I revered the ground he walked on. Often he would question me about my sporting life and about "the widow," as I called her. He took an unusual interest in me, not because I was such a good worker—I wasn't at all!—but because I was a rum bird, utterly unlike my fellow workers. Once, when the Xerxes Society, of which I was a member, rented a hall to give a dance, I invited Ray Wetzler to come—expressly to meet Pauline. The next day I was ravished when he told me she was beautiful and didn't look her age. He liked her Southern accent as well as her figure.

So, there I was a twenty-one. An athlete of sorts, a pianist, an utter romantic, starving, and tasting sex to the full. (At the time I believed I was in love with her.) She adored me, that I am positive of. Under the skin I was a Puritan. I felt guilty—imagine it!—for screwing this woman old enough to be my mother. One day I broached the subject of marriage. She didn't take to it very kindly. She tried to point out to me the absurdity of it, above all,

260

that it would never work. But I was oblivious to her arguments. I decided that I would broach the subject to my mother—which shows what a naïve idiot I was.

I remember that I was sitting at the kitchen table. my mother was busy preparing a roast for dinner. She had a big carving knife in her hand. I had hardly got the words out of my mouth when she leaped toward me brandishing the big knife. "Not another word out of you," she screamed, "or I'll plunge this into your heart."

I made no attempt to answer back. I knew my mother—knew she was capable of anything when enraged. When I recounted the incident to Pauline she said very simply, "I knew it wouldn't work Harry, I know what your mother thinks of me. It's too bad." And with that we dropped the subject.

Meanwhile the pregnancy was becoming a matter of concern. Pauline was letting the months slip by, not from carelessness but from inability to have someone perform an abortion. There was also the question of money. (Always the question of money.)

I was still holding my job at the Cement Co. I hadn't received a raise, nor did I expect any. Married men with children were not earning any more than I at the time.

One day on coming home from work, I found her lying a-thwart the bed with legs dangling over the side of the bed. She was deathly pale and there were blood stains on the bed and on the floor.

I knelt over her and asked—"What happened?" She motioned weakly with her hand and in a very weak voice said: "Look in the bureau drawer."

I rushed to the bureau, opened the second drawer and there I saw the body of a child wrapped in a towel. I spread the towel and beheld a perfectly formed little boy, red as an indian. It was my son. I choked on the realization of that fact. And from that to tears at the thought of what she must have suffered. It seems to be the lot of women to suffer. For the pleasures of the flesh they offer us men, we give then in return only pain. If the abortion itself was a horror the aftermath was even worse. The question was how and where to get rid of the body. The doctor, whoever he was—I never saw him—decided to chop the body into pieces and throw the pieces down the toilet. Naturally the toilet got clogged—and the landlady discovered all. She was not only irate but shocked and threatened to notify the police. How Pauline talked her out of doing this I don't know, but the result was that we were obliged to move on short notice.

Oddly enough, I never found out who the doctor was. I began to suspect that Michael, the man whom Pauline paid every week for the loans he made her, had had a hand in it. How else was she able to get the money required for an abortion, done in one's home? Michael kept his accounts in a little book. He was very cordial, very affable, and always willing to advance more money, if needed. What Pauline paid him was a trifle—never more than a dollar, it seemed to me. I doubt if such a system exists today, unless it be among the blacks and the Mexicans. But as I have often said, the poverty of poor whites has always been unbeliev-able in this land of plenty. I spoke of the piano being a threat to Pauline's love life. Even more were the books I was constantly reading. She was thoroughly mystified not only by the size of the books I brought home but by the quantity I devoured.

"What good is all that reading going to do you?" she would ask. And I would shake my head and reply—"I don't know, I just like to read." In those days there was neither radio nor television. Occasionally we would go to the movies, the *silent* movies, which cost about a dime then. What wonderful movies we saw, what great actors!

Coming home we had to climb two flights of stairs to reach our flat. I shall never forget the joy it gave me to follow behind her and goose her. As I stroked her she began to whinny, like a horse. The moment we opened the door to our flat we were in the kitchen and the kitchen table was waiting for us. She would lie on the table with her legs around my neck and I would sock it in like a monomaniac. I don't know any woman but one who enjoyed sex more than Pauline—and in a very natural way. She always seemed to be in a good mood, laughing and joking, during these bouts. No neurotic problems, no intellectual problems. "Easy does it."

To eke out an existence we finally took in a boarder. He was from Texas and worked as a motorman on a street car. He was a huge, pleasant, simple-minded individual with whom we had no trouble getting along. All he demanded was his round steak and fried potatoes and a bed to sleep in.

On the floor below us lived a married couple we saw quite a bit of. They were middle-aged. He was Lou Jacobs and she was Lottie. She was an inveterate cigarette smoker and he a pipe smoker. I was strongly attracted to Lou Jacobs for several reasons. First of all, he was like a father to me; second, he was a great reader, a reader only of great books; and last but not least he had a wonderful, if sardonic, sense of humor. He was such a person as I imagined Ambrose Bierce to have been. Cynical but kind, sardonic and religious, he was a philosopher and teacher both. Many were the authors we discussed when we were not playing chess. Like Marcel Duchamp, he was a fantastically good player, who did not play according to the rules but by instinct and intuition. With him as with René Crevel, "no daring was fatal." He would give me all manner of pieces, except of course his queen. He would often open a game by advancing a pawn on the rook's file. He was thoroughly unpredictable. Apparently he and his wife had had some tragic misunderstanding some years ago—I believe he had caught her in bed with their chauffeur. As punishment he never again made love to her. He treated her in a super-polite (mock) manner, as if she were the queen of the earth, but hewouldn't touch her. She seemed to have a great respect for him, despite his cruel treatment of her. As for Pauline, his manner toward her was always one of great deference admiration and sympathy. He thought her beautiful and very feminine. (I often wondered later what their astrological signs were. In those days one heard very little of astrology.)

From some people you learn this, from others you learn that. From Lou Jacobs I learned many things.

I had been going with Pauline for almost three years now. Soon it would be my twenty-first birthday. And soon America would enter the First World War. I was still a faithful member of the Xerxes Society and still in love with Cora Seward. (In fact I've never gotten over it.) More and more my pals would poke fun at me for going with "the widow." Little did they know the delights an older woman can offer a young man. For not only was Pauline my mistress, she was also my mother, my teacher, my nurse, my companion, everything rolled into one. Though my companions felt she was much too old for me, Lou Jacobs didn't, nor Tex the motorman, nor Ray Wetzler, my idol.

Just before August 1914, an old buddy of mine, Joe O'Regan, happened on the scene. As usual, he came with some dough he had accumulated during his last job. Joe, incidentally, didn't find Pauline too old either. In fact, he took a shine to her from the start. It was a godsend of course that Joe had happened along when he did. The money which he handed over to me was no mean sum; it meant we could eat porterhouse once in awhile instead of plain round steak. For awhile all was ducky, we got along together, all of us, fine and dandy. But Joe, who was always horny, began making advances to Pauline in my absence. One day I came home to find her with tears in her eyes. Joe had been after her again. "I know you're his best friend," she began. "He idolizes you. But he should show more respect to me. He shouldn't try to betray his best friend."

I did my best to make excuses for Joe. I knew him to the ground. He would fuck his own sister if given the chance. He was just made that way. But he was also a lovable, generous guy.

One day came the news that war had broken out. (We had yet

to join the holocaust.) The war seemed to change everyone's life, even ours though we were not yet participants. Everything became more serious, more stern and drastic.

I forget exactly how or why Joe disappeared, but he did eventually. Anyway, I had now made the acquaintance of an oculist who believed one could dispense with glasses if one exercised the eyes and led an outdoor life. Because of his talk I got the notion to give up everything and go West, become a cowboy. It was a lousy, a mean thing to do, but I left Pauline without telling her a word of my intentions. I believe I wrote her from the Garden of Gods in Colorado, explaining things as best I could.

Needless to say, I never became a cowboy. I found a job on a lemon ranch in Chula Vista, California, where I threw dead branches on a fire all day long. I never rode a horse—at best I drove a sled harnessed to a jackass.

After a few months of this drudge work I decided to return to Brooklyn. The decision was made imperative through a chance meeting with Emma Goldman, the anarchist. It happened in this fashion.

One night a cowboy friend at the ranch said he was going to town (San Diego) to visit a whorehouse he knew. He asked if I cared to go along and I agreed.

When we arrived in San Diego the first thing I espied was a huge poster announcing that Emma Goldman was lecturing that very night on European authors of renown. That decided it for me. I told my friend I would go to the whorehouse some other time.

It was a world-shaking event for me to hear Emma Goldman talk of the writers I so greatly admired—Nietzsche, Tolstoi, Gorky, Strindberg, et al. It changed the whole course of my life.

I left the lecture happy in the knowledge that I was not to be a cowboy but a man of letters.

But how to return home without losing face? Finally I hit upon an idea. I wrote Pauline to send a telegram to my folks, as if from California, saying "Sorry to hear of mother's illness. Leaving immediately. Signed Henry."

My mother of course was not fooled by the telegram. It was she who met me at the gate, with a look in her eye that told me everything.

For awhile I lived at home again, but visited Pauline every night and often stayed the night with her.

She was the same as ever. Her son George had died while I was away—of tuberculosis. I think Tex the motorman had left too.

Though everything was just the same, as I said a moment ago, still it was not the same. More and more I realized that I must break the tie. I no longer thought of Cora Seward, only of being free. What helped was that I had met the woman who was to become my first wife. She was my piano teacher.

I was going with her a few months when finally America joined the Allies against the Kaiser. I had left Pauline again, this time for good—and again without any explanation. A despicable thing to do, as I realized later, but typical of me at that time and even later.

One morning I awoke in bed with my piano teacher and it dawned on me with a rush that I might possibly be drafted for the bloody war. That was the last thing on earth I wanted to happen. I sprang out of bed shouting "We've got to get married!" and off I rushed to the barber for a shave and haircut. We were married in jig time and I felt fairly secure about not going to war.

It was a misalliance from the start. Constant bickering and quarreling. I missed the harmony and serenity of my days with Pauline.

One night, as I was taking a stroll all by myself, I came across a cinema in which they were showing a foreign film I very much wanted to see.

I pushed the door open to go in and whom did I see standing in front of me with a flashlight but Pauline.

"Harry!" she cried and dragged me inside. She was weeping. She escorted me to a vacant seat and in a minute or two she joined me.

The tears were now streaming down her face.

"How could you do that to me?" she kept repeating.

I mumbled a few inanities, too moved to say much. I felt deeply guilty, deeply penitent. I had no excuse of any kind to offer. Escorting her to her new abode, where she worked as a maid, I managed to explain that I had married since leaving her. This brought on fresh tears, fresh sobs.

I was so distraught on leaving her that on the way home I decided I would invite Pauline to live with us. Why not? She had been a ministering angel to me. Why could I not reciprocate?

I could hardly wait to break the news to my wife. I might have known what a reception she would give my naïve suggestion. She not only treated it with ridicule (as who wouldn't?) but she made me out to be not only an idiot but a philanderer. In her mind I had invented this story of meeting Pauline in the cinema. She suspected I had been seeing her while I was "courting" her. (sic)

Despite the irony of the situation I kept on pleading with her. To soften my proposal I assured her I had no intention of sleeping with Pauline. I just wanted to offer her shelter and a bit of human kindness. I found myself talking to a stone wall. I became bitter and rancorous. I never forgave her for her "cruelty," as I called it. But that did no good for Pauline. I felt so ashamed of my failure to retrieve the situation that I never looked her up, never phoned her, never saw her again.

I have often wondered how she ended her days, for certainly she could not have lasted this long. I hope that Fate was kind to her.

That I was a son-of-a-bitch of the first water there is no doubt. Perhaps some of the ills I suffered since that time were meant as punishment for my behavior.

The worst of it all is that her good influence affected me not at all in my succeeding marriages. I was not made for marriage, that seem obvious. I was born to be a creative individual, a writer, no less, God save the mark. The only lesson I have learned in all these affairs is that an artist should never marry.

Miriam Painter

Miriam was her Christian name. Miriam Painter. I thought it a beautiful name then, about seventy-five years ago, and I still think so today.

We used to get out of school about the same time everyday—different schools but not far apart. Hers was on Moffatt Street and Evergreen Avenue and mine on Covert Street and Evergreen Avenue. Her way home obliged her to turn up my street—Decatur Street—which meant that soon we were walking and talking parallel to one another, she on one side of the street, I on the other.

She was somewhat like a faun; she had a loping gait which obliged me to maintain a steady trot to keep pace with her.

We only walked this way about one long block, from Evergreen Avenue to Bushwick Avenue. There she made an abrupt turn and we waved good-bye to each other.

Our conversation from one sidewalk to the other was never of any consequence. I haven't the slightest recollection of its content today, all I recall is her natural ebullience, her charm, her gaiety *and* what I took to be a special interest in *me*. The fact that she was three or four years older than I was flattering to me.

Epreuve d'Artiste   Early Music   Henry Miller 1973

The other girls her age weren't nearly as friendly or, if I may put it that way, as approachable.

Having seen her and talked with her, the day was made for me. It was like a certain famous musician, Pablo Casals, who after his walk each morning sat down to the cello to play some Bach. That set *him* up for the day.

There were girls my age whom I knew and played with but by comparison with Miriam Painter they seemed coarse and vulgar. Miriam was destined to be "a lady," I was certain of it. Perhaps it was this factor which kept our daily intercourse the width of my street. We never touched, never kissed—only sidewalk to side-walk.

She has remained in my memory for about seventy-five years now. It was not a prolonged friendship either. I would say it lasted a year or two at most. Nor was it an infatuation which possessed me, as it did so often later. No, it was more like a scene on the stage. She simply went through a door that led nowhere and never returned. I was in love with her (or her image) but not infatuated. Everything was delightful and yet of no great import. That's what I think now. But, am I not deceiving myself? Was there not something very significant in this seemingly trivial relationship?

Could it have been that it was my introduction to the enchant-ing nature of the female? It seems that all through my life women have played a dual role. Usually an affair would begin by our being good friends. Later sex would enter and then there was the devil to pay. But almost always my loves have begun with a fragrance, with the simple seductiveness of creatures from another world. An instinctive reaction. I never knew much in advance of the woman who would later drive me mad.

If my memory serves me right there was at that time on the New York stage a woman named Painter—or could it have been Fay Bainter? That may have contributed to making her name so attractive. At the corner of Decatur Street and Bushwick

271

Avenue there was a rather large vacant lot. It was surrounded by a high fence on which large billboards advertising theatrical and musical stars frequently appeared. Sometimes just the title of the play stuck in my crop for years, like *Rebecca of Sunnybrook Farm*, which I never did see. Or it might be the name of a great singer, like Madame Schumann-Heink or Mary Garden. Or Laurette Taylor or Nazimova. For some reason their names alone were magical. Certainly they were never talked about at home nor by my chums in the street.

What's in a name? you may ask. And I answer, *"Everything!"*

Marcella

She was related to me in some way, probably as a second cousin. We got to know each other when we were in our teens. Usually we met on holidays or birthdays at one of the relatives' homes.

I had been playing the piano for five or six years and wherever I went where there was a piano I carried a roll of sheet music with me. The music I carried around was of two sorts—popular songs and classical music, such as Grieg, Rachmaninoff and Liszt.

Marcella, who was usually present at the festivities, thought I played beautifully. She had a good voice and was familiar with all the songs in my music roll. She was gay, buoyant, thoroughly alive.

One day I asked her if I could take her to a movie—in Manhattan. She readily accepted. Returning to her home we stood in the vestibule a few minutes kissing and hugging. As we did so I mumbled, "You know Marcella, I think I am falling in love with you."

It was shortly after this I ran across the widow and had an affair which lasted a few years. No more family reunions, no

273

birthday celebrations any more. I had definitely cut with all that nonsense. And of course I completely forgot about Marcella.

Through one of my relatives I learned that she had taken up with a boorish chap who sold cars. Apparently they didn't get along together very well. And, so I was told, Marcella had changed considerably in the interim. For one thing she had taken to drink. And it seems that now and then she drank so heavily that she passed out. Another strange thing was that she continued to go with this nobody but never got married—and she had been brought up a strict Catholic.

So, from time to time, I got rumors of her doings. Always surprising and always unpleasant or disheartening. Since we traveled in totally different circles we never had a confrontation. Not since that evening I had taken her to the movies—long ago. Then suddenly a death occurred in the family and who attended the funeral but Marcella. She had changed greatly over the years. She looked heavier, coarser, somewhat sluttish.

It was after we had left the cemetery and gone to a beer garden for refreshments and drink that I managed to corner Marcella alone for a few moments.

I went up to her, greeted her warmly and asked in all innocence whatever in the world had come over her to change so.

To my utter astonishment she calmly replied, "You! It's all *your* fault!"

"Me?" I gasped. "How do you mean?"

"You told me once that you loved me and I believed you."

"And so?"

"I kept waiting for you!"

"You kept waiting all these years without ever letting me know?"

She nodded.

"And so that's why you took to drink?"

She nodded again.

"That's downright stupid!" I exclaimed. She burst into tears.

274

I added: "You know, Marcella, ignorance is forgivable, but not stupidity." And with that off my chest I turned on my heel and walked off.

About a year later I learned that she had died—in the county hospital. She had become a hopeless alcoholic.

Silently I mumbled to myself—"And it was all your fault, Mr. Henry. Be careful next time you say 'I love you' to anyone."

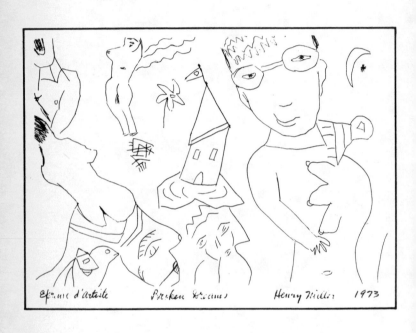

Épreuve d'artiste   Broken Dreams   Henry Miller   1973

Camilla

Her full name was Camilla Euphrosnia

Fedrant. She had black blood in her veins, or should I say white blood? I thought of her as a mulatto, a term one doesn't hear anymore for people of mixed blood.

At the time I was the employment manager of the messenger department of the Western Union Telegraph Company; in New York City. Camilla was my assistant. How she got this job I have completely forgotten. I *believe* that she had appealed to the president of the company. She had excellent qualifications—a college graduate and of a very good college, a refined manner, quick on the trigger and very good-looking. In addition a good talker.

She sat opposite me at a double desk. Often, when I had finished hiring for the day, I would just sit and chat with her. She was a most intelligent young lady who really had no need for the excellent college education she received.

Shortly after she became my assistant we began hiring women to deliver telegrams in the tall buildings in which a Western Union office was usually located on the ground floor. The management thought this would lend an added touch. There was no feminist movement behind the innovation.

One day Camilla said to me, "Mr. Miller, I think some of these women messengers are getting out of line. I have received a number of complaints from our clients."

"What are you getting at?" I asked.

"I mean, to put it bluntly," said Camilla, "that some of these women have taken the job to ply their trade—prostitution."

To my surprise I found myself saying, "I can't blame them. If I were in their place I might do the same thing. You know this is considered to be about the lowest job on earth."

To this she replied, "I can think of lower ones—dishwasher, garbage collector and so on. I am not condemning these girls, or women, but I think Mr. So-and-so (meaning the general manager) ought to be informed."

I disputed this. I went on to tell her how in the old employment office, I used to pretend to offer a woman a job and then screw her after hours in the clothing department.

"I think you were a cad," she said calmly, somewhat surprised by my easy sense of morality. She knew, on the other hand, how many boys I helped out of my own pocket. She knew that they venerated me and came to me with their problems.

"Don't let's talk about it anymore," I said. "How about having dinner with me tonight?" She readily agreed. We had been doing this for some time now. Usually I picked a cozy little joint in the Village where there was a dance floor and perhaps a trio of musicians. Between courses we would dance, if you could call it that. Actually what we were doing was having a dry fuck, as they called it. Camilla was what we would call "sexy" today. (I thought of her as a lascivious bitch.) I never knew exactly where she hailed from but surmised it was from Cuba or somewhere in the West Indies. I mentioned that she was a mulatto. She was so pale that she could pass for white. Besides her pale skin there was her speech and her deportment which was far superior to that of the American white woman, even the welleducated ones. If it was a pleasure to dance with her it was even more of a pleasure to converse with her. She was extremely well-read, not only in English, but in Spanish and French. I think she secretly felt that she had the makings of a writer in her.

Among the youngsters I hired and with some of whom I was on rather intimate terms was a chap called Blackie. He was fifteen or sixteen, handsome, intelligent, and somewhat ahead of his years. Without my telling him he guessed that I was rather fond of my assistant. One day he took me aside to tell me he had some interesting news for me. Just how it began I have forgotten. But in some bizarre way he had made the acquaintance of Camilla's girl friend, a white aristocrat from New England. And he had put the boots to her, young as he was. She was in her early thirties. He ended the story by wondering aloud if they could possibly be lesbians.

I noticed that Camilla did not show any liking for my little friend and so I never broached the subject to her.

It hadn't taken her long to observe that I was rather generous. When I did not have the means to lend some of my poor messengers money I would borrow the necessary from anyone in the office. Camilla wondered if I wasn't possibly too openhanded with these poor youngsters. I told her no, that one could never be generous enough with those in need. She was of a different opinion absolutely, which surprised me, since she had Negro blood in her veins and had come up the hard way. I tried to tell her that white people sometimes had it harder than Negroes. This she strongly doubted. I told her I had been a panhandler, a beggar, a bum. She said I was *different,* that I had stooped to such levels because I wanted to be a writer.

She was extremely kind-hearted, and often helped me in odd ways. Sometimes I would say, "That was mighty white of you!" to which she would always retort, "You mean mighty black!" She added that she thought it something of a weakness in her people to be so willing to lend a hand. I replied by observing that I had not noticed that black people were so helpful with one another. I

279

said I could not see that the blacks helped the blacks any more than the Jews helped the Jews or, for that matter, the whites the whites.

She seemed taken aback by my remarks. To make it worse I ventured to say that if I were pushed far enough I would not only steal but murder. This was too much for her Christian conscience. (She was Catholic, moreover.)

I mentioned these talks about black and white because thus far no one had openly said anything about Camilla's antecedents. One day, however, one of those rats who are to be found in every organization—ass-suckers is the name for them—discovered that my assistant was part Negro. And he promptly conveyed the information to my boss, who was the general manager. This was the man who had hired me and who always treated me with deference.

Over the telephone he told me what he had learned about Camilla, adding a hypocritical way, that "We all know the company has made it a rule never to employ black people. I think," he added, "we will have to let her go." He didn't say when or how.

I promptly told Camilla what had happened. Almost immediately she said, "Don't worry, Mr. Miller. I will go to see Newcomb Carlton," the then president of the company and the one I suspected who had hired her in the first place. "He wouldn't *dare* to fire me," she added.

Sure enough, the next thing I knew Camilla was offered a job in a Western Union branch in Havana—a better job with more money.

If my memory serves me right she refused the job and resigned. What became of her I never knew for only a few weeks later I quit my job myself.

Melpo

Shortly after I returned from Greece I became a guest at the home of Gilbert and Margaret Neiman in Beverly Glen. The house they occupied was just a little shack off the road. It was there I began making watercolors for anything you wanted to give me—a dollar or two, an old coat, a pair of shoes, anything whatever. I was in terrible straits due to the banning of the books I had written in France. The idea of taking a job never occurred to me. I just kept on writing and painting little watercolors at night. I was there only a couple of months when one day I received an unexpected visit from a Frenchman. He came to invite me to a reception being given by a Greek woman in some fashionable hotel a few miles away. He said she would send a chauffeur and limousine to fetch me. She was very eager to have me come as she had read my book on Greece and was deeply touched by it. He added that she was beautiful and generous. It wasn't difficult to convince me to accept the lady's invitation. The question was—what to wear? I had only the one suit for all occasions and it was worn threadbare. My shoes needed repairing. As I knew no one from whom I could borrow a suitable outfit I decided to go in what I had.

The hotel turned out to be rather a swanky one; the table was set outdoors, there was a dance floor and musicians and most of the guests had already arrived.

The moment I arrived Melpo came forward to greet me. She was all smiles and expressed her gratitude for what I had done for her country. (She meant writing *The Colossus of Maroussi*.) I was so flattered my head began to spin. This before having any champagne. To my astonishment she insisted that I sit beside her at the dinner table as the guest of honor.

She was not only beautiful as the Frenchman had said, but full of grace and delicacy. In many ways she reminded me of Anaïs Nin from whom I was now definitely estranged. Like Anaïs she appeared frail but was actually quite strong and healthy. She was also extremely amiable. I had thought I would be too shy and awkward but she put me at ease immediately. It seemed to me she was trying to apologize for her wealth and the seeming ostentation. I sensed that at bottom she was simple, direct and uneasy with her riches. The Frenchman had told me she was the wife of a prominent Greek ship-owner, a rival of Onassis. That had frightened me a bit when he mentioned it but now here I was in her presence, and feeling perfectly at home.

It didn't take me long to discover that she was most intelligent and extremely well-read. She spoke four or five languages to boot.

How she learned it I don't know but she was cognizant of the fact that I was down on my uppers. This fact only drew her to me more closely.

When the music started up she turned to me and asked if I would like to dance. She had already pushed her chair back. Out of politeness I said yes but quickly explained that I was not much of a dancer. She said it didn't matter. To my surprise I found myself doing very well on the floor.

Fortunately the dance music was old-fashioned. And I found I hadn't forgotten how to waltz or do the two-step. As we danced we talked; she volunteered or confided some surprising information about herself—to put me more at ease, I surmised.

Everything went beautifully. Before the evening ended she asked if she could accompany me home. She said she was a poor sleeper and used to being up all hours of the night. And so she escorted me to my dump in Beverly Glen.

On saying good-bye she asked if I minded if she were to drop by occasionally of an evening. She would like to take me for a spin and *talk* with me.

She would always telephone first to make sure I was free. Then her chauffeur and limousine would arrive to pick me up. Sometimes she would ask if she could have dinner with me. That always meant dining in some good modest restaurant. Before the meal was ended she would slip me the money to pay the bill under the table. It was usually double the sum needed. I said we loved to talk. She was an excellent conversationalist and always had plenty to relate. She had traveled over most of the globe—was equally at home in Rio as in London, Paris, New York or Tokyo. Our talk was always of books and places, two endless subjects. During all this time, and even later, I never so much as kissed her or embraced her. I venerated her. In the beginning she was surprised to learn I didn't have a car. "How do you get around?" she asked. "I walk," I replied. What walks! Back and forth to the Village, with a laundry bag slung over my shoulders. Up into the Holywood Hills and back at three or four in the morning. Only once did a driver offer me a lift and that was a rather distinguished film director who was living with Marlene Dietrich at the time. The others who passed me by never game me so much as a tumble. I was just another bum to them, I guess.

Well aware of my poverty stricken condition, Melpo nevertheless pretended not to be aware of it. Until one day I received a telephone call from her. It was almost a monologue. The burden of it was that she could no longer bear to see me living in such poverty, I who was one of the greatest writers in the world. I who had done so much for her people, and she who was so wealthy and had need of nothing. What she wished to do for me and, she insisted, it was the *least* she could do, was to get me a car, some new clothes, and put a modest sum of money in the bank for me.

Needless to say, I was so overwhelmed by her suggestion (or request) that I was almost speechless. I begged her not to do anything immediately, but to let me sleep on it. And that night I had the strangest dream in all my life. I dreamt that God had deigned to talk to me. He was telling me not to worry, that He had an eye on me and that I would never again be in dire need. In fact, He added, you shall always have everything you need.

I don't mean to say that those were His exact words, but they were the gist of them. In a sense He told me much more, things I would blush to put on paper.

Naturally I awoke next morning not only stunned but jubilant. I called Melpo right after breakfast and related the dream to her, adding—"You realize now, I hope, that I can't accept your most generous offer. I don't really need a thing anyway. I have what most people lack and you know that. But I thank you from the bottom of my heart."

Shortly after this happening Melpo had to leave for New York to join her husband. A month or two later I had a letter from her from Paris. Once in a blue moon I hear from her. I believe she divorced her husband and was living with another man somewhere in the vicinity of Paris. We remain eternal friends. I hope she is still alive to read what I have written about her.

How wonderful, I think to myself, that I never attempted to make love to her. Could she possibly have offered me more by offering her body as well?

If it truly was God whom I spoke to in my sleep, then it most certainly was she who inspired God, sacreligious though this may sound.

Sevasty

I believe it was some time after knowing
Melpo that I fell into the clutches of Sevasty. A friend of mine
pointed her out to me at the library where she was working. He
added, as if to clinch it—"She's Greek."

Yes, Sevasty was Greek but born in America. Her mother,
who was about the same age as myself, happened to be also born
on December 26, my birthday. Her mother was thoroughly
Greek and somewhat fearsome—to me, at least.

The first mistake I made was to pronounce Sevasty's name
wrong. I called her (on the phone) Se*vas*ty instead of *Sev*asty.

I was still living in the little cottage (the Green House) in
Beverly Glen. I was still poor as a church mouse, and it goes
without saying, minus a car. Still footing it—no matter where.

Now Sevasty at that time lived somewhere in the Hollywood
Hills—a distance of at least seven or eight miles. I was courting
her assiduously and always on foot, as I have just remarked. It
was an endurance test. Often I did not get home until 4:00 in the
morning. Weary, footsore, and often defeated.

Yet we had great love scenes, either in the yard of her house
or in the rear of the Green House. Passionate love scenes, which

285

left both of us exhausted. Yet never any sexual intercourse, for Sevasty had an obsession about *not* making love. Seems she had only recently divorced a young Greek who was more like a stud horse than a human being. In addition she had undergone a hysterectomy and was mortally afraid of growing a beard and having piano legs.

I have not mentioned her looks or her figure—both ravishing and tantalizing. Essentially she was the embodiment of sex. Sometimes, in mushing it up with her, she would appear to swoon.

At this particular period there was also another guest (or freeloader) at the Green House and his name was Dudley. Tall, handsome, talented (he both wrote and painted). To Dudley my affair with Sevasty was something of a bad joke. He knew that she completely dominated me. And I made no bones about it. I was at her beck and call, as they say. One day when she had written or telephoned me to get in touch with her—I believe it was for 2:00 P.M. sharp—Dudley suggested that we go to a bar before calling her. At the bar he asked if I wanted to put up with her nonsense perpetually. And I of course answered "No!" "Then listen to me," he began. "See that big clock back of the bar? Let's wait till the hands say ten after two and then go home. Don't call her! Are you game?"

Though it was torture for me, I did as he had urged, and to my surprise, went back home with him feeling quite normal—in fact, I should say, *relieved*.

Next day I received a special delivery letter from her, just as Dudley had predicted, asking in sorrowful words if something had happened to prevent my telephoning her. She signed off "with much love." All of this was certainly a great *soulagement*, as the French say, but still I was under her spell. I ate, drank and slept Sevasty. It was Sevasty this and Sevasty that. Everyone in the neighborhood was aware of my infatuation.

Then one day, like out of the blue, appeared a perfect stranger who said he would like to help me, if I would permit him. I said "How?" And he replied: "I would suggest that you have a talk with Swami Prahbavanada." I recognized the name, having been invited several times by ardent disciples to visit the ashram where the Swami lived and lectured.

"Why don't you telephone and ask if the Swami will see you?" said the stranger.

Why not? said I to myself. And so a few minutes later picked up the phone and asked for the Swami. To my great surprise he answered the phone himself. "What can I do for you?" he asked immediately. I told him that I was in a desperate plight and needed very much to have a few words with someone like himself. To my utter amazement he responded by saying, "Come over at once if you can. I will be very happy to see and talk with you."

I made some excuse for not visiting him that afternoon and asked if he could possibly see me about ten o'clock the next morning. His reply was swift and cordial. "By all means," he said. "Come any time that suits you."

I went to bed that night somewhat elated. After all, the proposed meeting was exactly what I needed. I wanted someone to listen to me *seriously*.

Promptly at ten the next morning I knocked at his door. He opened it with a warm smile and started to shake hands with me. But I quickly informed him that I had only come out of politeness. I added that something had occurred during the night and my problem had disappeared. "I'm sorry," I said, "But I don't have any need of you now."

To which he quickly replied, "But how do you know *I* don't have need of *you*." And so saying he grasped my arm and led me into his quarters.

I found that I had no need to go into details about Sevasty. I simply told him the problem had resolved itself in my sleep of its own accord. What I forgot to tell him was that his words, his manner of speaking over the phone had probably been the trigger which produced my release.

And so, as I said, we wasted no time on Sevasty and my foolishness, but began to talk of things of greater import. I remember telling him of my great love for Swami Vivekananda and Ramakrishna among other great souls. We rambled on for about an hour, pretty much as if we had known one another all our lives.

I left his presence feeling I had made a real friend. I remember particularly that he had scrupulously avoided urging me to attend the meetings, that he had shoved nopropaganda on me. Instead he had accepted me just as I was, another human being.

A short time after this exhilarating event I found myself living in Big Sur, where I remained seventeen years.

I had married again and was the father of two wonderful children. After being in Big Sur about a year I received a letter from Sevasty asking if she could visit me. I naturally assented.

She arrived looking just as beautiful as ever but without the powers of seduction she had wielded before. I took her for a long walk through the woods, during which we engaged in a serious but most friendly talk. When she got ready to leave she turned to me with an expression I had never before observed and said, "You are not only a great writer but a great man."

The hero of the romance was of course the good Swami Prahbavananda. Bless his name!

Aunt Anna

I must have been twelve or fourteen when Aunt Anna, as my mother called her, first appeared on the horizon.

Actually she was not my aunt, nor my mother's. Perhaps she may have been something like a second cousin to my mother. In some mysterious way she was related to the woman my mother always referred to as a monster. And her brother was that half-wit whose arm had been bitten off by a horse—so the story went.

She was married to a local politician, a crude specimen, whom my mother detested. As a matter of fact, he was quite a decent sort, as I discovered later in life. Typical of the politician then and now. How he ever got to marry his angelic creature called Aunt Anna is beyond me.

There was something very special about Aunt Anna. (My mother, by the way, always referred to her as Annie, not Anna. Anna belonged to the aristocracy of Tolstoi's famous novel.) Anna's visits to our house were few and far between. My mother always seemed to spy her coming through the gate in the street. In an almost reverential tone, she would turn quickly to me and say: "O, Henry, Aunt Anna is here. Go to the door and open it for her!"

I of course would spring to my feet, only too happy to open the door for Aunt Anna. She would always embrace me warmly, which would make me blush. As I said, I was about thirteen and she was a woman in her late twenties. To me she had no age, nor sex either. She was simply angelic, not of this world. I suppose she was what is called beautiful, but I was impressed by other qualities which were not exclusively feminine. In short, she was of the airs, as the Greeks would say, a creature not only ethereal but possibly celestial.

All through her visit with my mother I would sit and stare at her. She was probably aware of my adoration for after she had finished talking with my mother she would address herself to me. And in a way that seemed (to me at least) very private. What we discussed I no longer remember but it seemed to be intimate, very confidential.

Before my eyes there sat a woman who was *different*. The difference was on the side of the angels. (This reminds me of seeing Greta Garbo many years after her stage and screen career had ended. It was one of her early films and I had brought with me an Israeli actress who had never seen a Garbo film. The moment Garbo appeared my young Israeli friend gave a gasp, as if she had been stabbed. As for me, the tears quickly came to my eyes. I wept silently and unashamedly. I wept because of her most unusual beauty and also for her grace and skill as a performer.)

At the age I was at the time, I was still too young to be stage struck by any celebrities. I had never entered a good Broadway theatre, only the cheesy local ones which left no impression on me.

Why was Anna so different from other women I knew? Unfortunately the only women I was cognizant of were my mother's friend or relative. Thinking of them (later) I remarked the differences in speech, in gait, in gestures, in posture. My mother's cronies were mostly Germanic, and in Brooklyn at that time the German element was not noted for grace and charm. Quite the contrary.

Yet Anna was of German descent and came from a most provincial suburb. But Anna spoke like an angel; Anna *looked* like an angel, if I may say so. Thoroughly feminine, there was the additional quality which set her off from others. Only a few years later and I would be stumbling on the works of that little known nineteenth century author, Marie Corelli. Anna belonged to the hierarchy of those extraordinary female characters whom Corelli invented out of the whole cloth. Most of them were tinged with divinity. Whence came these creatures whom we are destined to meet usually only once in a lifetime. Like those unknown and most invisible creatures who swarm all about us and whom we sense not, so there are these earthly-heavenly bodies who influence our whole lives yet we fail to acknowledge them. In certain European countries there are what is known as "the little people." No one but the mad or the insane have ever seen or spoken to one, yet there is a tacit agreement among the common people that these mythical creatures truly exist.

All my life I wittingly or unwittingly have used Anna as a yardstick to detect others of her ilk. I have even had the great good fortune to live with one or two. Just as we can spot a holy man by the lustrous spherical orbs in his head so we can detect the presence of the angelic ones, no matter how they dress or look or behave.

Are we not more powerfully affected by the things or beings we refuse to acknowledge as real? Is it not precisely the unknown which leads us ever onward and upward? Goethe called it *"das ewige weibliche"* (the eternal feminine). We have the eyes to recognize them but not the sight. They are here among us "on loan," so to speak.

Facing East — Henry Miller 1944

Florrie Martin

The Martins lived only a few doors away from when we lived in "the old neighborhood"—Williamsburg, Brooklyn. Their daughter Florence and Carrie Sauer brought me to the police station one day for using bad language. Only my mother and her mother called her Florence. Everyone else referred to her as Florrie, which suited her better.

When we moved from the old neighborhood to "the street of early sorrows" in the Bushwick Section, we were soon followed by the Martin family, which included Ole Man Martin and his son Harry who was a year or two older than I, but slightly retarded for his age. Ole Man Martin, as everyone called him, was a character. He made a living working for the big hotels in Manhattan, which is to say, keeping them free of rats and mice. To do this he used two ferrets, which he carried in the pockets of his tan overcoat, a coat that only came to the knees and was already long out of style. His wife was an ardent church-goer with a sad and pious expression most of the time. Like my parents, she was a Lutheran. But my parents never set foot inside a church whether Lutheran, Methodist, Catholic or Presbyterian.

I was now about sixteen or seventeen and Florrie Martin must have been twenty-three or twenty-four. She was attractive and very blonde. She would ask me to take her to the movies or to a dance or some festival or other. And always, in the vestibule of her home, she would give me a long, slobbery kiss. I was not used to that treatment from older women. It set me afire and made me a frequent visitor at the home of the Martins. It must have been my last year in high school for I was already a member of the celebrated Xerxes Society. I was also a pal of her brother Harry who was something of a trial to his parents—a "loafer" and a "good-for-nothing," they called him. Harry took a liking to me and showed me "the other side of life," so to speak. It was through him that I first saw a burlesque show, the type which no longer exists. I was thoroughly shocked and completely enchanted; in fact I became an habitué of burlesque from then on. (And have never regretted it.) Harry also taught me to shoot pool and throw dice for drinks at the bar. It amused him to see me catch on so quickly.

The family were very friendly to any and everyone, at least so long as he or she was a church member. They always invited me to have coffee and cake or ice cream.

The more I saw Florrie the more I adored her. She was always radiant, always helpful and never indulged in criticism as did my folks. Without realizing it I fell madly in love with her.

The Xerxes Society... It was customary for us to meet at one another's homes once every two weeks or so. This time it happened to be at my house. Somehow this evening things didn't go off as usual. There was an air of restraint among the twelve members, provoked probably by my admonition not to make too much noise. I urged this much against the grain, only because my mother had begged me to have more consideration for the neighbors.

During a lull one of the fellows asked me if I wouldn't play for them. He said he heard that I was making fabulous progress at the piano. I readily agreed and sat down to play Liszt's *Second Hungarian Rhapsody*, the only one of his I knew. I did it with verve and dash and to my amazement was roundly applauded. "Encore, encore!" they shouted. Flattered that they thought so well of my style, I consented to play another. This time it was either Schumann or Rachmaninoff. I forget which. I rather suspect it was Schumann because I remember that as I ended the piece I was in a very sober poetic mood—*hors de moi-même,* so to speak. Yes, I sat there a moment or two after the closing notes in a semi-trance. The music had enchanted me. This time the applause was less vehement. Suddenly the enchantment was broken by some raucous voice demanding to know if I still saw Florrie Martin and how was it going. This was followed by other voices, one asking me if I was getting my end in, another if she was a good lay. Soon all the club members began laughing hilariously. And with this I suddenly wheeled around on my piano stool and began weeping. Not just crying, but weeping and sobbing at the same time. One of the members came over to me, put his hand on my shoulder, and said—"Jesus, Hen, don't take it so hard; we were only joking!"

This brought on a fresh burst of tears and sobs. (Only two or three times in my whole life have I wept as I did that night.)

What had happened? What caused this display of emotion? Partly the music, I suppose, and partly the fact that my love for Florrie Martin was of a purity these callow idiots would never comprehend. But primarily, I would say, because I was an adolescent. And in many ways I have remained an adolescent all my life. (I didn't know until the other day, for example, that I was still capable of a similar show of emotion.)

"The age of puberty," I believe they call it. A period of total contradictions; one day hot, the next day cold; a fervid friend today, tomorrow a heartless son-of-a-bitch. And so on. The way older folk regard this period in their progeny is painful. They refer it to as "growing up," "becoming a man." Nothing could be farther from the truth. It is the period when one loses one of man's most precious qualities—*innocence*. And what a loss this is only poets know. To become a man in this stinking civilization is tantamount to becoming a rat. It means retrogression, not evolution.

All the knowledge and experience on which man sets such value seems to me like utter nonsense. Growth does not mean arterio-sclerosis. Growth means what the French call *èpanouissement*. Indeed, a French saying sums it up to a T. *Pourri avant d'etre muri*. Rotten before ripened.

How strange, when I look back on this incident, that the Puritan in me should later have given birth to books that shocked the world. And yet perhaps not so strange. There is a Greek word which a learned friend of mine left with me as a little token of affection. It is ENANTIODROMOS. It means the process whereby a thing turns into its opposite, as for example, love into hate, and so on. May it not also be possible that we are never one but always two? How otherwise can we explain a Gilles de Rais, the valiant supporter of Joan of Arc, and the monster who emptied whole villages of young men or boys whom he raped and then murdered?

Edna Booth

Edna was the first female writer in my
life. We met in the Catskills (the Borscht route today) in a town
called Athens where my parents had decided to spend the
summer vacation. Edna had a sister called Alice and I had a friend
named George from my neighborhood in Brooklyn. We were
about sixteen, the two sisters in their late twenties. We all
resided at a boarding house, which was the custom in those
days. It was the period of Rag Time and one of my favorite
pieces which I rendered fairly well was "The Maple Leaf Rag."

The difference in age between us boys and the two attractive
women didn't seem to matter except that no sexual intercourse
was permitted by the women. (We were much too young, in
their opinion.) But this did not prevent them from tongue kissing. Every night we met at the same secret place and held our
"orgies" there. Orgy it was for me. I had never had anything to
do with a woman as much older than I as Edna Booth. She was
an expert at manipulating her tongue. (I couldn't even touch her
boobs or her cunt—just this tongue kissing *ad nausseam* and a
warm embrace.) Sometimes we broke the routine and took the
girls (or women) for long walks during which Edna told us some-

thing about her writing and a great deal more about the books she had read.

And it is because of the books that I can never forget Edna Booth. Whether she had read the classics I don't recall, but she knew the contemporary best writers along with some of the nineteenth century ones like Balzac, de Maupassant, Ibsen, Strindberg, Gautier, Verlaine (not Rimbaud!) and so on. Her favorite American writer was Theodore Dreiser. She also knew a few of the great Russian writers, like Maxim Gorky and Gogol and Tolstoi, but not Dostoievsky. Nor did I at the time. This greatest of all writers (in my humble opinion) I only came to know a year or two later.

It was about five in the afternoon and the "event" took place at the corner of Broadway and Kosciuso Street, Brooklyn. I have told the story before, but I am not ashamed to repeat it. Mahler repeated himself, so did Chopin and Beethoven—why should I worry about what the "critikers" say? Anyway, I was passing a dress shop and in the show window stood a young man about my age who was dressing a model. He caught my glance and beckoned me to step in. Which I did. He gave me his name—Benny Einstein—and asked if I would wait a few minutes as he was quitting work and lived nearby. Maybe I would accompany him to his home? I readily agreed and in the space of a few minutes he suddenly popped the question—"Have you read Dostoievsky?" (He must have divined that I was a literary bloke!)

"Dostoievsky?" I repeated. "Never heard of him." I added that I *had* read some Russians but not this bird.

"You never read *Crime and Punishment*?" he blurted out. As if such a thing could not be. "No," I confessed. "What else did he write?"

And so Benny went on to name the leading ones: *The Brothers Karamazov*, *The Possessed* and *The Idiot*.

I didn't realize till some weeks later what a heavy dose he had given me. Dear reader, if I seem to be making a fuss over a trifle, believe me I am not. Just as I never tire of recounting my accidental meeting with Emma Goldman in San Diego, so I never tire of rehearsing this introduction to Dostoievsky.

Looking back on the episode it seems to me that that late afternoon in Brooklyn the sun must have stood still in the heavens for a few moments.

But to return to Edna Booth. She in turn was amazed at all the authors I had read. And I had read a good deal for a guy my age. Particularly *foreign* authors, in translation of course.

Her sister Alice was quite a different type. She had auburn hair and freckles. Edna looked more like an actress and despite her sexy attitude held herself with dignity. I shall never forget how one afternoon I encountered Alice as we both were making our way through a field of oats or barley. As I bent forward to give her a friendly kiss I noticed a look of terror pass over her features *and*—suddenly she bolted. I immediately gave chase. Now Alice didn't hold the slightest interest for me—in fact, I took her for a nit-wit—but running away as she did, as if I were threatening to rape her, got my dander up. I ran and ran until I caught up with her. Then I took her by the arms, looked her square in the eyes and said: "You idiot, what's wrong with you? Did you think I was going to rape you?"

She hung her head and answered meekly, "Yes."

This only enraged me the more. For one brief moment I dallied with the idea of throwing her down and giving her a good fuck.

It wasn't her virtue that preserved her but her stupidity. I gave her one long look of disgust and turned on my heel to walk quietly back to the boarding house.

A little later that afternoon I ran into Edna. I said nothing about the incident with Alice. Instead I invited her to play a game of croquet with me. Croquet was still in fashion then. It's a game that a woman or a youngster can often play as well as a man. Somehow the chase after Alice had set my sexual glands working. As we moved from one wicket to another, as Edna bent over to pick up a ball or place a good shot I would deftly and gently fondle her rump. To my surprise she made no resistance. Because she was so much older than I and so much wiser I never dreamed one could take such an approach with a young lady. It was an eye-opener for me. It struck me later that the motto for such behavior should be: "Do it first and apologize later."

But with Edna there was no need to apologize. She knew me inside out, better than I knew myself.

The vacation over, we all returned to Brooklyn. Edna and her sister lived in some more aristocratic part of town than did my folks. We exchanged a few "literary" letters, and that was all. And then one bitter cold New Year's Day while out New Year's calling with the other members of the club (The Xerxes Society), whom should I run across—in a trolley car—but Edna, her sister and father and mother. I was a bit embarrassed to be caught out with such louts and bounders but Edna gave it no never mind. She noticed that most of us carried musical instruments and so she graciously asked that we get out our fiddles and what not and play something we liked.

"What, *here* in the trolley?" we asked, or shouted rather, for we were all a bit lit up. "Certainly," she replied. "You're not breaking any law by playing music in a public conveyance." That said, we got out our instruments, tuned up and—"What will we play?" shouted one of the guys.

With that George Gifford struck up, "We are such fine musicians . . ."

It made a hit with the passengers in the trolley. "More, more!" they yelled. And like that for fifteen or twenty minutes we regaled the bunch.

We only stopped because we were nearing our destination. As we stood up to go Edna beckoned me to approach. As I leaned over her seat to shake hands and say good-bye she pulled me to

300

her and gave me a rousing smack on the lips. Then, under her breath, she added: "I've never forgotten Athens!"

Needless to say that did it for me. I drank like a fish everywhere we called that New Year's Day and tumbled into bed drunk as a pope.

I must add that much much later, when I visited the real Athens, I thought of Edna and the Borscht route. And of Dostoievsky whom she had not yet read.

Epreuve d'artiste   The Head   Henry Miller   1973

Louella

I don't think Louella was her given name, I think she christened herself Louella because her real name was so difficult to pronounce. She came from a strange part of the world, one that few Europeans or Americans ever get to. As a matter of fact it was somewhere in the vicinity of Gurdjiev's birthplace. As a consequence she spoke a number of strange tongues—Armenian, Arabic, French, Turkish, Bulgarian, Russian and so on. And English as well. Indeed, her English was superb; she had been educated in a college somewhere in Lebanon, I believe. I never met her in the flesh but we corresponded regularly.

It began by my receiving a fan letter (with a photo) from her, after she had read *Cancer* and *Capricorn*. It was a fantastic letter, thoroughly perceptive, sensitive and beautifully written, in English, with lapses into French, Spanish and Portuguese. When I had these foreign language parts translated for me I discovered that she was not only well read, highly sophisticated, but somewhat of a sex addict as well. In fact, these passages sounded more like the work of a man.

I said we never met. She was constantly traveling, it seemed.

And to the ends of the earth. One day I might receive a letter from Hokkaido, the next from Tasmania or Rio de Janeiro. Nothing surprised me anymore.

She had an ebullient nature, always enthusiastic about life, but rather disheartened about the career she had chosen. It seems she had tried a number of fields, all of an artistic nature, and had finally wound up as a sculptress. Unfortunately, as she put it. She had very little talent for sculpture. She thought she might have done better to be a belly dancer or a night club singer. She was lucky not to depend for a living on her earnings as an artist. Just how she managed I never really knew, but I suspected it was through men. She had the morals of a bitch. *She* picked up the men she slept with and not vice versa. Except in one notable case. She claimed to have had an affair with Gurdjiev, maintaining that he had bewitched her.

A great part of our correspondence was centered about her attitude toward men—her sex life. She was perfectly frank about her tastes, her desires, etc.

For a brief period she wondered if she ought not try writing instead of her "half-assed sculptures," as she called them. She had read several books by Joseph Conrad and especially admired his use of English, which as is generally known, was the language he knew least well, yet he decided to write his books in this language. She asked what I thought of her English, to which I honestly replied that it was excellent. But then I added that that was no reason to choose it forher work. In fact, I urged her to write in some little known language, one she was proficient in.

"And who would translate me?" she demanded.

I answered, "Some scholarly Englishman, most likely."

She didn't like the idea of being translated. Anyway, after a series of letters discussing the possibility of her becoming a writer, she suddenly dropped the thought completely.

In many ways she might well have been dubbed "the Queen of Baluchistan." She was beautiful, exotic, gifted and a perfect snare for men. She lived not so much by her wits as by her cunt. She believed, or professed to believe, that God has given women cunts for two reasons—one for enjoyment and the other for survival. If she found herself short of cash and needed to take a cab she would seduce the cab driver. If a cop tried to give her a ticket for a traffic misdemeanor she would say "Tear it up! Let's go somewhere when we can have a private fuck!" And so on and so forth. Though she fucked for money—for a half dollar even— there was nothing of the whore about her. She thought the world was composed largely of idiots, bigots, and sadists. It didn't matter to her how she went about the business of survival. Only, no 9:00 to 5:00 job, please! *That* she considered insane. And so, as they say in burlesque—first she danced on one leg, then the other; and between the two she made a living. She took excellent care of her pussy. She knew all about the danger of venereal diseases but also knew that today they were curable without too much fuss. She was thoroughly realistic and at the same time an idealist. for example, in any sex relation involving love or affection she always did the choosing. The man had not only to be handsome, but virile and intelligent—a cultured gentleman, so to speak. And since she traveled here, there, and everywhere it was not too difficult to meet a man with her requirements. Sometimes they would remain together for months, especially if he was well-heeled and had charm. The one thing she could not abide was vulgarity. She had been over a good part of the U.S. and thought Texas the worst state of all. "Dumb brutes," she called the natives. Or "arrogant ignoramuses."

One may wonder, since we conducted such a long, drawn-out correspondence, why she never visited me. All during this time I was married and the father of two delightful children. Louella did not want to throw a monkey wrench into my domestic life. (She knew I would fall for her immediately.) Little did she know that it was the unhappiest marriage I had yet been through. Instead of the bliss she pictured, my life was more of an Inferno à la Strindberg. The only thing that kept me from suicide were my two children whom I adored.

So Louella kept knocking about the world, meeting men, having adventures of all kinds—in short, living life.

After not hearing from her for some time there came one day a letter from Guadeloupe. In it she related how she had met a handsome young woman about her own age, of mixed blood like herself, named Georgiana. Part of her blood strain was Irish, another part Creole. Apparently they were divinely suited to one another and soon established a lesbian relationship. "After all," she wrote, "I've had a bellyful of men with the stiff pricks. It's a beautiful change to have a woman friend with whom one is so compatible." She went on to add that Georgiana had induced her to try writing as a career. Her first project was a book about the Polish writer Joseph Conrad. Unfortunately she knew no Polish, but what Russian she knew was of help.

There was not much sex in his tales of the sea. She was getting fed up with sex. After all, she possessed a mind as well as a cunt. Why not use it?

The language she had chosen to write in was Portuguese. She thought it a rich language; besides, she admired the Portuguese people. They ran themselves down instead of puffing themselves up.

Good! I congratulated her on her choice of subject and of language and waited to hear more.

An interesting thing about the choice of language was that she almost chose Arabic. It was good for sex and for cursing, she wrote. But then how few people in "our" world knew Arabic. It would have been time wasted.

Well, it took even longer for the next letter to arrive. She was no longer in Guadeloupe. No, she had run into a wealthy man whose business was book collecting. He was also something of a scholar: read in Greek and Latin as well as the romance languages.

He had fallen in love with Louella at first sight. He had been slightly suspicious of her relationship with Georgiana but Louella quickly dispelled that by urging her friend to make advances to him, thus throwing him off the track.

They had left Guadeloupe as he had urgent business in Geneva. And so, after a month or so, they all went to live in the Ticino region of Switzerland—Locarno and then Lugano. Indeed, it was from her picturesque descriptions of this famous region that some years later I made it my business to visit the region, staying in a modest hotel in Locarno. As I have said elsewhere it was a veritable Paradise. In fact, eventually I had to quit the place—it was just too good. This sounds like an improbable reason, and certainly very few people have the opportunity to put my words to the test. But one should never forget that Paradise is always more boring than Purgatory or Hell. We were not made to inhabit a Paradise; we are more at home in the hell we have created.

From here on our correspondence diminished. I assumed that if she were not head over heels in love with him she at least respected him, her husband.

After a year or so the husband suddenly died of a stroke. He left her his fortune, which was considerable. On her own now, and comfortably situated for life, she decided to resume her literary career. She finished the book on Joseph Conrad; it was translated into English, French and German. And from Conrad she went on to write of other prominent authors such as Hermann Hesse, Wasserman and Maxim Gorky.

About ten years later I received a cablegram from her friend Georgiana, saying that Louella had drowned in a swimming pool.

Ruth &
The Fur-lined Coat

I had a strong feeling for her, not just
because she was highly intelligent, an excellent reader, always
pleasant and agreeable, but because of her name—*Ruth*. Though
I have long forgotten the story of Ruth in the Old Testament,
the name still rings a bell.

And this Ruth, who happened to be Jewish, resembled the
Biblical Ruth for some reason. She was married to a dear friend
of mine, one of the few geniuses I have known in my life. I don't
think they were very happy together; they were temperamen-
tally unsuited to one another. I was too good a friend of my
genius friend to take advantage of the situation; I was content
merely to drop in on them occasionally and spend an hour or
two chewing the fat.

They were both great talkers. He could talk all night about art
(he was a painter himself) while she enjoyed discussing books
and authors. She knew I was trying to write and did all she could
to encourage me. Often our discussions lasted for hours, in
which case I was always invited to stay for dinner. In those days I

depended a good deal on these chance invitations to dinner. Always a good talker, on days when I was starving I waxed exceedingly charming and loquacious. I talked my way into a meal as easily as taking a walk around the block. A matter of survival. And thoughI was a sponger, I was always welcome, always well received. This habit of mine was put to good use during my early days in Paris, as I have recounted elsewhere.

In New York, especially when virtually penniless, it meant a great deal of walking as well as talking to get some food in one's guts. I have often remarked the similarity in this respect to Rimbaud's vagabond days. The amazing thing, now that I look back upon this distant past, was my ability to walk immense distances on an empty stomach, for often none of my friends were home when I called on them. The one object which stands out in my memory, like a scene from a nightmare, is the Brooklyn Bridge. How many times I walked it to and fro on an empty stomach! I was as familiar with the scenery at each end of the bridge as an artist is with his theme, whether writer, painter or musician. The worst was *returning home* on an empty stomach. Because that meant a deal of walking in Manhattan, going from one friend's house to another. Oftimes I began my return journey from somewhere in the 70th or 80th streets. Needless to say, in New York there was little hope of ever hitching a ride. As a matter of fact I never tried to beg a ride. Like the idiot that I was, I just put my head down thoroughly disheartened, thoroughly depressed.

All this by way of relating how one day toward evening, and knowing no way of getting a free meal, I took the last nickel I had and got in the subway headed for Ruth's place somewhere in the Bronx. (I was then living near Columbia Heights, Brooklyn.) Even by subway it was a long trip and during the ride I prayed to God that Ruth or her husband or his sister would be home when I arrived. (I never phoned people in advance of my coming for fear they would make some excuse to dodge me.)

Fortunately, they were all home and in good spirits. They were delighted to see me and immediately invited me to stay for dinner. That night Ruth cooked an exceptionally good meal, topped off by some excellent French wines.

Since Ruth and her husband were on good terms this evening, it was not difficult to launch into monologues and dialogues. We must have talked of everything under the sun. Ruth's husband was especially fond of the Russian writers—and *musicians!*—and spent considerable time praising their works. For her part, Ruth broke ground by talking of nineteenth century Yiddish writers whom she had read as a young girl. We were drunk not on the wine alone but on talk. (I think of this evening with fondness because such occasions are now a rarity.)

Needless to say, none of us ever looked at the clock. Suddenly I realized that I was a long way from home and made ready to go. It was mid-winter and I was wearing a fur-lined overcoat which one of my Hindu messengers had given me as a gift on returning to India. It was a bit heavy when walking any distance, but warm and snug.

I was still thinking of our discussions as I left the house and turned automatically in the direction of the subway. It was only when I got to the subway station that I realized that I had spent my last cent getting to the Bronx. I stood on the subway steps reflecting what do do. I should have returned to my friends and borrowed a nickel or a quarter but I felt ashamed to ask for anything after having been so royally regaled.

As I looked around me I noticed a cab rack at the curb. And with that I suddenly had an idea. I went up to the nearest cab, told the driver my story, and offered him the fur coat if he would drive me to my place in Brooklyn.

"*Do you mean it?*" he shouted, and with that he hopped out of the cab. I was already slipping out of the fur coat to see if it would fit him. He tried it on and it fit perfectly. He beamed all over.

Once again he said—"Are you sure you want to do this? Do you really mean it?"

I replied in the affirmative without a second's hesitation. After all I had another ordinary overcoat and a sweater at home.

"Okay" he chirped, "hop in!" Then, "Where did you say you lived? You'll have to show me the way once we cross the bridge," he said.

We rode a space, then suddenly he turned halfway round and exclaimed: "You know, Mister, you're a bit of a nut."

"I know that," I replied calmly.

"Are you a writer or something like that?" was his next query.

"Exactly!" I said. "You hit it on the head."

Silence for a while. Then he tallied off with this: "First I thought you might be gaga. But you talked like a gentleman and I couldn't find anything queer about you. Now that I know you're a writer I understand. Writers are queer birds. Maybe you'll make a story out of it one day..."

I answered: "Maybe."

Renate &
the Astrologer

I was met at the Hamburg airport by Rowohlt's secretary, a charming black-eyed, black-haired young widow with Italian blood in her veins. She was escorting me to my hotel because Rowohlt himself had been suddenly obliged to leave town.

The next evening I had dinner with her in a restaurant at the airport. Neither she nor Rowohlt lived in Hamburg. His very modern publishing house was located in Reinbek-bei-Hamburg, a village about ten miles distant.

It didn't take me long to fall in love with Renate. She was full of grace, beautiful to behold, and had a noble or aristocratic touch to her. Her forte, I soon discovered, was language. Not languages, although she spoke three, four or five fluently and often did translations. No, her interest was in language itself, how it got that way, so to speak. Etymology was her cocktail. Needless to say, I was all ears when she opened up on her passionate subject.

She, on the other hand, had read most of my work, both in

English and in French. In short, though something of a scholar, she did not present the typical picture of a German female.

I had gone to Germany to arrange for translations of *Tropic of Cancer*. I was also getting a rather handsome advance—for the first time in my life.

Everything seemed propitious and promising. Renate and I often ate out, and I must confess, tasked some excellent cuisines. The wines too were good.

It so happened that she had two sons about the same ages as my son and daughter who were now living with their mother in Los Angeles. Their mother had just divorced the man she ran away with when we were all living in Big Sur.

One day Renate asked me to go to Hamburg with her to meet a good friend who was an analyst *and* an astrologer. She thought I would find him rather interesting.

She was right. He was not only interesting but fascinating. Hitler had forced him to become one of his own astrologers. But not for long. Soon it was discovered he was giving Hitler false hopes. Suddenly he became an enemy of the Reich and had to flee the country. This fact, and his interest in Madame Blavatsky's work helped form a budding friendship with the man. I forget his real name, so will call him Schmidt. A couple of months later, so it seemed to me, Renate and I decided to share our lives, together with our children. Consequently, it was decided that I should make a trip around Europe—France, Italy, Spain, and Portugal more particularly—to see if I could find a good place to live.

My old friend Vincent happened to be in town and announced at once that he would be only too glad to act as my chauffeur, interpreter, and secretary. (He knew about five languages well, having been a pilot for a commercial airline for some years. He had seen a lot of the world to boot.)

We started off blithely, touring Germany for its scenery, then gradually visited the other countries. We were proceeding at a leisurely pace; for once in my life I was not short of money. I had written my own children about the project and kept sending postcards as we made our way along.

In the Midi or south of France I was offered several châteaux at modest prices. They they were all in a state of disrepair and besides I would have had to maintain a chauffeur and a retinue of servants, all out of the question. Each time we stopped at a village, no matter where, there was always something fascinating abut the place. (Even Austria, which was not really on our list for a home, proved highly attractive, particularly the countryside.)

Naturally at every stopover I immediately rushed to the Poste Restante (General Delivery) to see if there was mail from Renate. Usually there was. I of course wrote her abundant letters, describing our impressions and adventures.

When we entered Venice, Italy, for some unknown reason I was stricken by a deep depression. It was so serious and so seemingly unwarranted that I decided to write a lewtter explaining my plight to Herr Schmidt in Hamburg. Perhaps he could put a finger on the sore spot?

Needless to say, though we roamed the city from end to end I saw hardly anything of this fabulous city.

A few days elapsed and then one day at lunch in a modest restaurant I suddenly realized that the depression was leaving me. I happened to glance at the big clock on the wall and the hands read seven minutes after 12 noon. I go to my room and write Herr Schmidt another letter. "Don't worry. Depression gone as suddenly as it arrived." Etcetera, etc.

In two or three days I get a special delivery letter telling me that the depression had left me because he, Herr Schmidt, had been *praying for me!*!

Punkt!

We continued on to Portugal, where I almost decided to settle because the southern part of it reminded me strongly of Big Sur.

Letters from Renate were tapering off. Now, as we started homeward to Hamburg, without having found a home to live in, I grew more and more dubious about Renate and her great love for me. In fact, by the time we reached the German border, I was almost frantic. I was sure she had fallen in love with some other man. I also felt terribly guilty over my unsuccessful trip. When we finally got to Reinbek I found a Renate who had become as cold as an iceberg. No other man in evidence either. No explanation. Just that it was all over.

Alors, que faire? Put my tail between my legs and take the first plane back to California. Now I had good reason to be depressed. What would my children say—after all the glorious pictures I had drawn for them of a new home in dear old Europe?

Some ten to fifteen years passed during which time we exchanged a few friendly letters and then one day, out of the blue, came *the* letter. I read it over three times. It was simply unbelievable.

Here's what she related. First, that she had never ceased to love me; second, that the real reason for giving me the go-by was because the analyst-astrologer, Herr Schmidt, had warned her that a life with me would be disastrous.

The strangest thing about it all was that I agreed with him. I had been through five marriages. What guarantee was there that I could make a success of a sixth or seventh?

A little later it dawned on me why Herr Schmidt's reasoning was sound. Looking back on my "many marriages," I came to realize that I was always primarily in love with my work. I was hopelessly married to my work.

And so I consoled myself with the fact that an "artist" should never marry. Adding, by way of sauce, "Marriage is the death of love."

Brenda Venus

How shall I paint her? In silver, gold, ivory or what? After all the other portraits I have drawn of women what new can I add? Well, love is always new, even the hundreth time around. I said Love, not sex. One can include the other, but the other can exist alone, unnourished except by physical desire. Love is a flame that is nourished on all sides from all directions. Anything or anybody can inspire it. Sometimes life alone is sufficient. There is holy love and unholy love. All are legitimate. All are beseeching the same thing—a response. And even when there is no response, love can exist, a tortuous affair, but still a yearning, a beseeching. Perhaps the case of unrequited love is just as thrilling and terrifying as mutual love. I have known all kinds. I deem myself fortunate to know this latest love, Brenda Venus. It is a love which seems to be astrologically right. We meet at all intersections, all conjunctions, all eclipses. We love in our sleep as well as in our waking moments. We are made with love, to put it bluntly. How explain sunrise and sunset, flood and drought? Things just happen. They happen in an aura of mystery. Everything, every being is enveloped in mystery. We move from one mystery to another. Our very language is pure mystery, or pure magic, how you will. And the language of love is the most impenetrable of all. It does not ask to be understood, just to babble.

Brenda is from a small town in Mississippi, thank God. Not far from the delta. She spent a few years in a nunnery in Biloxi, not far distant. Biloxi happens to be one of my favorite American towns. The Southern states are my favorite states. I fight the Civil War over, in my mind, again and again. Each time I am fighting on the side of the "rebels." My chief is the one and only General Robert E. Lee. In my fantasies the South never lost the war. The South was simply crushed by the North. But the Southerners were better soldiers, nobler, more courageous, more daring and inventive.

All this apropos the South long before the intervention of Brenda. I speak of it to explain my seeming infatuation for the young lady from Hattiesburg. She has been out of the South for some years now, attempting to be a figure in the movies. She has her idols, her stars, her *vedettes* and she aims to be another one of them. All of which means we see each other infrequently. We live on dreams , letters, telephone calls, much like other lovelorn. Only we are not "lovelorn." Lovestruck perhaps, but not lovelorn. Hungry but not famished, Yearning but not whining.

We also know one another telepathically. We come to each other's rescue just in the nick of time. We know how to heal wounds, balm aches and pains, play Jesus, Mary and Joseph and Jehosaphat, what what! Sometimes we incarnate the Holy one and the Evil one. Sometimes we are just Adam and Eve. We are never out of tricks. No, there is always lurking somewhere the shades of Dixie Friganza. We wait at gas stations, bus stops, and subway exits, just like everyone else. But we wait in hope and peace. We know what we wait for. And it comes, sometimes by parcel post.

How did we meet? What matter, we met. And we have been meeting ever since.

What's more, our *souls* meet. They meet at will or haphazardly, but surely, truly, sublimely. We sustain one another. I keep her from falling apart; she keeps me from bursting at the seams. We mollify and jollify one another. We appreciate one another. She could drag me along the rich river bottom. I would not murmur. All I'd keep saying (to myself) is—"I love you, I love you." I have said it a thousand times to a few hundred women perhaps. It is one phrase that never wears out, never gets rusty. To wake up with words of love on one's lips—what bliss! Just to say "Brenda" puts me in ecstasy.

Sometimes she talks Southern fashion to me. Then it's all moonlight and roses, camellias, gardenias and water moccasins.

To love at the end of one's life is something special. Few women can inspire that sort of love. Brenda seems to anticipate my wishes, my very thoughts. She is not bashful in avowing her love. She has guts, is quick on the trigger, ingenious. And always smiling. Not that fatuous smile of the empty head. A noble smile, sometimes a smile tinged with joyous sadness. Yes, she is a bundle of contradictions. Like myself. Maybe that alone explains a great deal, why we get on so well together, why we seem to have been made for one another since way back.

Did I mention that among other strains she has Navajo blood in her veins? That accounts for much of her character as well as physiognomy. Her silence is always impressive. Not gloomy, but meditative and speculative. It can also be chilling, as with our American Indians. Above all, she has a sense of fortitude, of independence, of determination. She can stand alone. She can use weapons with skill. She is not afraid of animals. She could kill without batting an eyelash, if she were obliged to kill. She can love the same way. Alors, what more does one want?

Inside she is like a three-ring circus. Always planning, intriguing, concocting. A perpetual ferment at work. Works herself to the bone physically and mentally. Can eat like a tigress but can do without too. Loves luxury but needs little. Is always dressed

319

like a rainbow. Under the shower she sparkles. When snoozing, the dreams which float through her head keep her perpetually bedazzled. She is a volcano in restraint, a geyser holding back its stream of flame. Everything under control, yet wild as a tornado within.

Where will this strange creature lead me, I wonder? To what strange shores? I have put myself in her hands. Lead me, O blessed one, wherever!

FINIS